DATE DUE

~~NV 13 99~~		
~~AG 5 '99~~		
~~DE 6 00~~		
~~ND 26 01~~		
NO 20 02		
~~DE 10 02~~		
AG 9 07		

DEMCO 38-296

Civil Rights and
Race Relations in the
Post Reagan-Bush Era

Civil Rights and Race Relations in the Post Reagan-Bush Era

Edited by
Samuel L. Myers, Jr.

PRAEGER

Westport, Connecticut
London

Library of Congress Cataloging-in-Publication Data

Civil rights and race relations in the post Reagan-Bush era / edited
  by Samuel L. Myers, Jr.
      p.   cm.
    Includes bibliographical references and index.
    ISBN 0–275–95621–0 (alk. paper)
    1. Afro-Americans—Civil rights.   2. United States—Race
relations.   3. United States—Ethnic relations.   4. Affirmative
action programs—United States.   5. Afro-Americans—Employment.
I. Myers, Samuel L.
E185.615.C583   1997
305.8′00973′09049—dc21   96–37730

British Library Cataloguing in Publication Data is available.

Library of Congress Catalog Card Number: 96–37730
ISBN: 0–275–95621–0

First published in 1997

Praeger Publishers, 88 Post Road West, Westport, CT 06881
An imprint of Greenwood Publishing Group, Inc.

Printed in the United States of America

The paper used in this book complies with the
Permanent Paper Standard issued by the National
Information Standards Organization (Z39.48–1984).

10 9 8 7 6 5 4 3 2

Copyright Acknowledgment

The author and publisher gratefully acknowledge permission to use the
following material: The *Hungry Mind Review* Questionnaire on Race
originally appeared in *Hungry Mind Review*, no. 30, Summer 1994.
Reprinted with permission.

Contents

Preface   vii
Samuel L. Myers, Jr.

Chapter 1
Historical Roots of Contemporary Racial Inequality   1
Herbert Hill

Chapter 2
Race, Civil Rights, and the New Immigrants:
Nativism and the New World Order   11
Evelyn Hu-DeHart

Chapter 3
Fighting White Racism: The Future of Equal Rights in the United States   29
Joe R. Feagin

Chapter 4
Affirmative Action Policy Under Executive Order 11246:
A Retrospective View   47
Bernard E. Anderson

Chapter 5
Racial Differences in Employment Shares:
New Evidence from the EEO-1 Files   61
William M. Rodgers III

Chapter 6
Where the Jobs Went in the 1990-91 Downturn:
Varying (Mis)Fortunes or Homogeneous Distress?   99
M. V. Lee Badgett

Chapter 7
Foundation Connections to Black Workers and Labor Unions
Richard Magat   149

Chapter 8
Diversity in the Workplace: A Dialogue Among Corporate Executives   167

Chapter 9
A Local Conversation About Race   179

Chapter 10
Hungry Mind Review Questionnaire
Betsy Hubbard, Kathleen Kalina, Rebecca Kelleher-Reeth,
Dartrell Lipscomb, Reginald J. Mitchell, Sr., Michelle Revels   189

Chapter 11
"Don't Throw Trash in the Well From Which You Must Drink":
Black Demagogues, the Media, and the Pollution of Racial Discourse
Richard M. Benjamin   205

Chapter 12
The Political Assault on Affirmative Action:
Undermining 50 Years of Progress Toward Equality
The Honorable Gerald W. Heaney   217

Chapter 13
Is Affirmative Action a Quota System?
Barbara R. Bergmann   227

Chapter 14
Reparations
William A. Darity, Jr.   231

Chapter 15
Remedies to Racial Inequality   243

Afterword: The Future of Race Relations and Civil Rights   251
Samuel L. Myers, Jr.

Index   259

About the Contributors   267

Preface

Samuel L. Myers, Jr.

Affirmative action. Quotas. Reverse discrimination. Racial preferences in hiring and college admissions. These are some of the contentious issues surrounding the retrenchment of support for racial equality in America. Quite ironically, however, the language of this retrenchment embraces the very vocabulary of general equality used to support the civil rights initiatives of the 1960s. The first sentence of the California Civil Rights Initiative—a controversial constitutional amendment propelling a national movement to dismantle affirmative action and race preferences—seems on first impression to be a progressive reaffirmation of racial equality: "The state shall not discriminate against, or grant preferential treatment to, any individual or group on the basis of race, sex, color, ethnicity, or national origin in the operation of public employment, public education, or public contracting."[1]

Of course, the public knows better. There is no need to be coy. Authors and principals of the initiative, Glynn Custred and Thomas Wood,[2] two conservative opponents of affirmative action, cleverly juxtaposition the phrase "or grant preferential treatment to" against the benign admonition "shall not discriminate against" to lend the impression that this is a "civil rights initiative." The public and the press correctly understand this effort to be an *anti-civil rights* undertaking.

Efforts like the California Civil Rights Initiative are popping up all around the nation.[3] These efforts represent an all-out national attack on the principal *remedies* to racial and ethnic discrimination. These remedies—which range from innocuous goals and time-tables to more emboldened numerical requirements—are among the primary legal and administrative victories of the civil rights movement of the 1950s and 1960s.[4]

The 1970s largely was a period of experimentation and implementation of these variations on the theme of remedying prior racial discrimination by embracing *affirmative* efforts to increase the representation of members of historically disadvantaged groups in the social and economic fabric of our nation. Once the overt structures of discrimination were outlawed, the long and difficult process of enforcement and policy implementation began.[5]

That period of experimentation and implementation long ago came to an end. There now is open hostility to the use of many of the commonly embraced mechanisms for remedying current and past discrimination. There is widespread belief that these mechanisms not only are unfair to the majority but might even be harmful to the minority.[6]

The years of retrenchment from the goal of equality and the national commitment to affirmative action as a mechanism for achieving racial equality is known as the Reagan-Bush era. These were years of successive constitutional challenges to affirmative action in employment, in higher education, in public contracting and procurement, and in a wide variety of related economic activities.[7]

These were years of fundamental economic change. The gap between the top and the bottom widened.[8] Middle-class jobs or "good jobs" seemed to shrink.[9] Median real earnings of white males declined.[10] Earnings of white males in the middle fifth of the earnings distribution fell.[11] This while, at least in many people's minds, minorities prospered at the majority's expense.[12]

These were years of drastic political changes. Republican victories were seen in state and local elections.[13] Sizeable increases in conservative voting power occurred throughout the nation.[14] And, most important, the White House remained in the hands of conservative Republicans for twelve consecutive years.

And these years were years of dramatic demographic shifts.[15] No longer were African Americans the majority minority in many locales.[16] No longer did women, Asian Americans, Latinos, and American Indians see African Americans as unswerving allies in the fight for justice and equality. No longer were even blacks unified in their quest for economic gains. Demographic shifts meant widening gulfs between the black middle class and the black underclass; between African Americans and other people of color; between women of color and white women.[17]

Civil rights and race relations as we once knew them are dead and gone. This monograph seeks to pave the way for the next era: the post Reagan-Bush era.

The chapters that follow are the edited result of a national forum inaugurated at the University of Minnesota in 1994 to develop forward-thinking approaches to solving the mounting problems of racism and inequality. Under the leadership of the Wilkins Forum, a panel of distinguished researchers, scholars, community activists, business leaders, media professionals, and others, the National Conference on Civil Rights and Race Relations in the post Reagan-Bush era sought to lay out the terrain of the present problem: what to do in light of the crisis facing the civil rights movement. The purpose was to examine the historical backdrop of the current crisis, to outline some of the unexplored contours of the crisis, to explore the evidence of the effectiveness of prior policies, and to map out the alternatives available for the next era that we face.

One of the recurring themes in the pages that follow is the role of white privilege in framing the original discriminatory patterns that the civil rights era sought to dismantle and in forcing the policy debate once the remedy of affirmative action was solidly in place. It is perhaps a theme that gets lost in many conventional discussions about equality and democracy. Such discussions proceed as if slavery and its horrible aftermath are long gone and forgotten. These discussions typically include statements like "My parents and grandparents never owned slaves" or "The current generation cannot be held accountable for the sins of prior generations."[18]

This theme is detailed explicitly in the first three chapters. Herbert Hill, Evjue-Bascom Professor of African American Studies and Professor of Industrial Relations at the University of Wisconsin, Madison, reminds us in chapter 1, "Historical Roots of Contemporary Racial Inequality," that white privilege lies at the root of current opposition to affirmative action:

[O]pposition to affirmative action is based on narrowly perceived self-interest rather than on abstract philosophical differences about "quotas," "reverse discrimination," "preferential treatment," and the other catch phrases commonly raised in public debate. After all the pious rhetoric equating affirmative action with "reverse discrimination" is stripped away, it is evident that the opposition to affirmative action is in fact the effort to perpetuate the privileged position of whites in American society.[19]

The role of white privilege is central to understanding the rise of restrictive immigration legislation and codes designed to exclude Chinese immigrants in the late 19th century, as Professor Evelyn Hu-DeHart so clearly relates in chapter 2, "Race, Civil Rights, and the New Immigrants: Nativism and the New World Order." Dr. Hu-DeHart, who directs the Center for Studies in Ethnicity and Race in America at the University of Colorado at Boulder, describes in addition the rise in multiculturalism and the New World Order in reigniting white racism, nativism, and fascism.

Fighting white racism in the New World Order, however, will not be easy, as Professor Joe R. Feagin relates in chapter 3, "Fighting White Racism: The Future of Equal Rights in the United States." Feagin, who is Graduate Research Professor of Sociology at the University of Florida, diagnoses the problem of race relations as the disease of white racism that "afflicts the mind, the emotions, the behaviors, and the institutions of white Americans." Clearly, understanding both racial discrimination and white's hostility toward remedies to racial and ethnic discrimination requires an appreciation for the persistence of white privilege in America.

The next section of the monograph focuses on the labor market, one important component of the economy where anti-discrimination efforts have evolved and where much progress has been made in both the public and the private sectors. In chapter 4, Dr. Bernard Anderson, a prolific economist serving as the Assistant Secretary of Labor in the Clinton administration, writes of the history and evolution of Executive Order 11246, the backbone of workplace affirmative action in America. In chapter 5, William Rodgers III, an innovative economics professor at the College of William and Mary, debunks the theory that the rising flight of jobs to the suburbs explains the erosion of black wage and employment opportunities in the 1980s. Instead, the culprit appears to be the heightening of racial segregation within specific firms over the years. M. V. Lee Badgett, an expert on race and gender discrimination in labor markets who teaches at the University of Maryland's

School of Public Affairs, examines recession year data from large private firms reporting on the employment composition of their establishments in chapter 6. She demonstrates that not all minorities face identical experiences when recessions strike. Some gain; some lose. The old adage of last hired, first fired takes on a new meaning when the workforce is not just black and white, but various colors, races, and ethnicities. In chapter 7, Richard Magat, a visiting fellow at Yale University's Program on Nonprofit Organizations, examines the role of foundations in linking black workers and labor unions. This chapter provides a unique historical perspective on how private funding organizations have influenced important aspects of the dynamics of labor markets. The section concludes with chapters 8–10, edited versions of extensive panel discussions dealing with race relations and diversity in the workplace. The views and the perspectives of managers and corporate insiders reinforce the realities uncovered in the empirical and historical documentation in the preceding chapters.

The third section focuses on racial discourse, an underdeveloped area that may play an increasing role in the formation of new directions for race relations. Chapter 11 comes from journalist Richard Benjamin, who dissects civil rights rhetoric and black demagogues. It touches on the issue of homophobia and adeptly addresses the role of the "liberal media" in the formation of negative images of blacks. While Benjamin uncovers the bias in newspaper reporting of racial incidents, chapter 12 uncovers personal bias among liberal Americans, perhaps influenced by the very liberal press that Benjamin castigates.

The final section details a range of remedies for racial inequality. The discussion and debate that we reproduce from the actual conference deliberations provocatively highlight the divided plane on which we rest as we embark on new directions to race relations and civil rights. We can resurrect affirmative action and related race preferences and worry about the backlash later, as Barbara Bergmann, Distinguished Professor of Economics at American University, argues in chapter 13. We can adopt once-and-for-all redistribution in the form of reparations, a remedy examined in detail in chapter 14 by the prominent economic theorist and professor at the University of North Carolina at Chapel Hill, William A. Darity, Jr. Or, we could simply hope for the best by turning our attention to strengthening the moral fibre of minority communities, as one discussant suggests.

Chapter 12, by Federal Court of Appeals Judge Gerald Heaney, was written especially for this volume and was presented at the spring 1995 Wilkins Forum focusing on affirmative action. It underscores the work that remains to be done in the quest for full equality. It makes clear the central thesis of this book: that racial and ethnic inequality rests in part on continuing discrimination in many walks of life. And until all discrimination against historically disadvantaged peoples has been eradicated, there will remain at least a legal basis for redress of that discrimination. Having made that point, however, Judge Heaney then provokes the theme of the epilogue to this volume. Like it or not, past strategies for reducing racial and ethnic inequality run the risk of dividing persons of color, of creating divisions so sharply torn that only a balkanization of our racial and ethnic groups would suffice to prevent bloodshed and interracial strife. But that strife is unlikely to be between blacks and whites, who have drawn farther and farther apart in American society, and whose distance from one another is both physical and cultural. Instead, the strife could well be between and among people of color. This must not happen. The future agenda of civil rights and race relations in America must see to it that it does not happen.

Thus two central themes emerge in this book: one of white racism and white privilege; another of the changing terms and changing *color* of the debate about race relations and civil rights. There is no quixotic attempt to forge a political middle ground in these chapters. There is no idealistic effort to seek a broad consensus that could draw large majorities of whites, blacks, Latinos, American Indians, and Asian Pacific Islanders into a single melting pot of American nationalism. Readers who expect to find it will quickly discover why the search for the easy middle ground is riddled with roadblocks. The biggest roadblock is white racism itself.

The middle-ground view in America concerning white racism is that it is on the decline, that it is not the mainstream view, and that its outward manifestations—unequal rewards in society—no longer measure as prominently as they did in previous eras. Many good Americans adhere to this view. In a recent address on race relations, Senator Bill Bradley, New Jersey Democrat, summarized portions of this perspective: "I believe that most white Americans are not racist. Mark Fuhrman is, thank God, the exception, not the rule. Most white Americans easily reject the crude stereotyping and violent race hate of Fuhrman. . . . Most people are not brimming over with race hatred."[20]

In many respects, Senator Bradley is offering the most appealing, most unthreatening, and most neutral interpretation of race realities. The view is designed simultaneously to satisfy minorities by admitting that white racism does exist and the white majority by contending that few whites are racists. This appeal to a compromise position has much to its merit. It may induce whites and blacks (and other persons of color) to engage actively in discussions and heartfelt exchanges about race and racism. It may break down the walls that make it difficult for many whites even to discuss racism or racial discrimination. It may permit blacks and others to go beyond a narrow fixation with racism and to examine other causes of the plight facing minority communities. It may ultimately provide unique opportunities for finding genuine solutions to the festering problems that are correlated with race but on their face involve complex intervening social and economic forces. Certainly this view is one that might prevail should we achieve the total elimination of race—or at least the "declining significance of race"—in the operation of economic and social institutions.

If only the view were accurate. In offering this appealing reinterpretation of race and racism, Bradley is also offering an enormous lie. Regrettably, the evidence does not reveal that most whites are free of racist tendencies. Racism is so prevalent, so persistent, so deeply embedded in American society that it is nearly impossible for victims of racism and white people of goodwill to shake off its many manifestations.

Regrettably, the vast majority of whites hold views and perspectives that clearly and unambiguously are racist. The essay by Joe Feagin provides ample documentation for this unfortunate reality. He summarizes survey results showing that three quarters of whites agree with such racist sentiments as "Blacks prefer to accept welfare" and "Blacks have less native intelligence." In another survey, Feagin finds that almost half of whites believe that blacks are lazy. Survey after survey finds that whites believe that blacks are poorly motivated, are less intelligent, and do not have the willpower to pull themselves up from poverty. The majority of whites also deny that racism plays any role in the plight of blacks.

More compelling evidence is found from a survey of liberal, upper middle-class, educated persons living in Middle America. The survey, conducted by the *Hungry Mind Review,* underscores appalling and disturbing evidence of deeply rooted racist beliefs. Some of these beliefs are directly acknowledged and confronted by the survey respondents. Others are revealed in subtle ways. For example, these liberal respondents, while often in favor of affirmative action and racially diverse neighborhoods, nevertheless tended to associate violent crime, loud music, neighborhood deterioration, and low socioeconomic status with people of color. Precisely for that reason they were often reluctant to "live the ideal" of racially diverse neighborhoods even though they might deny that race was a factor in the decision.

An entire session of the National Conference on Civil Rights and Race Relations in the post Reagan-Bush era was devoted to discussion and evaluation of the *Hungry Mind Review* survey. The actual responses were mailed in large batches to a diverse set of scholars and researchers who pored over the long, detailed, and often troubling open-ended answers to the survey questions. A talented team of Humphrey Institute of Public Affairs graduate students at the University of Minnesota coded the responses, entered them into the computer, and performed a detailed descriptive analysis of the results. The lively discussion and the heated debate about the depth of white racist beliefs in Middle America, and particularly in the "liberal" upper Midwest, literally went on for hours both in formal sessions and in the breakout sessions, in the hallways, over dinner, and throughout the night in hotel lobbies. While it is not possible to do full justice to the range of views expressed in the few pages devoted to summarizing the panel and the *Hungry Mind Review* survey itself, the glimpse that appears in this volume confirms the substantial consensus among those who examined the survey. That consensus is that white racism is more solidly entrenched in American society than Senator Bill Bradley will have one believe.

Another myth exposed in Joe Feagin's chapter is that of the convergence of black and white economic and social status in America. Whites overwhelmingly believe that discriminatory barriers against blacks have largely disappeared; that equal opportunity is a reality; and that parity—particularly among better skilled blacks and whites—has been reached. An entire section of this book is devoted to refuting this myth empirically. Although the chapters use the technical tools of applied labor econometrics, the main results point to the fact that racial discrimination and racism continue to play prominent roles in explaining observed inequalities in economic outcomes.

In reading through the chapters of this volume, the sympathetic observer will be reassured that affirmative action and related remedies were well-intentioned, had some positive impacts, and probably are still needed in some form. But at the same time, the reader will wonder, "Why were we so unprepared for the onslaught of attacks on efforts to remedy prior discrimination?" It is unfortunate that the years of experimentation and implementation of affirmative action and similar remedies were not years when constant analysis and evaluation of which approaches worked and which did not were undertaken. It is unfortunate that the attack on affirmative action and similar remedies occurs when quite unrelated economic reversals to the middle class occur. It is unfortunate that the fortunes of the minority hinge so precariously upon the goodwill and support of the majority—two commodities in short supply.

The chapters in this volume are designed to help stimulate thoughtful discussion, debate, and discourse to reverse the negative and pessimistic tone of current voices heard on the future of race relations and civil rights. Of course, there still needs to be evaluation and analysis of what programs work and what programs do not work. Someone needs to do this; and perhaps readers of this volume will be inspired to undertake the long overdue task of reexamining prior efforts to reduce racial and ethnic economic inequality. Yet, the urgency of the task rests not in the fact that we know far too little about successful initiatives undertaken during the pre-Reagan-Bush era. It rests in the fact that increasing numbers of Americans question the fundamental logic of undertaking any initiative at all on behalf of racial and ethnic minority group members. This is the horrible residual of the civil rights and race relations retrenchments in the Reagan-Bush era. If the era that follows is to represent any improvement at all, if the post Reagan-Bush era is to signal a new vision and new direction in civil rights and race relations, then the issues raised in this book will have to be addressed head-on.

NOTES

1. See text of the 1995 Civil Rights Initiative (CCRI Home Page).

2. Glynn Custred, Professor of Anthropology, California State University, Hayward; Ph.D., anthropology, Indiana University. Thomas Wood, Executive Director, California Association of Scholars (CAS), Ph.D., philosophy, University of California, Berkeley.

3. A recent U.S. Court of Appeals decision ruled the University of Texas's affirmative action program unconstitutional. Pennsylvania and Arizona are trying to enact legislation to outlaw the practice. The Attorney General of Georgia has asked the state university system to abolish all race-based admission and financial aid policies. Louisiana's governor ordered an end to state affirmative action and set-aside programs. See William Honan, "Moves to End Affirmative Action Gain Support," *New York Times,* March 31, 1996, p. A30; William Honan, "New Attack on Race-Based Admissions," *New York Times,* April 10, 1996, p. B8; and Jack Wardlaw and Ed Anderson, "Foster Orders LA Agencies to End Affirmative Action; Few Programs Will Be Affected," *The Times Picayune* (New Orleans) January 12, 1996, p. A1.

4. See Mitchell F. Rice, "Government Set-Asides, Minority Business Enterprises, and the Supreme Court," *Public Administration Review,* Vol. 51, No. 2 (March/April 1991).

5. See chapter 4, this volume.

6. See *The Gallup Poll Monthly,* no. 354 (March 1995): 36.

7. For example, *City of Richmond* v. *Croson*, 488 U.S. 469 (1989), which struck down an affirmative action program that set aside 30 percent of the dollar amount of city construction contracts for minority-owned firms; *Fullilove* v. *Klutznick*, 448 U.S. 448 (1980), which upheld the validity of a federal minority business enterprise program; and *Wards Cove Packing Co.* v. *Atonio*, 109 S. Ct. 2115 (1989), which ruled that the plaintiffs in Title VII cases must prove that an employer had no legitimate business reason for employment practices that had an adverse "disparate impact" on minorities.

8. See Samuel L. Myers, Jr., "'The Rich Get Richer And. . . .' The Problem of Race and Inequality in the 1990s," *Law and Inequality: A Journal of Theory and Practice*, 11, no. 2, (June 1993).

9. See Samuel L. Myers, Jr., and William A. Darity, Jr., "The Widening Gap: A Summary and Synthesis of the Debate on Increasing Inequality," prepared for the National Commission for Employment Policy, April 1995.

10. Ibid.

11. Ibid.

12. See *The Gallup Report*, no. 224 (May 1984): 28.

13. See *America Votes 21: A Handbook of Contemporary American Election Statistics*, compiled and edited by Richard M. Scammon and Alice V. McGillivray (Washington, D.C.: Elections Research Center, Congressional Quarterly, 1995).

14. Ibid.

15. See *Statistical Abstract of the United States*, (Washington, D.C.: U.S. Bureau of the Census, eds. 102–113).

16. Ibid.

17. Ibid.

18. For sentiments like these, see Andrew Hacker, *Two Nations: Black and White, Separate, Hostile, Unequal* (New York: Ballantine, 1992), and Studs Terkel, *Race: How Blacks and Whites Think and Feel About the American Obsession* (New York: Doubleday, 1992).

19. See Herbert Hill, "Historical Roots of Contemporary Racial Inequality," p. 27, this volume.

20. "Race Relations in America: The Best and Worst of Times." Speech by Senator Bill Bradley. Town Hall Los Angeles, Los Angeles, CA, Jan. 11, 1996.

Civil Rights and
Race Relations in the
Post Reagan-Bush Era

CHAPTER 1

Historical Roots of
Contemporary Racial Inequality
Herbert Hill

From the beginning of the new nation on the North American continent, each generation has been confronted by the question "Who can be an American?" The original assumption that only Anglo-Saxons could be American, or "good Americans," or "real Americans" permeated the entire culture for many generations.

However, by the middle of the nineteenth century, after much conflict and struggle, a process of acculturation was under way that eventually included non-Anglo-Saxon Europeans as "good Americans." But the color line that was established at the inception still held fast; the intention was for the United States to be a white society.

This racist assumption was repeatedly declared as national policy, as for example, the Naturalization Law of 1790, which explicitly limited citizenship to "white persons"; the Fugitive Slave Acts of 1793 and 1850; and the Dred Scott decision of 1857, in which the United States Supreme Court held that blacks were not people, only "articles of commerce."[1] These are but a few of the legal monuments based upon and testifying to the assumption that the United States of America was a white man's country and that only whites had rights in the law. As a policy of genocide and sequestration was established for the Native American population, and a dehumanizing system of slavery was violently imposed upon blacks, race and racism became central factors in determining the direction of American life and culture.

With the ratification of the Thirteenth, Fourteenth, and Fifteenth Amendments in 1865, 1868, and 1870, respectively, and the adoption of the Civil Rights Acts of 1866, 1870, and 1875, a new body of law affirmed that justice and equal treatment were not for white persons exclusively, and that black people, now citizens of the nation, were entitled to "the equal protection of the laws." Although the Thirteenth Amendment legally ended the institution of slavery, it left unresolved the fundamental issues of land reform and the protection of black labor. The failure to "reconstruct" the South left newly freed black men and women without an economic base, and denied land and work, the roots of long-term black poverty took hold. Decisions of the federal courts reduced emancipated blacks to an inferior legal status, discriminatory practices were enforced by widespread violence, and the great hope of Reconstruction came to an early end.[2]

Almost a century later, as a result of direct confrontation with the system of state-imposed segregation, together with the emergence of a new body of constitutional law on race, a hope was born that the legacy of centuries of slavery and racism would finally come to an end. But, as before, that hope was not to be realized. The high moral indignation of at least part of the white population during the 1960s was evidently but a passing spasm that was quickly forgotten, and history was to repeat itself as the potential for a second Reconstruction came to an early end.

The old conflict between those interests intent on perpetuating racist patterns rooted in the past, and the forces that struggle for a society free of racism, continues in many contexts, but most sharply in the raging battle for and against affirmative action. A major manifestation of the turning away from the goals of justice and equality is to be found in the continuing attacks against affirmative action. The effort to eliminate the present effects of past discrimination, to correct the wrongs of many generations was barely under way when it came under powerful attack. And now, even the very modest gains made by racial minorities through affirmative action are being erased as powerful institutions try to turn the clock of history back to the dark and dismal days of a separate and unequal status for black Americans.

Judging by the vast outcry, it might be assumed that the remedy of affirmative action to eliminate racist and sexist patterns has become as widespread and destructive as discrimination itself. And once again, the defenders of the racial status quo have succeeded in confusing the remedy with the original evil. The term "reverse discrimination," for example, has become another code word for resisting the elimination of prevailing patterns of discrimination.

The historic dissent of Justice John Marshall Harlan in the 1883 decision of the Supreme Court in the *Civil Rights Cases* defines the constitutional principle requiring the obligation of the government to remove all the "badges and incidents" of slavery.[3] Although initially rejected, the rationale of Harlan's position was vindicated in later Supreme Court decisions, such as in *Brown* v. *Board of Education* in 1954[4] and *Jones* v. *Mayer* in 1968,[5] among others.

The passage by Congress of the Civil Rights Act of 1964 further confirmed this constitutional perception of the equal protection clause of the Fourteenth Amendment and reinforced its basic principles. I believe that what Justice Harlan called the "badges and incidents" of slavery include every manifestation of racial discrimination, not against black people alone but also against other people of color who were engulfed by the heritage of racism that developed out of slavery.

In this respect, an interpretation of the law consistent with the meaning of the Thirteenth and Fourteenth Amendments to the Constitution leads to the conclusion that affirmative action programs carry forth the contemporary legal obligation to eradicate the consequences of slavery and racism. In order to do that, it is necessary to eliminate the present effects of past discrimination, and the most effective remedy to achieve that goal is affirmative action. Justice Blackmun in his opinion in *Bakke* wrote, "in order to get beyond racism, we must first take account of race. There is no other way."[6]

By now it should be very clear that the opposition to affirmative action is based on narrowly perceived group self-interest rather than on abstract philosophical differences about "quotas," "reverse discrimination," "preferential treatment," and the other catch phrases commonly raised in public debate. After all the pious rhetoric equating affirmative action with "reverse discrimination" is stripped away, it is evident that the opposition to affirmative action is in fact the effort to perpetuate the privileged position of whites in American society.

In his dissent in *Bakke*, Justice Thurgood Marshall wrote, "The experience of Negroes in America has been different in kind, not just in degree, from that of other ethnic groups. It is not merely the history of slavery alone but also that a whole people were marked as inferior by the law. And that mark has endured. The dream of America as the great melting pot has not been realized for the Negro; because of his skin color he never even made it into the pot."[7]

I propose to examine some important aspects of the historical process described by Justice Marshall, since even a brief examination reveals much about the sources of contemporary racial inequality, especially in regard to basic economic issues. A major recomposition of the labor force occurred in the decades after the Civil War. By the end of the nineteenth century the American working class was largely an immigrant working class, and European immigrants held power and exercised great influence within organized labor. For example, in 1900, Irish immigrants or their descendants held the presidencies of over 50 of the 110 national unions in the American Federation of Labor.[8] Many of the other unions were led by immigrants or their sons, with Germans following the Irish in number and prominence; the president of the AFL was a Jewish immigrant. Records of labor organizations confirm the dominant role of immigrants and their descendants in many individual unions and city and state labor bodies throughout the country at the turn of the century and decades later.[9]

For the immigrant worker, loyalty was to the ethnic collective, and it was understood that advancement of the individual was dependent upon communal advancement. Participation in organized labor was a significant part of that process, and many of the dramatic labor conflicts of the nineteenth and twentieth centuries were in fact ethnic group struggles. For blacks, both before and after emancipation, the historical experience was completely different. For them, systematic racial oppression was the basic and inescapable characteristic of the society, in the North and the South, and it was the decisive fact of their lives. The problems of the white immigrant did not compare with the oppression of racism, an oppression that was of a different magnitude, of a different order.

Initially isolated from the social and economic mainstream, European immigrants rapidly came to understand that race and ethnic identity were decisive in providing access to employment and in the establishment of stable communities. They defined themselves as white, and for them, assimilation was achieved through group mobility and collective ethnic advancement that was directly linked to the workplace. The occupational frame of reference was decisive.

Wages and the status derived from steady work could be obtained only by entering the permanent labor force, and labor unions were most important in providing access to the job market for many groups of immigrant workers. In contrast to the white ethnics, generations of black workers were systematically barred from employment in the primary sectors of the labor market, thereby denied the economic base that made possible the celebrated achievements and social mobility of white immigrant communities.

An examination of amicus curiae briefs filed in the Supreme Court cases involving affirmative action reveal the active role these two historically interrelated groups, white ethnics and labor unions, have played in the repeated attacks against affirmative action. With some few exceptions, this has been the pattern from *De-Funis* in 1974[10] and *Bakke* in 1978[11] to the most recent cases. Given the context in which this issue evolved, the historical sources of the opposition to affirmative action are not surprising.

The nineteenth-century European migrations to the United States took place during the long age of blatant white supremacy, legal and extralegal, formal and informal; and as the patterns of segregation and discrimination emerged in the North and the South, the doors of opportunity were opened to white immigrants but closed to blacks and other nonwhites. European immigrants and their descendants explain their success as the result of their devotion to the work ethic and ignore a variety of other factors, such as the systematic exclusion of non-Caucasians from competition for employment. As white immigrants moved up in the social order, black workers and those of other nonwhite races could fill only the least desirable places in marginal labor, the sole places open to them.

Employers and white labor organizations joined together and locked blacks out of the working class, out of industrial employment. By the turn of the century the process of black job displacement, of removing black workers from jobs they had long held and replacing them with whites, was also prevalent in the North. Here, too, economic expansion and the quickened pace of industrialization gave rise to new and more attractive jobs to which blacks were denied entry. At the same time, the emergence of labor unions that excluded blacks on the basis of race also hastened the displacement of Northern blacks from skilled jobs.

Charles Hamilton Houston, the architect of the legal struggle against state-imposed racial segregation, described how in 1909 the Brotherhood of Locomotive Firemen and Enginemen and the Brotherhood of Railway Trainmen negotiated agreements with major railroads to prevent the hiring of black workers. Houston wrote in 1949: "For the past fifty years the Big Four Brotherhoods have been using every means in their power to drive the Negro train and engine service workers out of employment and create a 'racially closed shop' among the firemen, brakemen, switchmen, flagmen, and yardmen."[12]

Houston, who as general counsel for the Association of Colored Railway Trainmen and Locomotive Firemen, represented black workers in litigation against the all-white railway brotherhoods, described many examples of how the powerful railroad unions forced black workers out of employment.

Inch by inch, and yard by yard, down through the years, the brotherhoods have been choking off the employment rights of Negro train and engine service employees. In 1890 the Trainmen, the Conductors, the Firemen and the Switchmen's Mutual Aid Association demanded that all Negroes in the train, yard, and locomotive service of the Houston and Texas Central Railway System be removed and white men employed in their places. . . . In 1909 the Firemen's Brotherhood staged a bitter and violent strike against Negro firemen on the Georgia Railroad, demanding white supremacy and the replacement of Negro firemen by whites.[13]

A similar "history of aggression" against black workers also occurred in Northern states, and Houston concluded that the major railroad unions had established what he called "the Nordic closed shop" on American railroads.[14]

Very much the same pattern of black job displacement occurred in the building and construction trades, in shipbuilding, and elsewhere, as labor unions excluded nonwhites and refused to admit black workers into union-controlled apprenticeship and other training programs in a variety of skilled-craft occupations.[15] At a later period when manufacturing plants such as those in the steel industry were unionized, separate racial lines of promotion and segregated labor classifications were written into many industrial union contracts, with the result that black workers became even more rigidly limited to unskilled and menial job classifications.[16] The consequences of these patterns of discriminatory employment practices by organized labor and employers were a major factor in the barring of African Americans from full and equal participation in the economic life of the nation.

According to sociologist Robert Blauner, there is

clear evidence that immigrant groups benefited from racism. When blacks began to consolidate in skilled and unskilled jobs that yielded relatively decent wages and some security, German, Irish, and Italians came along to usurp occupation after occupation, forcing blacks out and down into the least skilled, marginal reaches of the economy. . . . Without such a combination of immigration and white racism, the Harlems and the South Chicagos might have become solid working-class and middle-class communities with the economic social resources to absorb and aid the incoming masses of Southerners, much as European ethnic groups have been able to do for their newcomers.[17]

The elimination of traditional patterns of job discrimination was required by Title VII, the employment section of the Civil Rights Act of 1964.[18] Therefore the act adversely affected the expectations of whites, because it compelled competition with black workers and other minority group members where none previously existed. White workers' expectations had become the norm, and any alteration of the norm was considered "reverse discrimination." When racial practices that have historically placed blacks at a disadvantage are removed to eliminate the present effects of past discrimination, whites believe that preferential treatment is given to blacks. But it is *the removal of the preferential treatment traditionally enjoyed by white workers at the expense of blacks as a class* that is at issue in the affirmative action controversy.

In many different occupations, including a variety of jobs in the public sector, white workers were able to begin their climb up the seniority ladder precisely because nonwhites were systematically excluded from the competition for jobs. Various union seniority systems were established at a time when racial minorities were banned from employment and union membership. Obviously blacks as a group, not just as individuals, constituted a class of victims who could not develop seniority status. A seniority system launched under these conditions inevitably becomes the institutionalized mechanism whereby whites as a group are granted racial privileges.

After long delay and much conflict, a new comprehensive body of law emerged that had great potential and gave hope to women and racial minorities in the labor force.[19] By 1986, affirmative action, the most effective remedy to eliminate the present effects of past discrimination seemed solidly established, but once again the forces of reaction prevailed as Ronald Reagan achieved one of his major goals, hastening the end of the Second Reconstruction. Reagan and Bush not only succeeded in reducing the protection of civil rights laws but also transformed the federal judiciary, once the foremost champion of minority rights, into a dangerous threat to civil rights.[20] And as the gains of the 1960s continued to be eroded, the nation became even more mean-spirited and self-deceiving on racial issues.

A major reason for the retreat on race was that after substantive civil rights enforcement began in the 1960s, there was intense opposition by Northern whites to compliance with the law, especially in regard to affirmative action, school desegregation, and job seniority. These and other issues now clearly affected the lives of urban whites. Earlier civil rights struggles were largely concentrated in the South, and advances were for the most part of a limited, symbolic nature that required no change in the daily lives of white people, especially those living in Northern cities. But after 1964, institutional change in the status of blacks directly impinged on the lives of whites, who sought to maintain their traditional race-connected privileges.

Racism in the history of the United States has not been an aberration. It has been systematized and structured into the functioning of the society's most important institutions. In the present as in the past, it is widely accepted as a basis for promoting the interests of whites. For many generations the assumptions of white supremacy were codified in the law, imposed by custom, and often enforced by violence. While the forms have changed, the legacy of white supremacy is expressed in the continuing patterns of racial discrimination, and for the vast majority of black and other nonwhite people, race and racism remain the decisive factors in their lives.

The civil rights movement of the 1960s registered many gains for African Americans, and especially successful was the historic struggle to eliminate the legal basis of racial segregation. But the movement failed to eliminate the great disparity in the economic status of blacks and whites, or to successfully confront the institutionalized patterns of job discrimination.

The potential of the 1964 Civil Rights Act, and indeed of the entire body of civil rights law, has not been realized, not only as a result of administrative and judicial nullification by administrations hostile to civil rights progress but also because of profound social and economic changes that have had a devastating impact upon the once stable black working class.

It is all too clear that the elimination of legal racism does not mean the elimination of racist patterns deeply embedded in the basic institutions of the society. It is also evident that there are powerful forces beyond the reach of legislative and judicial processes. The full awareness of these factors will certainly inform the civil rights movements of the future as they give the highest priority to economic issues, to confronting the institutional structures that are responsible for the permanently depressed economic status of African Americans. Now, forty years after *Brown* v. *Board of Education* and thirty years after the Civil Rights Act of 1964, race remains the great and enduring division of American society.

NOTES

1. *Scott* v. *Sandford*, (60 U.S. 393 (1857).
2. The literature on Reconstruction is extensive. The classic work is W.E.B. Du Bois, *Black Reconstruction in America, 1860–1880* (New York: S. A. Russell, 1956), reprint of original 1935 ed. Joel Williamson, *After Slavery: The Negro in South Carolina During Reconstruction* (Chapel Hill: University of North Carolina Press, 1965), is a valuable contribution. The major recent study is Eric Foner, *Reconstruction: America's Unfinished Revolution* (New York: Harper & Row, 1988). See also Julie Saville, *The Work of Reconstruction: From Slave to Wage Laborer in South Carolina, 1860–1872* (Cambridge: Cambridge University Press, 1994).
3. *Civil Rights Cases*, 109 U.S. 3 (1883), Harlan in dissent.
4. *Brown* v. *Board of Education*, 347 U.S. 483 (1954).
5. *Jones* v. *Alfred H. Mayer Co.*, 392 U.S. 409 (1968).
6. *Regents of the University of California* v. *Bakke*, 438 U.S. 265 (1978), Blackmun concurring in part and dissenting in part.
7. Ibid. Marshall concurring in part and dissenting in part.
8. *Harvard Encyclopedia of American Ethnic Groups*, edited by Stephan Thernstrom, (Cambridge, Mass.: Harvard University Press, 1980), p. 538.
9. For statistical data, see Warren R. Van Tine, *The Making of the Labor Bureaucrat: Union Leadership in the United States, 1870–1920* (Amherst: University of Massachusetts Press, 1973) pp. 9–28; Gerald Rosenblum, *Immigrant Workers: Their Impact on American Labor Radicalism* (New York: Basic Books, 1973), pp. 67–86. For an interesting discussion of the ethnic composition of Chicago's working class in 1890, see Hartmut Keil, "The German Immigrant Working Class of Chicago, 1875–90: Workers, Labor Leaders, and the Labor Movement," in *American Labor and Immigration History, 1877–1920's*, edited by Dirk Hoerder (Urbana: University of Illinois Press 1983), pp. 157–76.
10. *DeFunis* v. *Odegaard*, 416 U.S. 312 (1974).
11. See note 6, above.
12. Charles H. Houston, "Foul Employment Practices on the Rails" (based on a report to the Fortieth Annual Convention of the NAACP, Los Angeles, July 1949), *The Crisis*, October 1949, pp. 269–272. See also "The Elimination of Negro Firemen on American Railroads—A Study of the Evidence Adduced at the Hearing Before the President's

Committee on Fair Employment Practices," *Lawyers Guild Review*, 4 (1944): p. 321; and Herbert Hill, *Black Labor and the American Legal System* (Madison: University of Wisconsin Press, 1985), pp. 343–372.

13. Houston, "Foul Employment Practices on the Rails," p. 271.

14. Ibid.

15. The literature on this subject is extensive and includes Charles H. Wesley, *Negro Labor in the United States, 1850–1925* (New York: Russell and Russell, 1967), repr. of 1927 ed.; Sterling D. Spero and Abram L. Harris, *The Black Worker* (New York: Columbia University Press, 1931); Herbert R. Northrup, *Organized Labor and the Negro* (New York: Harper & Brothers, 1944); Philip S. Foner, *Organized Labor and the Black Worker* (New York: Praeger, 1974); and Herbert Hill, *Black Labor and the American Legal System*, (Madison: University of Wisconsin Press, 1985). See also Frank E. Wolfe, *Admission to American Trade Unions* (Baltimore: Johns Hopkins University Press, 1912), pp. 100–112. For a discussion of the racial practices of the United Mine Workers, see Herbert Hill, "Myth-Making as Labor History: Herbert Gutman and the United Mine Workers of America," *International Journal of Politics, Culture and Society* 2, 2, (Winter 1988): 132–200.

16. A typical example is *United States* v. *Bethlehem Steel Corp.*, 446 F. 2d 652 (2nd Cir. 1971). In this case involving the United Steelworkers of America in the Buffalo, New York, area, a federal court stated: "Job assignment practices were reprehensible. Over 80 percent of black workers were placed in eleven departments which contained the hotter and dirtier jobs in the plant. Blacks were excluded from higher paying and cleaner jobs." The court observed that discriminatory contract provisions were embodied in nationwide master agreements negotiated by the Steelworkers Union in 1962, 1965, and 1968. The court also stated: "The Lackawanna plant was a microcosm of classic job discrimination in the north, making clear why Congress enacted Title VII of the Civil Rights Act of 1964." On October 14, 1971, the court issued a decree defining as members of the affected class some sixteen hundred black steelworkers, members of the union, who were entitled to receive benefits as a result of the court's decision. It is significant to note that in the Bethlehem Steel case, the Court of Appeals for the Second Circuit commented on the expectations of white workers who benefited from discriminatory collective bargaining agreements: "their seniority advantages are not indefeasibly vested rights but mere expectations derived from a bargaining agreement subject to modification. . . . If relief under Title VII can be denied merely because the majority group of employees, who have not suffered discrimination, will be unhappy about it, there will be little hope of correcting the wrongs to which the Act is directed." The federal courts did not hesitate to apply the same approach in litigation involving other industrial unions.

17. Robert Blauner, *Racial Oppression in America* (New York: Harper & Row, 1972), p. 64.

18. Title VII of the Civil Rights Act of 1964, 42 U.S.C. 2000 (e) to 2000 (e-17). For a discussion, see Herbert Hill, "Black Workers, Organized Labor, and Title VII of the 1964 Civil Rights Act: Legislative History and Litigation Record," in *Race in America: The Struggle for Equality*, edited by Herbert Hill and James E. Jones, Jr. (Madison: University of Wisconsin Press, 1993), pp. 263–341.

19. Among the many instances where federal appellate courts sustained affirmative action remedies in cases involving employment discrimination are: *Contractors Association of Eastern Pennsylvania* v. *The Secretary of Labor*, 442 F.2d 159 (3rd Cir. 1971); *Associated General Contractors of Massachusetts, Inc.* v. *Altshuler*, 490 F.2d 9 (1st Cir. 1973); *Fullilove* v. *Klutznick* 448 U.S. 448 (1980); *United Steelworkers of America, AFL-CIO* v. *Weber*, 443 U.S. 1993 (1979); *Local 28, Sheet Metal Workers International Association* v. *EEOC*, 478 U.S. 421 (1986); and *Johnson* v. *Santa Clara County Transportation Agency*, 480 U.S. 616 (1987).

20. In commenting on a ruling by the U.S. Court of Appeals for the Fifth Circuit that threatened affirmative action admission policies by universities, Ted Shaw, associate director of the NAACP Legal Defense and Education Fund, stated, "This is a disturbing, troubling ruling, that's part of a pattern we're seeing in which some judges who were appointed by very ideologically conscious administrations are really emboldened to try to dismantle the entire body of case law in the area of race discrimination." Peter Applebome, "Ruling Threatens College Policies on Racial Entries," *The New York Times*, March 21, 1996, p. 1. Two of the three judges on the panel were appointed by President George Bush; the third was appointed by President Ronald Reagan.

SELECTED BIBLIOGRAPHY

Bell, Derrick. *And We Are Not Saved: The Elusive Quest for Racial Justice*. New York: Basic Books, 1987.
———. *Faces at the Bottom of the Well*. New York: Basic Books, 1992.
Blauner, Robert. *Racial Oppression in America*. New York: Harper & Row, 1972.
Du Bois, W.E.B. *Black Reconstruction in America, 1860–1880*. New York: S. A. Russell, 1956. Reprint of original 1935 edition.
———. *The Negro American Artisan*. Atlanta University Publication 17. Atlanta: Atlanta University Press, 1912.
———. *The Negro Artisan*. Atlanta University Publication 7. Atlanta: Atlanta University Press, 1902.
Foner, Eric. *Reconstruction: America's Unfinished Revolution*. New York: Harper & Row, 1988.
Foner, Philip S. *Organized Labor and the Black Worker*. New York: Praeger, 1974.
Fredrickson, George M. *The Black Image in the White Mind*. New York: Harper & Row, 1971.
Hacker, Andrew. *Two Nations*. New York: Charles Scribner's Sons, 1992.
Hill, Herbert. "Black Labor and Affirmative Action: An Historical Perspective." In *The Question of Discrimination: Racial Inequality in the U.S. Labor Market*. Edited by Steven Shulman and William A. Darity, Jr., Middletown, Conn.: Wesleyan University Press, 1989.
———. *Black Labor and the American Legal System*. Madison: University of Wisconsin Press, 1985.
———. "The Problems of Race in American Labor History," *Review in American History*, 24 (1995): pp. 189–208, no. 2.
———. "The Racial Practices of Organized Labor—The Age of Gompers and After," in *Employment, Race and Poverty*, Edited by Arthur M. Ross and Herbert Hill. New York: Harcourt, Brace & World, 1967.
Hill, Herbert and James E. Jones, Jr., eds. *Race in America: The Struggle for Equality*. Madison: University of Wisconsin Press, 1993, pp. 269–272.
Houston, Charles H. "Foul Employment Practices on the Rails." *The Crisis*, October, 1949.
Lieberson, Stanley. *A Piece of the Pie: Blacks and White Immigrants Since 1880*. Berkeley: University of California Press, 1980.
Northrup, Herbert R. *Organized Labor and the Negro*. New York: Harper & Brothers, 1944.
Omi, Michael and Howard Winant. *Racial Formation in the United States*. Second edition. New York: Routledge, 1994 .
Ransom, Roger L. and Richard Sutch. *One Kind of Freedom*. Cambridge: Cambridge University Press, 1977.

Roediger, David R. *The Wages of Whiteness*. London: Verso, 1991.

Rosenblum, Gerald. *Immigrant Workers: Their Impact on American Labor Radicalism*. New York, Basic Books, 1973.

Saville, Julie. *The Work of Reconstruction: From Slave to Wage Laborer in South Carolina, 1860–1872*. Cambridge: Cambridge University Press, 1994.

Saxton, Alexander. *The Rise and Fall of the White Republic*. London: Verso, 1990.

Spero, Sterling D. and Abram L. Harris. *The Black Worker*. New York: Columbia University Press, 1931.

Steinberg, Stephan. *Turning Back*. Boston: Beacon Press, 1995.

Thernstrom, Stephan, ed. Harvard Encyclopedia of American Ethnic Groups. Cambridge: Harvard University Press, 1980.

Wesley, Charles H. *Negro Labor in the United States: 1850–1925*. New York: Russell and Russell, 1967. Reprint of original 1927 edition.

Williamson, Joel. *After Slavery: The Negro in South Carolina During Reconstruction*. Chapel Hill: University of North Carolina Press, 1965.

Wolfe, Frank E. *Admission to American Trade Unions*. Baltimore: Johns Hopkins University Press, 1912.

CHAPTER 2

Race, Civil Rights, and the New Immigrants: Nativism and the New World Order

Evelyn Hu-DeHart

HISTORICAL BACKGROUND

The idea of "immigrants" and "immigration" has been central to the project of writing the dominant narrative of American history, and undergirds the construction of the American identity. "We are a nation of immigrants," children are taught to intone from an early age, a mantra reinforced by the powerful symbol and image of the Statue of Liberty in the New York harbor beckoning immigrants—the poor, tired, huddled masses of Europe—to come to America and begin life anew.

This construction of America as a nation of immigrants who succeed once they are in this land is powerfully evoked by the Yale historian Donald Kagan:

Except for the slaves brought from Africa, most came voluntarily, as families and individuals, usually eager to satisfy desires that could not be met in their former homelands. They swiftly become citizens and, within a generation or so, Americans. In our own time finally—African Americans also have achieved freedom, equality before the law, and full citizenship. . . . What they have in common and what brings them together is a system of laws and beliefs that shaped the establishment of the country, a system developed within the context of Western Civilization. (Kagan 1990)

This dominant, official narrative is informed by a "triumphalist" view of American history, which is characterized as an unbroken string of successes, a relentless march toward freedom and democracy for all—all informed by the traditions and values of Western civilization. Indeed, America—meaning the United States—becomes the ultimate embodiment of Western culture, its most triumphant moment. Moreover, this version of American history would have been impossible without making the immigrant central to its narrative, because it was the immigrant who introduced Western civilization to the New World.

Triumphalists are reluctant to deal with the inconveniences of their historical construction, although Professor Kagan had to admit a caveat for the millions of Africans brought over as slaves. Even ardent triumphalists are hard put to characterize slaves as "voluntary immigrants," but remain generally unwilling to acknowledge other inconsistencies. What about Native Americans? How do they fit into this picture of immigrants building America around Western values? What about the first Mexican Americans, who were incorporated into America when the Treaty of Guadalupe Hidalgo was signed in 1848, giving the United States approximately half of Mexico's national territory and all the people living on it? They did not have to take one step while the international boundary was redrawn around them.

That left one group of non-Europeans who could reasonably be characterized as "immigrants"—the Chinese coolies who came first to California, then spread out to other mining states of the American West—in that they were not slaves, nor were they incorporated territorially. Consisting almost exclusively of men, the early Chinese immigrants provided cheap and docile labor for the mines and railroads of the Western states. But by 1882, responding to pressures mounted against the Chinese by Irish and other white immigrant workers who had made their way to California, attracted by its dynamic "frontier" economy, Congress passed a law denying further admission to Chinese laborers. Forty years later, in 1924, the Second Quota Act announced that "no alien ineligible to citizenship"—meaning all Asians (Japanese, Koreans, South Indians, Filipinos)—would be allowed into the country.

This ban made explicit the racialist construction of citizenship that had always been implied by the U.S. Naturalization Law, by which immigrants gained citizenship and thereby all civil and constitutional rights. Enacted shortly after the Republic was founded, in 1790, this law offered citizenship only to "free white persons." In other words, Asians, even while permitted to enter this country, formed a peculiar category of immigrants, those deemed "ineligible for citizenship."

Once this official differentiation between those immigrants who were always meant to become citizens (i.e., immigrants from Europe and heirs to Western civilization) and immigrants ineligible for citizenship is exposed, the triumphalist version of history can be challenged. Indeed, an alternative narrative has been forcefully presented by the historian Alexander Saxton:

America's supposed openness to newcomers throughout most of its history has been racially selective. By the time of Jefferson and Jackson the nation had already assumed the form of a racially exclusive democracy—democratic in the sense that it sought to provide equal opportunity for the pursuit of happiness by its white citizens through the enslavement of African Americans, extermination of Indians, and territorial expansion at the expense of Indians and Mexicans. If there was an "American orientation" to newcomers, *it was not toward giving equal opportunity to all but toward inviting entry to white Europeans and excluding others.* It is true that the United States absorbed a variety of cultural patterns among European immigrants at the same time that it was erecting a white supremacist social structure. *Moderately tolerant of European ethnic diversity, the nation remained adamantly intolerant of racial diversity*. It is this crucial difference that has been permitted to drop from sight. (Saxton 1990: 10; italics added)

In short, Saxton compels us to open our eyes to this critical separation between white, European immigrants deemed potential citizens, and nonwhite immigrants —Mexicans and Asians—grudgingly allowed into this country at various moments of territorial and economic expansion to fulfill labor demands, but never meant to become citizens and, hence, permanent members and of full participants in society. In the words of immigration historian Reed Ueda: "The founders assumed that persons of European ancestry would constitute the community of citizens. Thus they did not seek equal citizenship for blacks or naturalization rights for those who were not 'free-white person' (Ueda 1994:18).

U.S. immigration laws of the early-to-mid-twentieth century, which were based on national origins quotas, confirmed, reinforced, and consolidated this racial (and racist) dichotomy between the two groups of immigrants. The U.S. Naturalization Law, which was ideologically consonant with the immigration laws, remained in effect until after World War II.

There was, however, one serious crack in this otherwise solid edifice erected to keep out the undesirables from gaining a permanent foothold in American society. What of the children born to parents ineligible for citizenship, given the existence of the Fourteenth Amendment to the U.S. Constitution, which granted citizenship strictly on the basis of birth on U.S. territory, regardless of race? One bright light in this otherwise bleak period for Asian immigrants was the ruling by the U.S. Supreme Court in the case of *United States* v. *Wong Kim Ark* in 1898, which ratified the citizenship of second generation Chinese Americans, thus bringing "the Constitution squarely into conflict with the federal naturalization law making race, not place of birth, the touchstone of naturalization" (Ueda 1994: 28). On the other hand, in 1922 the Supreme Court confirmed the "white-only" principle for citizenship in *Ozawa* v. *United States*, declaring once and for all that Japanese aliens were not white, and hence not eligible for American citizenship. We shall return to this point of citizenship for children born in the United States to noncitizen parents later on in this chapter.

Even as Chinese, then other Asians, were being excluded from admission to the United States, Mexicans began crossing the international border in larger numbers, in many ways replacing Chinese as labor migrants in mining, railroad construction, and agriculture. The original one hundred thousand or so Mexican Americans came with the territorial incorporation in 1848; most of them were Spanish-speaking mestizos, that is, people of mixed European and indigenous heritage. Indigenous tribal communities, such as the Tohono O'odham (Papagos) of Arizona, whose traditional homeland straddled the border, were permitted to go back and forth without documents (Silko 1994: 414). During the nineteenth century, documents such as visas were not required, and most Mexicans moved back and forth, reflecting the vicissitudes of the border economy.

From the Liberal ascendance to power in Mexico through the turbulent years of the Mexican Revolution (1910–1917), Mexicans were driven by loss of land and livelihood, then by civil wars and economic devastation, to seek employment in the United States By the early twentieth century, they had ventured well beyond California and the Southwest, attracted by agriculture, fishing, lumbering, and other industries in the Northwest, and by agricultural, railroad, and factory jobs in the Midwest (in time making Chicago, after Los Angeles, the site of the second largest concentration of Mexicans). During World War I, the acute labor shortage made Mexican workers especially vital, causing the United States to lift all barriers to Mexican entry, including bans on contract labor. The government also experimented with a "guest worker" program that granted "temporary passes" to Mexican workers, and with relaxing head tax and literacy tests required by the Immigration Act of 1917.

While Asians were kept out and Mexicans were allowed in, the country also experienced the largest wave of European immigrants from 1880 to 1920. Up to twelve million southern and eastern Europeans—Italians, Slavs, and Jews— settled mainly in the East and Midwest. Although considered much less desirable than their western and northern European (Anglo and Protestant) predecessors, on the ethnic hierarchy of immigrants based on the criterion of "assimilability," they were nevertheless placed clearly above the Asians and the Mexicans, groups deemed inherently inferior and immutably "foreign."

Notwithstanding, the Palmer raids of 1919 and the early 1920s (which rounded up some six thousand suspected immigrant supporters of politically radical causes, five hundred or so of whom were eventually deported), the most serious nativist movement in the early twentieth century was directed toward Mexicans. During the Depression years of the late 1920s and early 1930s, hundreds of thousands of Mexicans and Mexican Americans (U.S.-born Mexicans, hence U.S. citizens according to the Fourteenth Amendment) were rounded up by government agents and deported to Mexico. A well-orchestrated, state-sponsored anti-Mexican hysteria, blaming Mexican workers for massive unemployment, justified this unprecedented act of deportation. By then, the use of Mexicans as a reserve supply of labor for U.S. capital had become firmly established. In addition, the deployment and manipulation of this reserve, so readily available and poised on the long border with Mexico, produced a "revolving door" strategy that saw the United States not only *alternating* between letting Mexicans in and keeping them out but also, at times, *simultaneously* deporting and importing them. Such was the case during the Depression, when the Department of Agriculture intervened on behalf of the California growers to ensure their supply of cheap Mexican laborers (Cockcroft 1986: 60–61).

Paradoxically, deportation and importation of Mexicans occur simultaneously and for identical reasons: to provide scapegoats for society's economic problems; to guarantee a large surplus of workers in the labor pool, in order to meet production needs or to hold the general wage level down; to deter other workers from seeking better wages or work conditions by implying that they can always be replaced; and to make things difficult for potential labor organizers while assuring a pool of potential scabs. In sum, the deportation-importation of Mexicans serves to keep workers intimidated, divided, and confused (Cockcroft 1986: 42).

By the twentieth century, the United States began to keep track of "illegal" immigrants from Mexico, a problem the government made sure to correct with their next major initiative regarding Mexican labor migration.

Relatively few immigrants came to the United States after the 1920s, when the last surge of European immigration had peaked. Asian immigration continued to be severely restricted by exclusionary laws and national origins quotas. Recurrent labor demands, however, did open the borders to labor migrants from Canada; about 1.25 million arrived between 1920 and 1950s. The U.S. territory of Puerto Rico became another new recruitment ground for U.S. capital. But it was Mexico that once again came to the rescue.

To meet high wartime demands in 1942 and for over two decades afterward, the U.S. government devised an official labor contracting system ostensibly to regulate and control the entry and supply of Mexican workers for the U.S. agriculture and industry. The bracero program admitted farmworkers on short-term contracts that were supposed to guarantee work and living arrangements. Mexicans admitted under this program were classified as foreign laborers, not as immigrants. By the end of the *bracero* program in 1967, 4.7 million Mexicans had entered the United States under its terms (Ueda 1994:3 3–34). During this time, the revolving door continued to operate, for the bracero program did not function continuously; rather, it was halted and restarted numerous times as labor demand in the United States ebbed and flowed. The tide of illegal immigration did not subside, however, as Mexicans overstayed their permits once admitted as braceros; others—the *mojados* (wetbacks)—simply preferred to enter and seek work on their own terms, to elude the restrictions of the official bracero program.

Following the well-established revolving door strategy, the U.S. government continued to deport "illegals" even as it recruited braceros. The fear of illegals reached a feverish pitch in 1954, in the midst of the bracero program, when the government launched "Operation Wetback," a dragnet that indiscriminately rounded up one to two million Mexican-looking people, regardless of citizenship or immigration status, for deportation to Mexico. The terror instilled in Mexicans limited the accessibility of labor organizers to Mexican workers. "In other words, the U.S. was sending a double message: Mexicans get out; Mexicans come in. The door revolved, Mexicans were harassed, wages held steady or dropped, and labor stability was assured for at least another decade" (Cockcroft 1986:78)

U.S. immigration history took the next dramatic turn in the late 1960s, as the Vietnam War began to wind down. By then, a number of fundamental changes in the U.S. immigration and naturalization laws had taken place. First, in 1943, the United States repealed the Chinese Exclusion Act of 1882. In 1952, the McCarran-Walter Act repealed the race-based naturalization law, although it retained national origins quotas for immigrants first established in 1924.

In 1965, major immigration reform finally abolished national origins quotas, which had severely limited immigration from the Third World. This change occurred within the context of the emerging civil rights and antiwar movements, which challenged race and racism at home and abroad.

Beginning with actions taken during World War II, followed by the Korean War and the Vietnam War, later the class-based social revolutions of Central America, the United States firmly took its place on the world scene as an economic and political global power, the main bulwark against capitalism's nemesis, communism and the Soviet Union. Unable to distinguish the genuine, intense and internally generated desire by colonies of Western imperial powers for national liberation from the expansionist needs of Soviet communism, U.S. political and military intervention in hot spots all over Asia, Latin America, and the Caribbean, and to a lesser extent in Africa, created a new kind of immigrants pressing on American borders. These were refugees fleeing their ravaged homelands. With few exceptions, most came from the Third World, the source of immigrants previously defined as "ineligible for citizenship."

Even more numerous than refugees were immigrants—individuals or families—from Third World countries previously excluded from moving to the United States until the 1964 immigration reform removed those barriers. The increasingly globalized economy after World War II produced surplus populations (on both the high and the low end of the educational and economic scales) in dependent capitalist societies. From 1965 to 1990, a totally unexpected immigration surge of unprecedented numbers has appeared. Totaling over ten million, this influx has seemingly caught the nation by surprise. Certainly, the framers of immigration reform in the 1960s had no way of predicting the character and scope of this new wave, 90 percent of which are non-European, and therefore nonwhite.

THE NEW WORLD ORDER

When the Soviet Union collapsed during his watch, President George Bush declared the dawn of the New World Order. What he meant by this was not made clear, but anyone observing the world and the domestic U.S. scenes can certainly point to a number of new developments, realignments, and rearrangements. First and foremost was the end of the Cold War, which meant that the world no longer revolved around the East-West, capitalist-communist axis. The end of this ideological war had immediate repercussions on the economies of the superpowers and, indeed, worldwide. For the United States, it meant making a transition from a heavily defense-driven economy to a "peace" economy, one based on other imperatives, such as trade. Thus, both President Bush, a Republican, and President Clinton, a Democrat, were intent to get NAFTA—a North-South trade relationship—passed. Similarly, both presidents were willing to suspend human rights considerations to retain trade relations with China, the world's most populous nation. No state is as central to this transition, yet more caught in its difficulties, than California, now in the midst of persistent post-Cold War recession. The California economy is the country's second weakest, having experienced four years of budget shortfalls.

During the boom years of the war and postwar era, California experienced a population explosion induced by internal migrants from elsewhere in the United States, as well as by the refugees and new immigrants from Asia, Mexico, and

Latin America as described above. In addition to a rise in sheer numbers, the nature of the population became even more diverse. Because 90 percent of the new immigrants come from Third World countries, they swelled the numbers of U.S. minorities already in California, making it a "majority minority" state by 1990. As the gateway for Asians crossing the Pacific and for Mexicans venturing across the U.S.-Mexican border, California has absorbed some 40 percent of the newcomers: refugees, asylum seekers, and immigrants.

According to the 1990 census, foreign-born citizens and residents of the U.S. number 19.7 million, constituting 8 percent of the total U.S. population, a proportion considerably smaller than the 15 percent foreign-born at the turn of the twentieth century. The vast majority—85 percent—of the newcomers are legal immigrants. Only 13 percent are undocumented (2.5 million), and they account for just 1 percent of the total U.S. population of 250 million (Cole 1994:410; Fix and Passel 1994:4, 21). One-third of the foreign-born have become naturalized citizens; half are legal permanent residents; 6 percent entered as "humanitarian" admissions, that is, as refugees or asylum seekers; and five hundred thousand to eight hundred thousand are here on temporary visas (students, businessmen, etc.).

Only about one-third of the undocumented are from Mexico, and slightly less are from Central America and the Caribbean. Putting it another way, four out of ten cross the U.S.-Mexican border illegally. Six out of ten enter legally and overstay their visas. Thirteen percent of the undocumented come from Europe and Canada, and 11 eleven percent from Asia (Fix and Passel 1994: 24–25).

These dramatic demographic changes are taking place within the context of a multicultural discourse that emerged in the wake of the civil rights movement, which in turn spawned a series of ethnic pride and empowerment projects: black power, brown power, red power, and yellow power. Multiculturalism has infiltrated every institution, from government to business (where it is best known as "managing diversity"), and especially higher education. But even as the rhetoric and politics of multiculturalism empower racial-ethnic minorities, they further destabilize the traditional white "majority," already shaken and shrunken by the rapidly changing demographics.

Another way of describing the demographic changes in California is that the historical white majority is no longer so. Moreover, not only is the white proportion in the population declining, but it is aging as well. In other words, along with the "colorization" of California there is the "graying" of white Californians. Californians of color not only are becoming the numerical majority, but they are heavily concentrated in the younger age categories. In many urban districts, they overwhelmingly predominate in the schools. The student bodies of leading universities in California—Berkeley, UCLA, Stanford—are at or near "majority minority" status. Minorities are also the majority of the labor force, both employed and unemployed.

The middle class has also become more integrated—Blacks, Latinos and Asians having joined its ranks—but the political and economic elite remains largely white. This elite and this middle class watched on TV, with horror and from behind locked doors in the comfort of their homes, as Los Angeles erupted into the nation's first multicultural urban uprising in April 1992 (Kwong 1991: 44–46; Mann 1993).

Besides the African American urban underclass—venting their frustration by looting and burning the shops of Korean immigrants, whose small businesses have helped revitalize the neighborhoods that were abandoned by white businesses after the Watts riot of the late 1960s—new immigrants from Mexico and Latin America also joined in the melee. In fact, half of those arrested were Latinos. While the Koreans concentrated on building small businesses in poor neighborhoods, Latinos took many of the recently created, low-paying manufacturing and service jobs. In this new urban economy of Los Angeles, the longtime black minority was left out (Davis). The L.A. uprising further destabilized an elite and middle class already made insecure by the post-Cold War recession that California seems unable to move out of.

THE RISE OF NATIVISM IN CALIFORNIA

The search for a way to explain California's diminishing quality of life landed on the defenseless backs of the new immigrants. Particularly singled out for scrutiny and opprobrium are the undocumented immigrants, or, as the media, politicians, and anti-immigrant forces prefer to call them, "illegal aliens." The need to scapegoat some group in our midst for society's ills has given rise to a new nativist movement in California, one that will surely spread across the West, the Southwest, and the nation.

Technically speaking, anyone crossing the border into the United States without proper documents, or anyone overstaying an authorized visit to the United States, becomes an illegal immigrant. They come in all races, colors, and ethnicities, and from all corners of the world. In New York, for example, the largest groups of illegals are Irish, Italians, and Poles (Sontag 1993).

In California, Texas, and Arizona, however, illegal aliens have become practically synonymous with Mexicans, and secondarily Asians and other immigrants from the non-Western world. The racialized illegal immigrant is clearly evident in current political discourse and well planted in popular public perception. The category of "illegal alien" is more than just a legal question; it is equally a social construction with definite racial overtones.

Illegal aliens attained national notoriety in the late 1980s, when Congress debated a new round of immigration reform. The major thrust of the Simpson-Mazzoli bill, later incorporated into the 1988 Immigration Reform and Control Act (IRCA), was to deter illegal immigration by denying such persons employment through "employer sanctions." In other words, it attempted to shift the burden of proof on to those who did the hiring, by holding employers responsible for ascertaining the immigration status of job-seekers. The mechanism did not work well, however, for employers risked fines in order to hire cheap laborers, and the state of California under Governor Wilson never enthusiastically enforced it.

IRCA also contained an amnesty plan for illegal aliens. For a brief period of time, illegal aliens who could prove continuous residence in the United States for five years—by showing such evidence as pay stubs, rent and utility bill receipts, precisely the kind of records that the undocumented are unlikely to have or to save—could regularize their status, become legal permanent residents, and eventually citizens. The point of this measure was to further isolate, marginalize, and criminalize the vast majority of undocumented immigrants, who were unable to provide proof of continuous residence.

From the enactment of IRCA into the mid-1990s, the social construction of illegal aliens as an unsavory and very undesirable social element continued to take shape. In short time, illegal aliens ceased to be merely those who enter the country without proper documents. They are the dark-skinned Arab/Muslim religious fundamentalist and terrorist who blows up the World Trade Center in New York City; the black Caribbean sociopath who shoots innocent passengers on the Long Island commuter train; the pregnant Mexican welfare cheat who crosses the border to San Diego to have babies who then become U.S. citizens and in turn enable the mother to claim welfare benefits; the unassimilable Southeast Asian war refugees too eager to take any job at any wage, thus depressing the wage scale and stealing the livelihood of bonafide, longtime Americans; the Mexican and Asian youth gangs contributing to urban crime problem; the single Hispanic men loitering on suburban street corners, urinating in the streets, sleeping under bushes in residential yards; they are the children crowding into the urban public schools, demanding bilingual education and other special services; the families without insurance who jam our public hospital emergency rooms. Television and the print media provide numerous other examples of what one commentator has termed "nativist paranoia" (Cole 1993). The image and rhetoric invasion a century ago, has been especially effective (Kadetsky 1994; Rodriguez 1993; Weintraub 1994).

In short, illegal aliens are terrorists, criminals, welfare cheats, and freeloaders, social burdens who exacerbate our urban crime problem and severely strain the public resources that our taxes support. Gone is the idea that immigrants have built this country and exemplify prized American virtues of family and hard work. In fact, when some immigrants work too hard, that is turned against them, because their work ethic depresses wages and deprives American citizens of their livelihood. A common refrain is "Asians are unfair because they work too hard" (Rodriguez 1993).

Local, state and national politicians, notably Governor Wilson of California, Governor Chiles of Florida (faced with a unique flood of undesirable black Haitians and more desirable "white" Cubans), Senators Feinstein and Boxer of California, and a host of other elected officials, have seized on the illegal alien problem for political gain. They figure it is a no-lose proposition for them, since illegal aliens cannot vote and have no voice. In contrast, by getting tough with illegal aliens, they have everything to gain with those who do vote, by providing them with a convenient, ready scapegoat for their frustrations. In the 1994 elections, incumbent governor Pete Wilson won reelection with his anti-immigrant stance by closing a twenty-point gap with his opponent, Kathleen Brown, who was more reluctant to use the illegal alien issue in her campaign. On the national level, the Commission on Immigration Reform (CIR), chaired by former Texas congresswoman and professor Barbara Jordan (who died in 1996), Speaker Newt Gingrich and the Republicans' "Contract with America," and President Clinton himself have all entered the ring with their boxing gloves on. As Democratic political consultant Mark McKinnon noted rather sadly during the 1994 elections, when he saw Governor Ann Richards jump on the immigrant-bashing bandwagon: "Immigration is a potential powder keg kind of issue. It plays to the politics of fear, and the politics of fear can be very persuasive" (Berke 1994).

Indeed, in this New World Order of financial instability and political insecurity, at what price to the human rights of illegal aliens, and the civil and constitutional rights of all other Americans, immigrants and citizens alike, are we willing, as a nation, to solve a problem allegedly caused by 1 percent of the population? In order to exclude those among us designated foreign and undesirable, are too many Americans willing to create a fascist or police state built on racialist constructions and racist notions? A close examination of Proposition 187, also known as the "Save Our State" ballot initiative, which passed by a two to one margin in California in November 1994, and which is now certain to spread across the nation, sheds light on these troubling questions.

PROPOSITION 187: PLAYING THE "IMMIGRATION CARD"

Building on the theme first sounded by presidential candidate Pat Buchanan during the 1992 presidential campaign, when he proposed building a "Berlin Wall" on the U.S.-Mexican border, liberal incumbent Senator Barbara Boxer and gubernatorial candidate Kathleen Brown advanced ideas to militarize the border, such as posting members of the National Guard along its two thousand miles.

Indeed, a pilot project of this kind was already underway with "Operation Hold the Line" in El Paso, Texas, where a beefed-up Border Patrol force of four hundred armed agents claimed to have reduced monthly crossings from ten thousand to two thousand. Of course, the eight thousand who were unable to cross at El Paso merely went to other crossing points. So, in late 1994, at the San Diego crossing in California a similar plan was launched named "Operation Gatekeeper." Most recently, in February 1995, the Nogales border crossing in Arizona was promised additional armed agents, because by then it had become the new "hot spot" (Ayres 1995). In time, according to the Berlin Wall logic, a new Iron Curtain will rise in the New World Order, this time along a North-South divide.

Champions of the border militarization strategy do not, of course, admit that the premises on which it rests are highly disputable: that most illegal immigrants arrive via the U.S.-Mexican border, which is simply not true, as already noted in this chapter that this long border can be permanently and seamlessly sealed, which is questionable, given the cost; and that sealing the border would deter Mexicans from crossing. There is also the question of NAFTA, which, after all, guarantees an open border for trade between Mexico and the United States, not to mention the fact that reverse crossings—U.S. citizens freely entering into Mexico for vacations, vacation homes, babies to adopt, servants—is taken for granted (Rodriguez 1993).

Another simplistic but emotional notion that politicians have successfully planted in the popular imagination is the need to remove the "welfare magnet" as an incentive for illegal immigrants. The assumption here is that generous social benefits available in California have motivated Mexicans to invade the state. "Why does the U.S. Government continue to reward illegal immigration . . . at such costs to the American people?" Governor Wilson plaintively asked in his open letter to President Clinton (Wilson 1993).

These ideas for immigration control were embodied in the "Save Our State" initiative, or Proposition 187, which California voters approved by a two to one margin in November 1994. So popular was this initiative that Governor Wilson came from behind and won reelection on its coattails, and phantom senatorial candidate Michael Huffington nearly unseated incumbent Dianne Feinstein. Proposition 187 contained these major provisions:

- Deny children of illegal immigrants access to public education; those in school would be expelled immediately.

- Deny illegal immigrants nonemergency medical care and police assistance.

- Require teachers, school administrators, doctors and other health care and social workers to report anyone merely suspected of being an illegal immigrant to Immigration authorities, in effect, forcing them to act as informants for the government.

In addition to the above restrictions that became Prop. 187, Wilson had advocated two other even more extreme measures that could not be included because their enactment would fall under federal jurisdiction. First, he argued for a constitutional amendment to deny U.S. citizenship to children born on U.S. soil to illegal immigrants. Because this clearly contravened the Fourteenth Amendment, Wilson offered the rather lame rationalization that the Fourteenth was enacted only to validate the citizenship of former slaves and their children. He was either ignorant, or simply denied the existence, of the Supreme Court case *United States* v. *Wong Kim Ark* (1898), in which the United States affirmed the application of the Fourteenth Amendment to a U.S.-born child of Chinese immigrants who were themselves denied citizenship under the U.S. Naturalization Law (Wilson 1994; Tamayo 1993)

The second drastic measure Wilson advocated was the use of tamperproof I.D. cards to identify "legal U.S. residents." Thus, anyone caught without one could be presumed illegal. This idea presaged the one that Barbara Jordan's Commission on Immigration Reform proposed one year later, which was a national computer registry of the names and social security numbers of all citizens and aliens authorized to work in the United States, so that employers could check the status of job applicants (CIR News 1994; Pear 1994). Again, anyone not in the registry can be presumed illegal.

So uncharacteristically radical were these proposals that to even to many conservatives, such as A. M. Rosenthal of the *New York Times*, erstwhile presidential candidates William Bennett and Jack Kemp, and Linda Chavez of the

Manhattan Institute, mandatory I.D. cards and a national registry constituted "immigrant-hunting computer banks and work licenses that cut away at every American's liberty" (Rosenthal 1994), or smacked of totalitarian "big government meeting the information age" (*The American Experiment* 1995). In fact, to these conservatives, all of Prop. 187 is an overreaction, a "nativist abomination," in the words of conservative columnist William Safire (Safire 1994).

These otherwise powerful conservative voices found their objections falling on deaf ears, for the anti-immigration movement had gathered much too much momentum to be sidetracked. Apparently nobody bothered to check key underlying assumptions in Prop. 187 against the facts. Will people really stop trying to come to the United States if we exclude them from schools, welfare benefits, and health care, or even from citizenship? Or will they keep coming to rich and developed nations of the world as long as theirs remain poor and underdeveloped? Do immigrants—legal and illegal—really take out more from society in benefits than they contribute in taxes and job creation? Will people in general, or even government authorities, really take care to distinguish between legal and illegal immigrants once the punitive measures are put in place? Will California and the nation prosper again once there are no more illegal immigrants? Are illegal immigrants in particular, and immigrants in general, becoming a superfluous population, no longer required by our economy as a reserve labor force? In other words, can we really shut the "revolving door" that is the U.S.-Mexican border?

Although the impetus for Prop. 187 came from a range of grassroots middle class groups in southern California, intellectual guidance and resources came from a well known, anti-immigrant national organization. Feeding much of the hysteria and mis/disinformation behind Wilson's gubernatorial campaign and Prop. 187 was the Federation for American Immigration Reform (FAIR), whose well known agenda is to significantly curb all immigration to the United States. Cofounded by former Colorado governor Richard Lamm, a longtime proponent of Zero Population Growth, FAIR membership numbers some fifty thousand, and the organization's operating budget is $2.5 million. Its California director is Alan Nelson, Immigration and Naturalization Service (INS) commissioner under Reagan. He wrote the "Save Our State" ballot initiative with former INS colleague Harold Ezell, who coordinated the many grassroots anti-immigrant groups into the successful Prop. 187 campaign. Among large financial donors to Prop. 187 was state Senator Don Rogan, well known for his association with the white supremacist Christian Identity movement (Kadetsky 1994).

FAIR's national director, Dan Stein, knows exactly how to fan the fears of its largely older white male membership, whose insecurity has deepened with the state's worsening economy. In a FAIR publication, he pointed to a "bloody political battle" if immigration was not immediately curtailed, and predicted that if the problem was not settled by "effective political leadership," it would be "settled in the streets." Such alarmist sentiments, Frank Sharry of the National Immigration Forum stated, smacked of Nazi and skinhead pronouncements in Nazi Germany (Kershner 1993). Journalist Mark Cooper agreed, noting that what Rodney King did to bring out and heighten black-Asian tension, Prop. 187 did for black-Latino tension. Its passage "has already—and perhaps irreversibly—deepened the racial divides that rip this state like so many seismic faults and portend an almost unimaginable chain of political earthquakes in years to come" (Cooper 1994).

Sharry also criticized FAIR's Alan Nelson, who praised Wilson for taking a "brave stand on illegal aliens," at the same time feeding him dubious "facts" and wildly exaggerated "statistics" about borders out of control, invasions of undocumented immigrants, and their excessive use of social services. In addition to presenting claims of the cost of illegal immigrants to the California economy, Wilson criminalized the immigrants by the calculation that they alone "could fill eight state prisons to design capacity" (Wilson 1993).

Sharry countered Wilson's and Nelson's allegations with research conducted by the Urban Institute of Washington, D.C., and other independent scholars. First, he noted that most undocumented immigrants, fearful of being discovered and deported, tend not to use social services and in any case are ineligible for most. Even legal immigrants are barred from receiving cash benefits for three years. For example, during IRCA's amnesty program in the late 1980s, less than 1 percent of those who sought legalization received general assistance, such as Social Security, supplementary security income, workers' compensation, or unemployment insurance. Less than 0.50 percent received food stamps or Aid to Families with Dependent Children.

Sharry further noted that the vast majority of the legalized immigrants were working—83 percent compared to with 77 percent of the general population. Men and women of the legalized population worked more hours per week than other men and women in the workforce, usually with no overtime pay. Moreover, even those legalized under IRCA's amnesty plan were barred from receiving most social benefits for five years. Sharry concluded: "These figures make clear that undocumented immigrants are not the burden on our country that Mr. Nelson portrays them as being, nor is illegal immigration so great a problem as he states" (Sharry 1993). He vigorously protested FAIR's unscrupulous tactics of perpetuating ideas that immigrants drain resources and fanning fears that they diminish California's quality of life (Kershner 1993).

Precise, careful research undertaken at the Urban Institute researchers suggests that immigrants, legal and illegal, contribute much more in taxes paid than they cost in services received. They also create more jobs than they fill, directly by starting new businesses and indirectly through expenditures on goods and services. According to the 1990 census, total immigrant income in 1989 was $285 billion. Subtracting estimated cost of services received, Michael Fix and Jeffrey Passel of the Urban Institute calculated a positive net balance of $25–30 billion. In other words, immigrants "add up to an economic boon to America" (Rosenthal 1994; Fix and Passel 1994: 47–51). These researchers also discerned no appreciable negative effect by working immigrants on wages, and no more than 1 percent displacement by immigrants of native American workers. If immigrants displaced anyone, they conclude, it is likely to be other recent immigrants (Fix and Passel 1994: 47–51). At the end of their careful study of the issues surrounding immigrants, legal and illegal, Fix and Passel suggested that, contrary to growing popular perception that immigrants are a drag on the economy, they "may be a key factor in future job creation and improving the Unites States' competitiveness in an increasingly global economy" (Fix and Passel 1994: 71).

Since the November 1994 elections, immigrant bashing did not abate; in fact, it soon spread to national politics. Republicans on the national level and President Clinton himself have chimed in with anti-immigrant measures. Ostensibly concerned only with illegal aliens, Clinton reiterated a number of popular myths about them in his State of the Union address of January 1995:

The jobs they hold might otherwise be held by citizens or legal immigrants. The public services they use impose burdens on our taxpayers. That's why our administration has moved aggressively to secure our borders more, by hiring a record number of new border guards, by deporting twice as many criminal aliens as ever before, by cracking down on illegal hiring, by barring welfare benefits to illegal aliens (Clinton 1995).

Going one step further was the Republicans' "Contract with America," which moved against its next target: "immigration itself, the concept of America as a haven for refugees and a place of economic hope for some of those who stupidly fail to be born in America" (Rosenthal 1994). Its welfare reform clause included a provision to exclude legal immigrants from over sixty federal programs, including education loans and scholarships, housing, immunization, Medicaid-Medicare, and school breakfast and lunch programs (Dong 1994).

In California, illegal alien bashing may have reached new heights immediately after the election. Refusing to concede defeat to Democrat Dianne Feinstein for the Senate seat, Republican candidate Michael Huffington aired a radio ad with the incredible claim that he had "evidence that the recent election of California was riddled with illegal alien voting." Prop. 187 author Harold Ezell set up a Voter Fraud Task Force phone number (800 FRAUD 90) (Claiborne 1994). All this seemed to have been another inflammatory tactic to stir up and maintain anti-immigrant fervor after the elections.

In the end, of course, no amount of immigrant bashing can deny the fact that California growers continue to rely on Mexican and other immigrant labor. Despite their silence on 187 during the campaign because "you don't want to offend the governor," Ed Angstadt, president of the Grower-Shipping Vegetable Association of Central California, admitted as much: "We need all those people. You can't take a position against people you rely on to work for you" (Chavez 1994). In fact, Wilson knew that as well, otherwise, why would he have expressed support for a guest worker program during a speech at the Heritage Foundation (the conservative policy think tank) just before the November elections? "It makes sense—it has in the past, it may well continue to do so in the future" (Chavez 1994). In other words, Wilson proposed reviving some version of the bracero program that had kept the revolving door on the border functioning so well.

And no amount of policing the border, no amount of welfare denial, can permanently halt the movement of Mexicans across the border. California writer Richard Rodriguez, son of Mexican immigrants, can attest to that: "Any coyote in

Tijuana can tell you that illegal immigration is inevitable, as long as distinctions between rich countries and poor, developed countries and the Third World, are not ameliorated" (Rodriguez 1993). And so it was that with the recent sudden and sharp drop of the Mexican peso, more Mexicans were massed on the border, ready to cross at the opportune moment, undeterred by the beefed-up border patrol.

CONCLUSION

Militarizing our border; denying citizenship to children born on U.S. soil; requiring teachers to spy on their students and doctors on their patients; registering all Americans in a computer bank—all these are strongly suggestive of fascist or police state tendencies. How could the new immigrants in general, and illegal aliens in particular, have provoked such intense revulsion that so many Americans are willing to approve so many unconstitutional, anti-human rights and anti-civil rights measures to rid ourselves, ostensibly, of just 1 percent of our population? The draconian solutions seem entirely out of proportion to the scope of the problem. As one commentator put it: "If all the problems of your country are attributable to this minuscule population, then your system's really in trouble" (Sontag 1993).

The answer, I believe, lies in America's growing insecurity about its preeminent position in the world, its global economic competitiveness, and its national identity as a people, a nation, and a culture. The new immigrants, because they are predominantly non-European and nonwhite, reinforce the contemporary multicultural challenge to the triumphalist construction of America as an English-speaking, culturally European nation that is the embodiment of the superiority of Western civilization. Seen in this light, immigrant bashing is part of the backlash against multiculturalism. Immigrant bashing also has resurrected the race-based dichotomy between immigrants destined to become citizens and immigrants ineligible for citizenship.

The new immigrants also exemplify the new globalism. They are part of an international phenomenon of labor migration and mass population movements that began with the postwar decolonization of the Third World, and continued through the breakup of the Soviet empire. They represent activities in the new global economy, in which capital, jobs, and labor are internationalized and increasingly acquire transnational characteristics.

The New World Order has precipitated the rise, once again, of nativism and fascism, as reaction and response to changes that we don't yet comprehend and thus cannot quite accept. What's next? Already there are clues, again in California. A new ballot initiative has been organized, this time to attack and ban affirmative action across the board (Johnson 1995). Insidiously named "Californians for Civil Rights" by its organizers, it would mandate the removal of affirmative action guidelines in hiring and education. The Republicans in Congress have already picked up on its political appeal. Presidential candidate Bob Dole, for example, declared his discomfort with "reverse discrimination," and vowed to undertake a thorough examination of affirmative action on the federal level (Minzesheimer 1995).

The destabilized white power structure will soon re-focus all its attention from Third World immigrants to longtime Americans of color. Together with welfare reform and the crime bill, elimination of affirmative action means launching a full frontal attack on the numerically growing but increasingly vulnerable minority populations of this country. And the race war will accelerate.

BIBLIOGRAPHY

The American Experiment, Winter 1995. Center for the New American Community. The Manhattan Institute.

Ayres, B. Drummond, Jr. "Flow of Illegal Aliens Rises as the Peso Falls." *New York Times*, February 4, 1995, A6.

Berke, Richard. "Politicians Discovering an Issue: Immigration." *New York Times*, March 8, 1994, A14.

Chavez, Lynda. "More Mexicans, More Profit." *New York Times*, December 8, 1994, A19.

CIR News. Newsletter of the U.S. Commission on Immigration Rights. May 1994.

Claiborne, William. "Loser Huffington Seeks Voting Fraud Evidence." *The Washington Post*, December 2, 1994, A10.

Clinton, William J. "State of the Union Address." *New York Times*, January 26, 1995, A11.

Cockcroft, James. *Outlaws in the Promised Land. Mexican Immigrant Workers and America's Future*. New York: Grove Press, 1986.

Cole, David. "Five Myths About Immigration." *The Nation*, October 17, 1994, 410–11.

————. "The Scapegoats." *The Nation*, July 26–August 2, 1993, 125.

Cooper, Marc. "Prop. 187's True Colors." *The Village Voice*, December 6, 1994, 13–16.

Dong, Steven. "Contract with America: War on Poverty Becomes War on Immigrants." *AsianWeek*, January 20, 1994, 2.

Fix, Michael, and Jeffrey Passel. *Immigration and Immigrants: Setting the Record Straight*. Washington, D.C.: Urban Institute, 1994.

Johnson, Kevin. "Affirmative Action as Next Target in California." *USA Today*, January, 1995, A1.

Kadetsky, Elizabeth. "'Save Our State' Initiative: Bashing Illegals in California." *The Nation*, October 17, 1994, 416–22.

Kagan, Donald. Text of speech to incoming freshmen class. *Yale Alumni Magazine*, November 1990.

Kershner, Vlae. "A Hot Issue for the 90s. California Leads in Immigration—and Backlash." *San Francisco Chronicle*, June 21, 1993, A1, A6.

Kwong, Peter. "The First Multicultural Riots." *The Village Voice*, October 15, 1991, 45–46.

Mann, Eric. "Los Angeles—A Year Later (II)." *The Nation*, May 3, 1993, 586–90.

Minzesheimer, Bob. "Affirmative Action to Get Review from Republicans." *USA Today*, February 7, 1995, 6A.

Pear, Robert. "Federal Panel Proposes Register to Curb Hiring of Illegal Aliens." *New York Times*, August 4, 1994, A1, A7.

Rodriguez, Richard. "Immigrants Threaten California's Myth About Itself." *AsianWeek*, September 10, 1993, 4.

Rosenthal, A. M. "Hunt Them Down." *New York Times*, October 4, 1994, A17.

Safire, William. "Self-Deportation?" *New York Times*, November 21, 1994.

Saxton, Alexander. *The Rise and Fall of the White Republic*. London: Verso, 1990.

Sharry, Frank. Letter to Editor. *New York Times*, September 1, 1993, A10.

Silko, Leslie Marmon. "America's Iron Curtain: The Border Patrol State." *The Nation*, October 17, 1994, 412–46.

Sontag, Deborah. "Analysis of Illegal Immigrants in New York Defies Stereotypes." *New York Times*, September 2, 1993, A11.

Tamayo, William. "Putting Politics Before Principles." *AsianWeek*, October, 1993, 2.

Ueda, Reed. *Postwar Immigrant America: A Social History*. Boston: Bedford Books of St. Martin's Press, 1994.

Weintraub, Daniel. "Wilson Sues U.S. over Immigrants' 'Invasion.'" *Los Angeles Times* (Orange Country edition), September 23, 1994, A3.

Wilson, Pete. "An Open Letter to the President of the United States on Behalf of the People of California." *New York Times*, August 10, 1993, A11.

CHAPTER 3

Fighting White Racism:
The Future of Equal Rights in the United States
Joe R. Feagin

THE FUNDAMENTAL PROBLEM

To use a medical metaphor, if we seek an appropriate remedy for a societal problem, we must accurately diagnose the problem. The basic racial problem in the United States is white racism. White racism is a social disease that afflicts the minds, emotions, behaviors, and institutions of white Americans. White racism pervades every nook and cranny of U.S. society. It has been our major problem since at least the 1600s, and it is the one national problem that could possibly destroy the United States as we know it over the next several decades.

The first step toward a remedy for white racism is becoming aware of its reality. Unfortunately, many white Americans currently are in a condition of denial of its reality. Recently, I searched for the phrase "white racism" in the headlines of several million articles and reports in more than seven hundred magazines, newspapers, newsletters, and wire service releases in Mead Data Central's Nexis database, for the time period 1978–1995. Only twenty-eight of the millions of articles on U.S. issues published since 1978 had a headline that included "white racism." Of these, *not one* was a serious, in-depth look at white racism in U.S. society by a white editor or reporter. Most were articles in black magazines, articles on black statements about racism, or relatively brief references to the role of white racism in a particular incident.[1] Since the late 1970s, it appears, no white journalist or editor in a mainstream periodical has taken the central part that whites play in modern racism seriously enough to do a major article on the subject. Very few in the white economic, political, or media elite see white racism as a major, persisting problem for the United States. Most appear to agree with this recent *Chicago Sun-Times* editorial: "In the 1950s, white racism was blacks' major problem. In the 1990s, the problem is urban violence, fueled by guns and gangs."[2] Today, it would appear that most whites prefer not to think about racial matters, and especially not about the "r" word (racism).[3]

When whites as a group are forced to focus on racial matters, such as after major racial incidents, they tend to view the U.S. racial problem as one of mutual group relations, not of the racism of the dominant white group. For example, the May 18, 1992, issue of *Newsweek* had two cover headlines: "Rethinking Race and Crime in America" and "Beyond Black and White." We see the word "race" here, but not "white racism." Similarly, *Time's* cover headline was: "Why Race Still Divides America and Its People."[4] Again the title does not mention white racism, nor is it made clear in either issue's articles that the racist ideas and discriminatory practices of many white Americans are central to the "race problem" in the contemporary United States.

White racism is the responsibility of all white Americans, but those whites in authority bear the greatest responsibility to deal directly with the societal cancer of racism. Yet, as a nation, we have been misled in recent years by a gaggle of right-wing and mainstream analysts and pundits who have told the American people that the primary cause of persisting racial tensions and problems in this country is not white racism but the violent black underclass, or "dysfunctional" black families, or black "dependency" on welfare. Many of these apologists for the persisting racial divide blame the underclass for its immorality or black middle-class people for not taking responsibility for the underclass. A favorite idea in this analysis is the "declining significance of race." A denial of white racism and a blaming of the black victims of racism have become intellectually fashionable in the last two decades.

THE OVERWHELMING EVIDENCE OF WHITE RACISM

The evidence for white racism in the contemporary United States is over-whelming. Let us briefly examine major dimensions of white racism—attitudes, emotions, actions, and institutions—in turn.

The Racial Attitudes of White Americans

White racism is expressed in white prejudices and stereotypes. In a 1995 national survey the Anti-Defamation League found that most whites subscribed to one or more antiblack stereotypes. Evaluating a list of eight stereotypes of African Americans, including "prefer to accept welfare" and have "less native intelligence," three-quarters of the whites agreed with one or more, and just over half agreed with two or more. No less than 30 percent agreed with four or more of the stereotypes.[5] Moreover, in a 1994 National Opinion Research Center (NORC) national survey whites were asked to evaluate on a scale (1–7) how work-oriented blacks are. A small group, 16 percent, ranked blacks at the hardworking end; just under half chose the lazy end of the spectrum. Asked about whites, only 7 percent placed whites in the lazy ranks, and the majority ranked whites in the hardworking ranks.[6] In a similar 1990 NORC survey, whites were asked to rank blacks and whites on preference for welfare aid (versus being self-supporting); over half the whites ranked blacks toward the welfare preference end of the spectrum. Asked to rank blacks on intelligence, 29 percent of whites placed blacks toward the unintelligent end of the continuum.[7] A majority of whites still stereotype black people as inclined to go on welfare and as not hardworking—and a substantial minority still stereotype black Americans as unintelligent.

Today, a majority of whites also refuse to view racial discrimination as a major barrier for people of color. In the 1994 NORC survey, whites were asked, "On the average blacks have worse jobs, income, and housing than white people. Do you think these differences are mainly due to discrim-ination?" More than six in ten said *no*. When asked if the differences were mainly due to the fact that most blacks "just don't have the motivation or willpower to pull themselves up out of poverty," the majority said *yes*.[8] Over the last decade a number of other surveys of whites have revealed a similar victim-blaming pattern. In addition, a substantial minority of whites actually defend overt racial discrimination. The same 1994 NORC survey found that 35 percent of whites believe that a white homeowner should have the legal right to refuse to sell his or her home to a black person, which is contrary to existing federal law.

The implications of these survey data are serious. Today, there are about 150 million white Americans over the age of 17. A rough extrapolation from these various survey data (conducted on whites over the age of seventeen) suggests that more than 100 million of them hold antiblack prejudices and stereotypes—and that some 45–60 million Americans are extreme in their white racism, even to the extent of defending their right to engage in racial discrimination in areas like housing. Since there are only 35 million black persons in the United States, the probability that many African Americans will encounter a *very racist* white adult on a given day is quite high.

Nonetheless, in spite of this overwhelming evidence of widespread white prejudice, stereotyping, and propensity to discriminate, little political, legislative, scholarly, or media attention has targeted white racist attitudes toward African Americans or other people of color as a major societal problem for discussion or redress in the 1990s.

The Emotional Side of Racism

White racism entails much more than cognitive images and stereotypes; it is also about antiblack emotions. Some survey data hint at the substantial level of racialized emotion that lies behind white attitudes. For example, in the 1990 NORC national survey, two-thirds of whites said that they would have a negative reaction if a close relative married a black person, whereas only 5 percent said they would have a positive response. It is important to note that the only characteristic given to the respondents was that the person marrying into the family was black. Most whites quickly responded and did not even opt for the choice of "don't know" or "not sure." In addition, about a sixth of white Americans nationally, and a much larger proportion in the Deep South, favor a law banning marriages between blacks and whites.[9]

The deep emotional reactions of many whites come through even more clearly in longer interviews. For example, in several research projects I and my graduate students have conducted in-depth interviews with whites on racial subjects, including the issue of interracial dating and marriage. In their comments whites often reveal visceral and deep feelings. One example is this response from a white businessperson, when asked a question about his adult child dating a black person:

I'd be sick to my stomach. I would feel like, that I failed along the way. I'd probably take a lot of the blame for that. I would feel like probably I failed out on the job along the way or they would not have those tendencies to do that. I'd feel like I probably failed as a father, if that was to happen. And it's something that I could never accept. I would probably be in big-time trouble over that. It would truly be a problem in my family because I could never handle that, and I don't know what would happen because I couldn't handle that, ever.[10]

In such reactions we see how for whites, their views on racial matters are not just about their images of the black outgroup but also about their views of themselves, including, in this case, their views of what makes a good parent. This white man is talking not only about his racial attitudes but also about their deep personal and emotional roots.

The strength of white feelings about African Americans may also be expressed in declining white support for equal-rights programs and efforts. Today, the majority of white Americans believe black Americans have fully equal opportunities. For instance, in a recent survey done for the National Conference of Christians and Jews, a large majority (69 percent) of whites felt that black Americans currently have an equal opportunity for a quality education, and another 63 percent believed black Americans have equal opportunities for skilled jobs. A majority also felt blacks have an equal chance to get decent housing. (Similar views were expressed by whites about the opportunities available for Latinos and Asian Americans.)[11] Moreover, in a 1994 *Times-Mirror* survey, 51 percent of the white respondents agreed that equal rights have been pushed *too far* in the United States, a proportion up from 42 percent in 1992.[12] Thinking about this response, a question comes to mind: Is it possible to push equal rights too far in the United States? Given the lack of civil rights enforcement efforts in recent years, the white answers here suggest an emotional response, perhaps conditioned by statements of conservative white analysts and political leaders in the media, rather than a response built on reasoning about actual events in the United States.

WHITE RACISM AS DISCRIMINATORY ACTION

Discrimination in Employment

The most serious form of white racism is racial discrimination. Discrimination is about practices that directly harm people. To take one major example, workplace discrimination by white Americans targeting people of color, particularly African Americans, is widespread in all areas of the United States. For example, in 1994 the federal Equal Employment Opportunity Commission had 90,000 complaints of discrimination, mostly from women and people of color, from all areas of the country. Still, these complaints are the tip of the iceberg. Research on discrimination in employment suggests there is much more than these numbers suggest.

For example, in a 1990 study of discrimination in hiring in Washington, D.C., and Chicago, the Urban Institute sent pairs of black and white men, matched in terms of biographical characteristics, to apply for entry-level jobs in services, retail sales, and manufacturing. Twenty percent of the black men received unfavorable and differential treatment; they did not advance as far in the hiring process as their matched white counterparts.[13] And the measured discrimination here was for only a small part of the employment process in firms hiring working-class applicants.

In interviews with African American professional and managerial women, another major study found that 42 percent had personally experienced discriminatory treatment, especially in regard to promotions and wages.[14] In addition, a 1993–1994 Los Angeles random-sample survey of more than one thousand African Americans, six in ten reported having faced some workplace discrimination, such as being refused a job because of their race or suffering racial slurs from a supervisor, within the past year. The most frequent discrimination, reported by nearly four in ten of the respondents, was the denial of a job because of their race. Moreover, about 30 percent reported suffering two or more different types of racial discrimination in the workplace during this period. The Los Angeles study found that there was a direct correlation between educational level and experience with discrimination. While just under half of those black workers with less than a high school degree reported workplace discrimination in the last year, eight in ten of those with a college degree, and *almost all* of those with postgraduate work. These barriers face other people of color as well. The Los Angeles study also found that a majority of highly educated Asian and Latino workers reported workplace discrimination.[15]

Given these and similar findings for all other aspects of employment for African Americans and other people of color, a reasonable estimate is that there that there are millions of serious cases of employment discrimination by whites in the United States each year. Inclusion of more subtle cases of discrimination, such as being channeled into "ghettoized" jobs within workplaces, would probably increase this number to more than 10 million cases.

In interviews with more than 400 working-class and middle-class African Americans in five separate studies since the late 1980s, I have found that some type of racial hostility and discrimination is frequently confronted by many African Americans in various work and business settings. In a major study of 209 African Americans interviewed in numerous cities across the country, I encountered many instances of discrimination like the following. A black female manager at a large corporation discussed a performance evaluation involving her white male supervisor:

We had a five scale rating, starting with outstanding, then very good, then good, then fair, and then less than satisfactory. I had gone into my evaluation interview anticipating that he would give me a "VG" [very good], feeling that I deserved an "outstanding" and prepared to fight for my outstanding rating, knowing my past experience with him and more his way toward females. But even beyond female, I happened to be the only black in my position within my branch. So the racial issue would also come into play. And he and I had had some very frank discussions about race specifically. About females, but more about race when he and I talked. So I certainly knew that he had a lot of prejudices in terms of blacks. And [he] had some very strong feelings based on his upbringing about the abilities of blacks. He said to me on numerous occasions that he considered me to be an exception, that I certainly was not what he felt the abilities of an average black person [were]. I was of course appalled and made it perfectly clear to him. . . . But, when I went into the evaluation interview, he gave me glowing comments that cited numerous achievements and accomplishments for me during the year, and then concluded it with, "So I've given you a G," which of course just floored me. . . . [I] maintained my emotions and basically just said, as unemotionally as I possibly could, that I found that unacceptable, I thought it was inconsistent with his remarks in terms of my performance, and I would not accept it. I think I kind of shocked him, because he sort of said, "Well I don't know what that means" when I said I wouldn't accept it. I said, "I'm not signing the evaluation." And at that point, here again knowing that the best way to deal with most issues is with facts and specifics, I had already come in prepared . . . I had my list of objectives for the year where I was able to show him that I had achieved every objective and I exceeded all of them. I also had my sales performance: the dollar amount, the products, both in total dollar sales and also a product mix. I sold every product in the line that we offered to our customers. I had exceeded all of my sales objectives. As far as I was concerned, it was outstanding performance.[16]

Understandings of racial discrimination on the part of African Americans typically are grounded in recurring experiences with whites over a long period of time. We see here that this women had prior experience with the white male supervisor and knew about his negative racial attitudes. This knowledge led her to be prepared to take countering action against possible discrimination. Such cases show the linkage between white attitudes and actions. The presence of these whites in decision making positions points to the need for active affirmative action programs and vigorously enforced civil rights laws.

African Americans in business settings face a range of discrimination problems. In another research project that involved focus group interviews with black professional businesspeople in a Southern area, we found that they face a variety of types of racial discrimination from whites at their job sites. For example, one black manager discussed an experience with a blatant racist joking:

My mind goes back to one [racist joke] in particular that I heard, a few years ago on my job. A [white] manager asked "What is a Pontiac to a black man?" And I thought about it for a while, and he said (speaking in a very rhythmic, stilted, monotone), "The poor old nigger thinks it's a Cadillac." . . . And that was the start of my day. And I know exactly what you're saying. You can fight, and just totally blow up. And then you've got a difficult day, and difficult week, because you can't win those battles. You can maybe straighten him for that particular day, but then you're labeled as "overly sensitive" or whatever.

Some analysts of racial discrimination underscore the point that since the civil rights laws of the 1960s, much racial discrimination has become covert or subtle. However, numerous cases like this indicate that considerable overt racism still plagues the lives of African Americans, including those who venture into the predominantly white business world. Everyday problems of doing one's jobs, which are difficult enough for members of groups until recently excluded from that white world, are made worse by racial hostility and discrimination that crashes in constantly and, often, unexpectedly.

Discrimination in Other Arenas

Public accommodation is yet another area where African Americans suffer much discrimination, which ranges from exclusion to poor service. The high energy cost of racial discrimination can be seen in the following account, from an African American news director at a white-owned TV station. She and her boyfriend had gone to a professional basketball game, then decided to eat at a historically white restaurant:

He was waiting to be seated . . . he said, "You go to the bathroom and I'll get the table. . . ." He was standing there when I came back; he continued to stand there. The restaurant was almost empty. There were waiters, waitresses, and no one seated. And when I got back to him, he was ready to leave, and said, "Let's go." I said, "What happened to our table?" He wasn't seated. So I said, "No, we're not leaving, please." And he said, "No, I'm leaving." So we went outside, and we talked about it. And what I said to him was, you have to be aware of the possibilities that this is not the first time that this has happened at this restaurant or at other restaurants, but this is the first time it has happened to a black news director here or someone who could make an issue of it, or someone who is prepared to make an issue of it. So we went back inside after I talked him into it and, to make a long story short, I had the manager come. I made most of the people who were there (while conducting myself professionally the whole time) aware that I was incensed at being treated this way. . . . I said, "Why do you think we weren't seated?" And the manager said, "Well, I don't really know." And I said, "Guess." He said, "Well I don't know. Because you're black?" I said, "Bingo. Now isn't it funny that you didn't guess that I didn't have any money?" (And I opened up my purse and I said, "Because I certainly have money."). "And isn't it odd that you didn't guess that it's because I couldn't pay for it, because I've got two American Express cards and a Master Card right here. I think it's just funny that you would have assumed that it's because I'm black."[17]

The hostile tactic here was not the "no Negroes" exclusion of earlier legal segregation, but rejection in the form of no service. This is a case that might appear to be subtle discrimination from the point of view of many white observers, but to this black couple it appears as blatant and is interpreted as a clear violation of their civil rights.

Discrimination pervades every area of U.S. society. Housing is a basic human need, and the search for housing in historically white residential areas often brings African Americans into contact with hostile whites. There are millions of cases of discrimination targeting African Americans and other people of color each year in the United States. In a federal survey involving 3,800 test audits in twenty-five metropolitan areas, African American renters faced some type of discriminatory treatment *about half the time*, while black home seekers faced discriminatory treatment *59 percent* of the time in their initial-stage encounters with whites. Latino testers encountered discrimination at a similar rate.[18] If we were to go beyond this initial-stage discrimination and examine later-stage housing discrimination such as in mortgage lending, and if we extrapolated these data to housing searches by people of color across the nation, we could reasonably estimate there are at least 3 million cases of housing discrimination by white Americans each year across the United States. Indeed, Roberta Achtenberg, assistant secretary for fair housing at the U.S. Department of Housing and Urban Development in the early 1990s, has argued that the actual number could be as high as ten million cases of housing discrimination annually.[19]

Then there is the educational arena. This has been a site of much debate about affirmative action in recent years. The ideal image of colleges and universities has been that they are unique places of enlightenment, open-mindedness, and tolerance of diversity. However, most recent studies of the campus racial climate at universities from Princeton on the East Coast to the University of California (Berkeley) on the West Coast have found a significant proportion of black students reporting racial problems or discrimination on campus. Life for most African Americans on a major university campus takes the form of a daily acid rain of racism falling into their lives. For that reason, many African American students at historically white colleges and universities have considered dropping out.

In a recent research study involving interviews with black juniors and seniors at a predominantly white university, we received many detailed accounts of racial hostility and discrimination by whites targeting black students. Black students reported being called "nigger" by whites (including white students) on or near campus, closer surveillance of black student parties and of black men walking across campus by campus security personnel than of white students, white students' telling derogatory racial jokes, encountering the white "hate stare" and looks signaling "What are you doing on this campus?," white professors making fun of African cultures, black students frequently being singled out as the spokespersons for their group, and black students graded down when they write papers on African history or literature. For example, one student noted how a white student reacted to him:

I was walking to class by [a certain] House. It was about twelve noon, and I had my backpack. I'm a black student, right. And there was this white girl in the car, and she pulled in the parking space, right. And she's about to get out. And, you know, I'm walking up. I'm not even paying attention to her, and the next thing I hear is "click, click." And she's looking at me like I'm going to rape her.[20]

With his student dress and backpack, this young black man should have been seen by the white student as a legitimate member of the campus community.

However, many whites view black men as unwelcome intruders in white spaces. In the same campus study another student noted how his light skin color gave him a glimpse of the white side of the racial wall:

I run into white people. . . . I can hear them going, "Those black people, this." And it's like the time—it's amazing you sit there, and they think I'm Hispanic . . . you'd be amazed what people are saying when they don't think there are black people in the room. They're like, "Oh I can't stand that black guy." And they'll be saying "Nigger this, Nigger that." But when the black people are around, it's like, "Hey Bob. What's up, bro?" And they play like this nice little role. It's like there's no way. I'm kind of like weird in the sense that I can sit in between and I can see all this happening. . . . There's only one black person that I see on a consistent basis in any of my classes in science, and it's like I barely know him because we're not like doing anything. So most of the people I know—it's like if they can't handle the fact that I'm black, then I'm probably not going to be friends with them. And it's like the whole issue's always a big deal. . . . I've run into it a lot, and it's like I hear complaints about what other black people do on campus.[21]

Out of the sight of most black Americans, many whites still think and act in very racist ways, even in places thought to be bastions of enlightenment and tolerance. In the backstage situation the use of racist epithets not only reveals white prejudices but also suggests that a bonding process between whites is taking place, one in which hostile comments toward the racialized other highlight the shared white identity. Whiteness is defined against the reality of the racial "other."

THE SOCIETAL IMPACT OF RACIAL DISCRIMINATION

The racial discrimination described above has a very serious impact on its targets and on U.S. society. We have noted above some of the effects on particular victims of racist actions. We hear the pain and anger in the black voices that recount instances of racial discrimination. We see the effort and energy that must be expended to deal with white racism. We see the lost chances for equal opportunities and achievement because of white-imposed barriers.

The impact of these barriers on achievement is obvious in much data on U.S. society. For example, white men still dominate and control every major U.S. institution, from Fortune 1000 companies and major public and private universities to the U.S. presidency and major leadership positions in both state and federal legislatures. Indeed, one 1980s' analysis of top positions in the major economic, political, and educational organizations in the United States found only 20 black people and 318 nonblack women in the 7,314 most powerful positions.[22] More recent studies show the same dominance of the white male minority. The clearest evidence of the corporate world's failure to promote meritorious black employees is the fact that in 1994 not one of the Fortune 1000 companies had an African American as its head. (There were only two white women at the helm of these companies.) According to a recent report of the federal Glass Ceiling Commission, about 95 percent of the holders of top corporate positions (vice president and above) are white men. Yet, today, white men make up about 39 percent of the adult population in the United States.[23] It appears that the most successful "affirmative action" program in U.S. history is the one that sees to it that white men are greatly over represented in the society's most powerful positions.

Constant encounters with racist barriers in every U.S. institution bring serious negative consequences for African American families and communities. Note white racism's long-term, cumulative impact: Blatant discrimination combines with subtle and covert discrimination, over years and lifetimes, to have a negative impact on individuals and on the family members with whom they share their oppressive experiences. In this way the pain of one individual becomes part of the pain, and the collective memories, of extended families and larger communities. This negative impact requires the expenditure of much individual, family, and community energy to develop coping strategies to deal with white racism.

One can measure the societal impact of racism in other ways. A country's general quality of life decreases as a result of racial discrimination. For example, in 1993 the United Nations released a Human Development Report with chilling statistics on the world's nations. The report calculates a Human Development Index (HDI) that measures overall quality of life in a country; the HDI includes measures of life expectancy, education, and income for each country and for certain racial-ethnic subgroups within certain countries. According to the report, U.S. "Whites rank number one in the world (ahead of Japan), blacks rank number 31 (next to Trinidad and Tobago), and Hispanics rank number 35 (next to Estonia)."[24] The quality of life for African Americans and Latino Americans is quite low by the standard of white Americans. The impact of 376 years of discrimination on the resources and wealth of African Americans has been devastating.

THE MYTH OF "REVERSE DISCRIMINATION"

It is commonplace for white male Americans to counter discussions of traditional racism with the argument that government programs to remedy discrimination have actually created discrimination against white men on a large scale. However, this relatively new idea of "reverse discrimination" was intentionally developed as part of an ideological attack against government attempts to remedy centuries of racist discrimination directed by white Americans against people of color. It is obvious on examination that the term "reverse discrimination" is a grossly inaccurate label for government remedial practices. From the beginning, affirmative action programs were devised by *white men* in Congress, corporations, and other bureaucratic organizations, and they have often been implemented by white men. No major government affirmative action policies were created or crafted primarily by African Americans or other people of color.[25]

Recall, too, that white racism has entailed omnipresent patterns of discrimination by whites in all major institutional areas of U.S. society—in public accommodations, housing, employment, business, education, health services, and the legal system—for nearly four centuries. Over this period millions of whites have actively discriminated against many millions of African Americans. White Americans, including those who stood on the sidelines or who came to the country recently as immigrants, have benefited enormously from this discriminatory process through the intentional blocking of African Americans (and other people of color) from participating in the resources and opportunities of the wider society. The total cost to African Americans of this exploitation and discrimination is doubtless much more than a trillion dollars in today's currency.

Given this portrait of centuries of racist oppression, the exact reversal ("reverse racism") would have to mean this: Over several hundred years, massive institutionalized discrimination would be implemented by dominant black groups against most white Americans. Some significant segment, if not all, of U.S. housing, educational institutions, and employment would be controlled by African American decision makers, and a disproportionate number of lower-level officials would be black. In addition, decision-making blacks would implement much discrimination targeting whites. Because of this widely institutionalized system of reverse discrimination, over many years hundreds of millions of whites would suffer billions of dollars in economic losses, lower wages, unemployment, widespread housing segregation, and inferior school facilities. This situation of institutionalized racism directed against whites would be close to real "reverse discrimination." It has never happened.

Interestingly, recent research studies indicate that the cases of white men suffering serious discrimination, even at the hands of other whites in connection with affirmative action decisions, are relatively rare. One recent Labor Department report by Alfred Blumrosen examined about three thousand federal district court decisions on discrimination for 1990–1994. Out of this total, Blumrosen found fewer than one hundred reverse discrimination cases, less than 4 percent. "Of that one hundred, there are maybe 20 percent that—20 to 30 percent that—the plaintiffs win and the other . . . 70 percent the plaintiffs lose. The cases in which they lose are mainly cases in which they've claimed that they were better qualified than the black or the woman who got the job, and after the trial was over the judge decided they were not better qualified."[26] In addition, discrimination complaints by white men make up only 1.7 percent of EEOC's inventory of charges of discrimination.[27] It should also be noted that most of these cases are not about true "reverse discrimination," in which a black person discriminated against a white male; most involve *other whites* taking action against white men. Documented claims of "reverse discrimination" affecting white men are very uncommon, in all sectors of U.S. society.

THE REMEDIES FOR RACIAL DISCRIMINATION

Today, white racism is not close to being on the action agendas of white business, political, and educational leaders in the United States. More than 90 percent of these leaders are white men with little concern about making the massive changes necessary to eradicate the various forms of persisting white racism. Nonetheless, it is definitely in the long-run interest of all white Americans to bring major changes in the structure and patterns of white racism. Whites are but a small minority of the world's population; and by 2060 they will be only a statistical minority in the United States. White racism is perhaps the most wasteful problem —in human terms—facing the United States today and is the most consequential for the nation's future. White racism has the potential to array white and black Americans against each other in ways that could eventually devastate the social and political structure of the United States. Over the last decade we have had major riots in Miami and Los Angeles, the latter a billion-dollar riot in 1992 that took more than fifty lives. Moreover, in the 1960s, before affirmative action programs and certain major civil rights laws were substantially implemented, we had hundreds of civil disturbances in cities across the nation.

Today the rage over pervasive racial discrimination has grown to very intense levels in the nation's communities of color.[28] Nationwide upheaval and civil disorder can take place again if white policy makers ignore the rage of the oppressed and continue to move backward on major commitments to the ideals of liberty, justice, and equality for all Americans.

What can be done? There is much action that will help rid the United States of white racism and its many consequences. The consequences of long-term racial discrimination, such as poor jobs, poor family incomes, and poor housing, can be met with a multibillion-dollar Marshall Plan for the cities, an idea that has been proposed many times over the last few decades. Government social programs can be made to work, as Head Start and Social Security clearly show, if there is the political will to fund them well and over a long period of time. Guaranteeing a decent-paying job for every American who wants to work, and the training for such a job, will over time largely rid this nation of much of the potential for major urban rebellions and increasing street crime.

What about civil rights laws? State, local, and federal governments can take much action to reduce racial oppression, beginning with the vigorous enforcement of existing civil rights laws. During the 1960s the civil rights movement pressured Congress to pass legislation banning discrimination in employment, voting, and housing, and over the next decade some effort was put into government enforcement of these laws. Yet these civil rights advances were stopped by the white backlash of the 1980s and 1990s. The Reagan administration destroyed or weakened federal civil rights enforcement agencies. Until 1987 the U.S. president's budget included an appendix, called Special Analysis J, that reviewed the federal civil rights enforcement effort. That appendix was discontinued in the Reagan years. Interestingly, the 1987 budget appendix reveals that the budget authority for the principal civil rights activities of the U.S. government was only $350 million out of a total budget of nearly a trillion dollars. Moreover, much of that funding was not for direct enforcement of civil rights laws. The discussions in the 1987 appendix reveal small-scale government efforts to enforce civil rights laws, with very few major investigations or lawsuits being pursued in the areas of criminal interference with civil rights, voting rights, equal employment rights (only 537 cases in active litigation in 1985), and housing (only 3,308 complaints processed in 1985).[29]

For the most part, President George Bush continued this negative approach to civil rights. Both Reagan and Bush appointed conservative justices to the Supreme Court, and Court decisions since the 1980s have restricted discrimination victims' ability to sue for redress. In the late 1980s a new civil rights bill was proposed to overcome the limitations of some of these conservative Supreme Court decisions. Bush at first opposed the bill, but after a long congressional struggle and some weakening of the bill, he finally signed the 1991 Civil Rights Act into law. In 1993 the Clinton administration finally began to enforce the civil rights laws somewhat more vigorously.

Today, however, government enforcement of civil rights has not recovered from the anti-civil rights actions of the Reagan-Bush "revolution." Indeed, there is not yet any regular report on the federal civil rights enforcement effort by any federal agency. The issue is not on the political agenda of white policy workers. The destruction of the U.S. Commission on Civil Rights by presidents Reagan and Bush could still be seen in the 5-3 conservative majority on the commission in 1994, a majority that has been able to pack the commission with conservative employees and to pursue conservative political agendas. In addition, in the mid-1990s some employees of the various federal agencies authorized to enforce civil rights laws were still left over from the Reagan-Bush years and had a conservative view of civil rights.

It is clear that strong civil rights laws do not guarantee real equality of opportunity in everyday settings. They must be vigorously enforced. Few of the many millions of cases of racial discrimination perpetrated by white Americans each year against African Americans and other people of color are countered by effective private or government remedies. Indeed, U.S. government agencies have neither the resources nor the staff to aggressively enforce antidiscrimination laws. Because of under funding, federal agencies such as the Equal Employment Opportunity Commission (EEOC) typically have such a large backlog of cases that most victims of discrimination cannot achieve timely remedies through the federal government. Sharply increased enforcement efforts are necessary, and it is time to press the federal government for much additional funding and effort in this area.[30]

It is important to remember that most affirmative action policies stem from 1960s' presidential executive orders, 1960s' and 1970s' court orders, and independent efforts in the private and public sectors aimed at increasing opportunities for women and people of color. As I noted earlier, in almost all cases white male officials originally fashioned these generally modest or token affirmative action programs. For a time, many programs were effective in bringing some people of color and women into historically white institutions, and many white male decision makers would have taken no action to desegregate workforces without these affirmative action pressures. According to a Labor Department report, an estimated five million workers of color and six million women are in higher occupational classifications today because of these affirmative action programs.[31]

There is much talk these days about eliminating the old affirmative action programs. However, getting rid of affirmative action programs would have a serious negative effect on people of color. We can note one example from business set-aside programs. William Taylor, chair of the Citizens' Commission on Civil Rights, has summarized the national effects of the Supreme Court's 1989 *Croson* cases striking down a business set-aside program for African American businesses in Richmond, Virginia. He reports that in the city of Richmond, minority business construction declined from about 40 percent of the city's dollars to about 15 percent shortly "after the lower court first struck down the program." And the percentage fell to less than 3 percent by 1988. In addition, "In Tampa, minority business participation dropped from 22 percent to 5.2 percent in the quarter following suspension of the 25 percent goal in March 1989; in Philadelphia, public works subcontracts awarded to minority- or women-owned firms was 97 percent less in May 1990 than in May 1989, with minority business rate participation falling to 1.92 percent in November 1990."[32] Without active remedial programs, many white male decision makers will continue to discriminate, openly or covertly, against women and people of color.

Even a cursory reading of U.S. history books makes it quite clear that preferential treatment for whites has long been legitimate in the United States. It is the preferential treatment to remedy past and present discrimination against people of color that becomes controversial. Even though new civil rights laws and remedial action plans will bring increased racial tensions, because they involve some redistribution of resources and power, they are necessary to preserve not only the democratic ideals of the United States but also, over the next few decades, the United States itself. Remedial programs at their best are designed to improve equality of opportunity and thereby to help reduce housing, employment, and income differences between white and black Americans.

Still, we need more than a few new civil rights laws and better enforcement of civil rights and affirmative action provisions of existing laws. In my considered view, we need a new constitutional convention. In the 1776 Declaration of Independence, the young Thomas Jefferson penned, "We hold these truths to be self-evident, that all men are created equal, that they are endowed by their Creator with certain unalienable Rights . . . Life, Liberty, and the pursuit of Happiness." He envisioned here not only legal rights but also the basic rights people have solely by reason of being human. He and his fellow revolutionaries declared that the American minority of the British empire had rights that derived not from British law but from natural law. Ever since, these revolutionary ideas have inspired similar statements of basic human rights by many other groups, including those disenfranchised by the original U.S. Constitution.[33]

One of the most important of these statements, the Universal Declaration of Human Rights, passed by the United Nations in 1948, stipulates that "all human beings are born free and equal in dignity and rights" and that "all are equal before the law and are entitled without any discrimination to equal protection of the law." Article 8 of this international agreement asserts: "Everyone has the right to an effective remedy . . . for acts violating the fundamental rights." The Universal Declaration affirms that human beings have rights independent of the particular societal and governmental conditions in which they live, and it presses governments to incorporate all basic human rights into their legal and political systems. In the United States this comprehensive task remains to be accomplished. Thus, we need a new constitutional convention, a possibility envisaged by the founding fathers. I propose a thoroughgoing revision of the present Constitution, this time by representatives of *all* the American people. For all its possible difficulties, a new constitutional convention seems required not only to address the basic human rights of previously excluded groups but also to ensure that the fundamental governing document of this democracy is actually produced by representatives of all Americans. The egalitarian and democratic provisions already in the Constitution would be retained, and new provisions could be added to strengthen these provisions and to move the country forward to a more democratic reality.

Finally, there is a huge educational task to be accomplished. Gideon Sjoberg and Ted Vaughn have pointed out that the human capacity to "take the roles of others and to recognize another's humanity and commonality with oneself is an essential step in recognizing the rights of others."[34] An important step in securing everyday equality for African Americans will be for a majority of whites to develop the ability to empathize with African Americans as equal human beings. Human beings have the ability to reflect critically on their behavior, a reflection that is essential if white Americans are to move beyond racist perspectives and practices. Perhaps we could create a cradle-to-grave educational program for all Americans, but especially for white Americans, that teaches the real racial history of the United States, including genocide, segregation, and present-day discrimination. We could create many television programs in prime time to teach white Americans about their sordid racial history, about their own prejudices and acts of discrimination, and about strategies for eliminating that racism. Most white Americans still deny that they are racist or that there is much serious racism in America. We should educate white Americans to see the racism in their attitudes and actions and to recognize that racism in others.

In addition, it is clear that real change will require the creation of new political alliances and coalitions. Somehow, we must develop in this nation a large group of white anti-racists who fight aggressively against the racism they encounter in their daily lives. These anti-racist whites could build new coalitions with oppressed African Americans and other people of color. The Reagan-Bush era brought a collapse in the critical civil rights coalitions that once included black and white Americans. Today, the enforcement of civil rights laws and the impetus for advances in their content and scope lack the broad support of such coalitions. New coalitions that bind together various racial and ethnic groups are essential for future action to eradicate the cancer of racism destroying the United States.

NOTES

For the most part, I focus on black-white issues in this chapter. However, most of my arguments can be extended to white relations with other people of color (for example, Asian and Latino Americans).

1. There was one 1980 article about a white professor speaking of the costs of racism for whites. There were a few articles noting books or programs dealing with white racism. A search for all articles using "white racism" at least three times in the space of two hundred words yielded only a few more articles, with the same basic pattern of neglect. *Jet* magazine, a black periodical, had the best articles.

2. "Rights Still Are Under Attack," *Chicago Sun-Times*, September 5, 1994, p. 15.

3. A prominent black journalist recently told me that she could not use the "r" word in articles because of the often negative white reactions.

4. These distinctions were first made in Derrick Z. Jackson, "Missing from the LA Coverage: the Word Racism," *Boston Globe*, May 13, 1992, p. 19.

5. Anti-Defamation League, *Highlights from an Anti-Defamation League Survey on Racial Attitudes in America* (New York: ADL, 1993), pp. 18–25.

6. National Opinion Research Center, "1994 General Social Survey." Tabulation by author.

7. National Opinion Research Center, "1990 General Social Survey." Tabulation by author.

8. National Opinion Research Center, "1994 General Social Survey." Tabulation by author.

9. National Opinion Research Center, "1990 General Social Survey."

10. Joe R. Feagin and Hernan Vera, *White Racism: The Basics* (New York: Routledge, 1995), p. 149.

11. "Survey Finds Minorities Resent Whites and Each Other," *Jet*, March 28, 1994, p. 14.

12. Cited in Richard L. Berke, "The 1994 Campaign; Survey Finds Voters in U.S. Rootless and Self-Absorbed," *New York Times*, September 21, 1994, p. A21.

13. Margery Austin Turner, Michael Fix, and Raymond J. Struyk, "Opportunities Denied: Discrimination in Hiring," Report 91–9. (Washington, D.C.: Urban Institute, August, 1991.)

14. Elizabeth Higginbotham and Lynn Weber, *Workplace Discrimination for Black and White Professional and Managerial Women*, in *Women and Work: Ethnicity and Class*, edited by Elizabeth Higginbotham and Lynn Weber (Newbury Park, Calif.: Sage, forthcoming).

15. Lawrence Bobo and Susan A. Suh, "Surveying Racial Discrimination: Analyses from a Multiethnic Labor Market," unpublished research report, Department of Sociology, University of California, Los Angeles, August 1, 1995.

16. Joe R. Feagin and Melvin P. Sikes, *Living with Racism: The Black Middle-Class Experience* (Boston: Beacon Press, 1994), pp. 145–47.

17. Feagin and Sikes, *Living with Racism*, pp. 40–41.

18. See Margery Austin Turner, Raymond J. Struyk, and John Yinger, *Housing Discrimination Study: Synthesis* (Washington, D.C.: U.S. Government Printing Office, 1991), pp. ii–viii.

19. "Civil Wrongs; As Blacks Go House Hunting, Too Often the Door Is Closed," *Chicago Tribune*, November 14, 1993, p. C1.

20. Joe R. Feagin, Hernàn Vera, and Nikitah Imani, *The Agony of Education: Black Students in White Colleges and Universities* (New York: Routledge, 1996) p. 502.

21. Ibid., pp. 65–66.

22. Thomas Dye, *Who's Running America?*, 4th ed. (Englewood Cliffs, N.J.: Prentice-Hall, 1986), pp. 190–205.

23. Glass Ceiling Commission, *Good for Business: Making Full Use of the Nation's Human Capital* (Washington, D.C.: U.S. Government Printing Office, 1995), pp. 12, 60–61.

24. The report is quoted in Carole Collins, "U.N. Report on Minorities: U.S. Not Measuring Up," *National Catholic Reporter*, June 18, 1993, p. 9.

25. This paragraph and the next two draw in part on Joe R. Feagin and Aaron Porter, "Affirmative Action and African Americans: Rhetoric and Practice," *Humboldt Journal of Social Relations* 21 (1995): 81–104.

26. Alfred Blumrosen, on CNN NEWS, April 4, 1995, Transcript # 909-10. See also Associated Press, "Reverse Discrimination Complaints Rare, Labor Study Reports," *New York Times*, March 31, 1995, p. A23.

27. Nancy Montwieler, "EEOC: Casellas Says New Litigation Procedure Will Free Commission for More Policy Work," *Bureau of National Affairs Daily Labor Report*, April 21, 1995, p. D5.

28. See Feagin and Sikes, *Living with Racism*.

29. "Special Analysis J," in *Special Analyses: Budget of the U.S. Government, Fiscal Year 1987* (Washington, D.C.: U.S. Government Printing Office, 1987), pp. J1–J11.

30. For a more extended discussion, see Feagin and Vera, *White Racism*, pp. 185–189.

31. The data are cited in Kevin Merida, "Reverse Discrimination Rejected; Study Finds Many Claims by White Men 'Without Merit,'" *Houston Chronicle*, April 1, 1995, p. A5.

32. William L. Taylor, Citizens' Commission on Civil Rights, testimony to Subcommittee on the Constitution, Committee on the Judiciary, United States House of Representatives, *Federal News Service*, April 3, 1995.

33. This paragraph and the next draw in part on Feagin and Vera, *White Racism*, pp. 188–193.

34. Gideon Sjoberg and Ted R. Vaughn, "The Ethical Foundations of Sociology and the Necessity for a Human Rights Alternative," in Ted R. Vaughn, Gideon Sjoberg, and Larry Reynolds, *A Critique of Contemporary American Sociology* (New York: General Hall, 1993), p. 135.

CHAPTER 4

Affirmative Action Policy
Under Executive Order 11246:
A Retrospective View
Bernard E. Anderson

Equal job opportunity is central to the enjoyment of many benefits of American society. Work provides the main source of income to support a family's standard of living and to secure it's economic future. The denial of employment because of race, sex, creed, national origin, or other factors unrelated to an individual's productive potential is one of the most disgraceful practices possible in a nation committed to equal opportunity and economic justice.

The nation's struggle to live up to its high ideals as a land of opportunity is reflected in the continuing effort to address the troublesome presence of race. W.E.B. Du Bois, the dean of black intellectuals, wrote shortly after the turn of the century that "the greatest issue of the 20th century is the problem of color line." History has shown the wisdom of Du Bois's judgment.

Over many generations in our national history, discrimination and the systematic exclusion of racial minorities and women from full participation in the economy became embedded in the attitudes, values, and behavior of virtually all institutions in American life. The labor market was replete with occupations in which the normal expectation was that no minorities or women would be employed. Moreover, job ceilings were imposed in occupations where minorities and women were permitted to work. America was widely heralded as the "land of opportunity," but that phrase was clearly understood to apply almost exclusively to white men.

The civil rights movement, often called America's second revolution, began to change the status quo by challenging the denial of basic rights and insisting upon the protection of equal opportunity. Beginning with the U.S. Supreme Court's epochal decision in *Brown* v. *Board of Education* (1954), the nation was forced to abandon its support of segregation and discrimination, and to begin to address the pervasive and stubborn barriers to full participation by minorities and women in American life. Institutions, attitudes, and behavior had to be changed in ways that allowed the previously excluded to make their contribution to society.

In 1961, affirmative action was adopted as public policy to assure the full participation of minorities and women in the job market. Today "affirmative action" is subject to many interpretations, but essentially, it defines a set of special measures that take race and gender into account when decisions are made on hiring, promotion, and other aspects of employment. The consideration of such factors certainly is not new to the American experience. What is different about affirmative action is its use of personal characteristics as a device to assure, rather than to deny, equal job opportunity.

Government intervention in the labor market is indispensable to the protection of equal job opportunity. In the absence of government intervention, there are no "natural forces" that would lead automatically and inexorably toward the equalization of job opportunities for racial minorities and others.

Economic theory suggests that competition in the labor market will lead employers to hire and promote the most productive workers, in pursuit of profit maximization, without regard to race or gender. The theory, however, can accommodate discrimination. As Gary Becker observed in *The Economics of Discrimination*, employers might have a "taste for discrimination" that can be satisfied simultaneously while maximizing profits. That means an employer who discriminates is willing to forgo part of the monetary benefits of production in order to indulge the "taste for discrimination."

Under these conditions, discrimination in the labor market might continue indefinitely if no countervailing force is introduced to eliminate it. The persistence of racial inequality in the labor market before the adoption of public policies to protect equal job opportunity demonstrates the failure of natural competitive forces to prevent discrimination.

THE RATIONALE FOR AFFIRMATIVE ACTION

The unequal economic status of minorities, women, and majority group men is not solely the result of current discrimination in the labor market, and would not disappear immediately if discrimination ceased to exist. Interpersonal differences in occupational status, income, and other measures of economic well-being reflect a broad range of personal characteristics including, but not limited to, personal preferences, age, education, attitudes, and values. Observed differences in economic status among groups also reflect the present effects of past discrimination against members of particular groups based on their race, sex, and other personal characteristics. Thus, although current acts of discrimination might be widely condemned as incompatible with contemporary American values, and punished because they are unlawful, the mere enforcement of laws against discriminatory behavior will not assure equal opportunity. Something more is required to secure and protect the rights of all persons to participate fully in the economy.

As President Lyndon B. Johnson said in 1965:

You do not take a person who for years has been hobbled by chains, liberate him, bring him up to the starting line of a race and then say, "You are free to compete with all others," and still believe [that you are] being fair. It is not enough just to open the gates of opportunity. All of our citizens must have the ability to walk through those gates. This is the next and more profound stage of the battle for civil rights.

Supreme Court Justice Harry Blackmun recognized the same imperative when he observed in the *Bakke* case, "In order to get beyond racism we must first take account of race."

The use of race and gender identification for inclusionary, rather than exclusionary, purposes altered the nature of antidiscrimination policy. The rationale is that affirmative action helps make the distribution or availability of social goods and opportunities more equal and fair. Professor Richard Wasserstrom of the Department of Philosophy, University of California, Santa Cruz, captured the essence of the problem.

We are living in a society in which a person's race [and sex] is a socially significant and important characteristic. It affects both the way the individual looks at the world and the way the world looks at the individual. In our society, to be black is to be at a disadvantage in terms of virtually every conceivable measure of success or satisfaction—be it economic, political or social. Viewed from the perspective of our social realities, race [and gender] in our world is taken into account in a certain way in the context of a specific set of institutional arrangements and a specific ideology which together create and maintain a system of objectionable, oppressive institutions and unwarranted beliefs and attitudes towards those who are [racial minority and female] and in favor of those who are [white and male]. ("A Justification of Preferential Treatment Programs," Conference report prepared for the Rockefeller Foundation)

Affirmative action is aimed at the entrenched attitudes, behavior, and institutional arrangements that perpetuate the denial of equal opportunity to minorities and women. It is based on the reality that in the absence of conscious, deliberate efforts to assure equal opportunity, the legacy of past discrimination will be reinforced by contemporary actions. The expectation is that by pursuing the special measures of affirmative action, attitudes, values, and behavior will change in ways that redress the balance against population groups previously excluded from full participation in the job market.

IMPLEMENTING AFFIRMATIVE ACTION

When President John F. Kennedy issued Executive Order 10925, reauthorizing the federal government's program to assure nondiscrimination in employment among government contractors, he built upon the record established by his three immediate predecessors. Beginning with President Franklin D. Roosevelt's Fair Employment Practices Commission (FEPC), three successive agencies attempted to prohibit discriminatory practices in firms doing business with the federal government.

The experience of the three agencies was largely ineffective. The FEPC had only advisory powers, supplemented by the authority to hold hearings on the employment practices of defense contractors. With limited staff and even more limited political support within the Roosevelt administration, the FEPC operated with long delays in responding to charges of discrimination submitted by black workers and by civil rights leaders. The main objective of government policy makers during the FEPC years was the successful prosecution of the war effort; all other goals, including equal job opportunity, were assigned lower priority.

The Truman Fair Employment Committee had a relatively short life span, but President Truman acquired high credibility on equal employment opportunity (EEO) after he issued the executive order that desegregated the armed forces. Like its predecessor, however, the Truman committee was plagued with limited staff and little authority to investigate contractor employment practices and to act on findings of discrimination.

During the Eisenhower administration, the Committee on Government Contracts was headed by Vice President Richard M. Nixon. The committee staff was expanded beyond the level of previous committees, and an attempt was made to address the most obvious cases of employment discrimination. In response to evidence submitted by civil rights organizations, the committee, at times supported by the direct action of the vice president, intervened to correct discriminatory behavior.

One important feature of the committee's work was the collection of data documenting the employment practices of government contractors. Though limited in scope and coverage, the industry employment data revealed significant evidence of socially segregated occupational opportunity. But the lack of measurable progress toward equal job opportunity under the policies pursued by the Eisenhower, Truman, and Roosevelt fair employment committees led President Kennedy's civil rights advisers to recommend a more proactive policy aimed at rooting out the widespread job discrimination evident within the government contracting community. That was the main goal of Kennedy's President's Committee for Equal Employment Opportunity (PCEEO), which was chaired by Vice President Lyndon B. Johnson.

Indeed, the need for a stronger program than that implemented before 1960 was signaled in the final report of President Eisenhower's Committee on Government Contracts. It concluded:

Overt discrimination in the sense that an employer actually refuses to hire solely because of race, religion—is not as prevalent as is generally believed. To a greater degree, *the indifference of employers to establishing a positive policy* of non-discrimination hinders qualified applicants and employees from being hired and promoted on the basis of equality.

The direct result of such indifference is that schools, training institutions, recruitment and referral sources follow the pattern set by industry. Employment sources do not normally supply job applicants regardless of race, color, religion, or national origin *unless asked to do so by employer*. [italics added] (Final Report of the Committee on Government Contracts, Executive Office of the President)

Executive Order 10925, which created the PCEEO, introduced affirmative action as the device to get at the institutional racism and sexism—patterns of past discrimination built into institutional systems—described in the Eisenhower committee's report. "Affirmative action" was a term drawn from the field of labor-management relations, where employers found guilty of unfair labor practices regarding employee attempts to organize could be required to take steps to assure a work environment free of threats against future employee organizing activities.

As interpreted at that time, the affirmative action requirement for government contractors meant special recruitment and preemployment assessment policies aimed at producing more equal opportunity for available jobs.

The prototype for an affirmative action program was the agreement signed by the Lockheed aircraft company in 1961 after a complaint against its employment practices was filed with PCEEO by the NAACP. The company agreed to take special efforts to recruit and employ black workers in both white- and blue-collar jobs. Most importantly for future policy implementation, the company also agreed to record, and submit to the committee, periodic reports on the number of employees hired, by race, sex, and occupational group.

A number of firms signed similar agreements, called Plans for Progress, and proceeded to alter their hiring policies in order to increase black employment. The voluntary program, however, eclipsed the executive order's enforcement activity aimed at nonsignatory employers. Still, the special efforts seemed to produce modest gains. The 103 Plans for Progress companies increased the percentage of black employees from 5.1 percent to 5.7 percent within the first two years. That represented a gain of 40,938 of the companies' 341,734 vacancies—more than double the representation of black workers among those hired before Plans for Progress.

TOWARD GOALS AND TIMETABLES

When Title VII of the Civil Rights Act of 1964 was passed, the administration of the federal government's antidiscrimination contractor program was reorganized. The PCEEO was abolished, and its responsibilities were transferred to the U.S. Department of Labor's Division of Labor Standards. A new agency, the Office of Federal Contract Compliance (OFCC), was created to enforce the new Executive Order 11246.

The new office proceeded to develop regulations and procedures to assure equal job opportunity among government contractors. But the special problems with minority employment in the construction industry persisted, with increased difficulty. Such problems were exacerbated by frequent demonstrations by civil rights activists in local communities where government-supported construction proceeded with virtually all-white work crews in all-black neighborhoods. In an effort to generate greater responsiveness by construction contractors equal employment, OFCC introduced the requirement for employment goals and timetables as a device for measuring compliance with the executive order.

The goals and timetables were part of the Philadelphia Plan, an agreement with contractors performing federally assisted construction in that city. The plan stated explicitly that the goals were not to be considered quotas, but were guideposts for measuring the contractors' progress toward equal opportunity. The maximum requirement of the government's program was good faith effort to achieve the goals. There was no requirement to hire the unqualified, or to discriminate against nonminorities. What was important was the process that employers used to integrate their workforce. If an employer failed to meet the goals and timetables, the response of the government typically was to investigate the efforts used to achieve the goals. Although OFCC retained ultimate authority to withdraw a contract, or to refuse to award a future contract to an employer in noncompliance, that sanction was not applied until a decade later, when Secretary of Labor Ray Marshall withdrew a contract from a trucking company.

Goals and timetables were quickly introduced into contracts in nonconstruction industries, and were expanded to cover women under Revised Order Number 4, issued in 1971. "Goals" were stated as target proportions of minorities and women who might be expected to be employed in the various occupations, based on the proportion of such persons in the relevant population. The "timetable" was the number of years during which measurable progress toward the achievement of the goal should be made.

This enforcement device sparked widespread and vociferous opposition. Some critics refused to concede that goals and timetables were not synonymous with quotas, despite clear statements to the contrary in both the executive order and its implementing regulations.

One line of attack against goals and timetables focused on the comparison of the employment of minorities and women in various occupations against the presence of such groups in the local population. Thomas Sowell, a black conservative economist, argued that to elevate employment and population parity to a legitimate public policy goal is to make statistical variance a federal offense. He further observed that in no nation, at no time, has there ever been parity between the number of persons of various racial, ethnic, or religious groups in the population, and their presence in all occupations, industries, and other classifications of employment. To suggest that statistical parity should be the goal of equal opportunity, according to this criticism, is to make goals synonymous with quotas, despite protestations to the contrary.

Another critic of affirmative action, Glenn Loury, formerly of the Kennedy School of Government at Harvard, suggests that numerical information on racial and sexual employment practices can be useful in identifying firms that might warrant closer scrutiny as potential discriminators. Recognizing the limitations of a pure "color-blind" position as the foundation of equal employment opportunity enforcement, Loury concedes the value in comparing an employer's complement of minorities and women with their presence in the labor market.

But Loury is loath to adopt goals and timetables as a device for hiring or promoting members of the legally protected groups except in a finding of discrimination. In his view, to use goals and timetables except as a remedy against discrimination is to confer benefits on some minorities and women who are not entitled to such rewards. His view, then, is similar to Sowell's in rejecting the notion that statistical disparity between a group's employment and its population representation is a legitimate basis for setting goals to achieve equal opportunity.

While critics continue to debate whether goals are in fact quotas, employers have adopted affirmative action as a regular part of their personnel practices. The Dupont Corporation, for example, set internal hiring and promotion goals higher than those suggested by OFCC. The rationale for the practice is that the company pursues management by objectives, and considers goals and timetables for equal job opportunity a useful tool for measuring the results of affirmative action policy.

To be effective, however, the implementation of affirmative action, including the skillful use of goals and timetables, requires strong support from the chief executive and careful staff training and technical assistance. What seems apparent is that in the wake of increased criticism of goals and timetables by senior officials of the federal government, including the attorney general, the chairman of the U.S. Commission on Civil Rights, and others during the 1980s, some business firms abandoned their focus on numerical measures of compliance with antidiscrimination policies. Others, especially large firms, continue to adhere to goals and timetables, but many have integrated EEO objectives into regular human resource development strategies. The result is a widespread perception that affirmative action is less important today than before—a perception reinforced by the virtual silence of senior corporate executives on the importance of equal job opportunity and affirmative action. According to Christine Kramer, director, Affirmative Action Planning at CBS:

There is no question in my mind, having been in the field for 15 years, that affirmative action has changed significantly. One of the things that I find most frustrating is that [some] larger companies continue to use entry level hiring as a cop-out for meeting their obligations under the Executive Order Program. A lot of us tried to begin to institutionalize affirmative action with a long-range goal of doing ourselves out of jobs so that there wouldn't be a need for such a function, and that worked in a lot of companies, even in specific divisions and parts of companies. But I do see that changing. (U.S. House of Representatives, Committee on Education and Labor, *Final Report of the Advisory Group on Affirmative Action*)

AGGREGATE MEASURES OF IMPACT

The bulk of the statistical evidence supports the conclusion that the labor market position of minorities improved more rapidly after 1971 than might have been expected from earlier trends, general business conditions, or relative educational attainment of minorities. But females' earnings have not increased significantly relative to those of males. Whether such stability at a time of rising female labor force participation would have been predicted before 1970 has not been carefully studied. To discern the impact of affirmative action on the observed trends, the effects of the OFCCP and EEOC must be measured. Such research, while not conclusive, suggests that OFCCP has been a factor leading toward higher levels of employment of minorities than might have occurred without the agency, but that EEOC's impact is more difficult to measure.

Statistical studies of the impact of affirmative action often suffer from the lack of careful specification of precisely what in the operation of OFCCP or EEOC would produce higher levels of employment for minorities and women than otherwise might exist. But if the burden of proof is lowered to a level more commensurate with limitations imposed by incomplete data, more positive results of affirmative action emerge.

For example, a study by Finis Welch and James Smith, two Rand Corporation economists thought to be unsympathetic to affirmative action, concluded that "affirmative action has resulted in a radical reshuffling of black jobs in the labor force." They found that affirmative action shifted black male employment toward EEOC-covered firms and industries, and that it resulted in an increase in the representation of black male workers in managerial and professional jobs in such firms. As a result, "there has been a short-lived, but significant positive effect on wages of younger black workers," and "the main beneficiaries of affirmative action—in terms of income—have been young, college educated blacks."

An unpublished study conducted by OFCCP in 1984 concluded that companies subject to Executive Order 11246 from 1974 to 1980 showed more favorable employment gains for minorities and women than did nonfederal contractors, who, presumably, were obligated only to adhere to nondiscrimination—a less effective device for assuring equal job opportunity (U.S. Department of Labor, *Employment Patterns of Minorities and Women*). The 77,000 companies reviewed had over 20 million employees. During the six-year period, minority employment increased 20.1 percent and female employment 2.2 percent, while total employment grew by 8.2 percent. Moreover, the federal contractors had a smaller proportion of minority and female employees in the lower-paying jobs than did noncontractors, and contractors showed significantly faster growth of minorities and women in managerial jobs.

Professor Jonathan Leonard of the University of California, Berkeley, conducted one of the best-conceived and most thorough studies of the impact of the executive order and of Title VII on minority and female employment. He concluded that while the OFCCP program helped black workers, its impact on nonblack minorities and women was less conclusive. He also found that class-action litigation under Title VII had a relatively greater impact than affirmative action on black employment. Leonard's data, like that of the OFCCP study, showed that the greatest gains have been in the higher-paying managerial, professional, and craft occupations, although gains were recorded across a wide range of occupational fields. Significant gains were noted among black bus drivers and computer operators, as well as attorneys and psychologists.

A study conducted by the Bureau of National Affairs found that among 114 employers in a cross section of U.S. industry, women had achieved at least first-level management in almost 9 out of 10 firms, and executive positions in about half of the responding companies. Female gains exceeded similar progress among minority employees. Similarly, in 1986 the Korn/Ferry executive search firm conducted a seven-year follow-up study of senior-level executives in a broad range of industries. The results showed that of more than 1,300 respondents, 2 percent of the senior executives were women, a ratio that, although low, was still several times the level observed in 1970. But there was little representation of minorities in senior positions (less than 1 percent), a status unchanged over a seven-year period. Minorities, however, showed improved representation in middle management. The Korn/Ferry study suggests that despite government efforts to promote affirmative action, the impact on the race and sex composition of occupants of the executive suite has been minimal.

OFCCP IN THE REAGAN YEARS

During the 1980 presidential campaign, Ronald Reagan opposed affirmative action as an undesirable social policy. His public statements, including a major campaign speech delivered in Mississippi, equated affirmative action with quotas. Governor Reagan's position on the issue was buttressed by widely publicized statements made by prominent black conservatives, such as Thomas Sowell, Clarence Thomas, and Clarence Pendleton, who, because of their racial identity, lent legitimacy to the attack on affirmative action.

Shortly after the Reagan administration took office, a determined campaign was launched to reverse the policy on affirmative action for government contractors and to weaken the enforcement power of OFCCP. Only days after the inauguration, the Department of Labor suspended the new executive order regulations adopted in the eleventh hour by the Carter administration. Over the next two years, a new set of regulations was drafted to bring the executive order's implementation more in line with the policy preferences of the new OFCCP leadership.

Specifically, the new regulations (a) raised the dollar threshold for coverage to $250,000 per contract, thereby reducing the number of contractors required to adopt an affirmative action plan; (b) cut the amount of paperwork involved in reporting on compliance with affirmative action plans; (c) declared that goals and timetables were to be used solely as guides to action and not as measures of compliance; (d) changed reporting on utilization from monthly to quarterly; (e) measured "underutilization" within a 10.0 percent variance between the contractor's employment and the availability of minorities and women in the area's population; and (f) measured the availability of minorities and women by occupation and skill level as well as by population. In addition to these regulatory changes, a recommendation was made to withdraw OFCCP's authority to invoke back pay penalties for findings of discrimination; the back pay remedy would be limited to EEOC.

OFCCP's proposed regulations were strongly endorsed by the Department of Justice, where William Bradford Reynolds, the assistant attorney general for civil rights, had launched a major policy and media campaign against affirmative action. The Justice Department was joined in its campaign by a congressional group led by Senator Orrin Hatch of Utah, who attacked affirmative action and threatened to offer legislation prohibiting the requirement that contractors adopt goals and timetables.

Civil rights advocates marshaled a defense of affirmative action and aimed their attention at the House of Representatives, where OFCCP allies, such as Congressman Augustus Hawkins, chairman of the Education and Labor Committees; and Don Edwards, chairman of the Judiciary Subcommittee on Civil Rights, used their influence to thwart the publication of the proposed regulations. The regulations also ran up against the political clock as the 1982 midterm congressional elections approached. The Reagan White House did not want the regulations to be a lightning rod issue that would energize the president's political opponents.

Business Support

One of the interesting, and highly significant, aspects of the controversy over OFFCP policy was the support for affirmative action by major segments of the business community. By the early 1980s, many business firms had institutionalized affirmative action as a regular part of their human resources management policy. They had little inclination to change such practices, notwithstanding the preferences of the Reagan administration. Indeed, several prominent members of the Business Roundtable, the Fortune 500 business group, publicly declared their intention to continue to practice affirmative action, and to use goals and timetables even if OFCCP changed the rules. Such business executives argued that affirmative action helped them to manage the workforce better; to get the best employees, especially women; and to improve their competitive position. Also, at that time, there were few complaints from white males.

Legal Environment

At the same time efforts were made to weaken enforcement of the executive order, the federal courts announced several major decisions affecting the scope of affirmative action. In 1979, the U.S. Supreme Court announced its decision in the *Bakke* case, in which affirmative action in college admissions was upheld, but only under conditions that avoided injury to white male applicants. Other court decisions during the 1980s attempted to define the limits on the use of affirmative action while not prohibiting the policy entirely as a device for assuring equal job opportunity.

OFCCP Operations

While the Reagan administration was thwarted in its efforts to rewrite the rules for administering Executive Order 11246, a concerted, and more successful, effort was made to reduce enforcement through administrative measures. For example, during the first two years of the new administration, the number of OFCCP compliance officers was reduced from 735 to 430. Also, the number of conciliation agreements dropped from 1,121 to 849.

Unable to issue new regulations, the OFCCP political leadership attempted to change the policy direction through other means. Program leaders adopted the "podium policy," communicating directives not in writing but through telephone calls, staff meetings, and public events with employers. Policy was also communicated to career staff through notes written in the margin of conciliation agreements, rather than in formal policy memoranda. Through these, and other unusual and irregular devices, field staff soon learned that the preferred approach to enforcement was to do little, and not rock the boat.

A review of OFCCP performance data suggests that there was continued emphasis on conducting compliance reviews—the key enforcement tool. In fact, during the first Reagan term, the number of reviews increased by 1,890, or 60 percent. During the second Reagan term, the number of reviews grew by an average of 257 per year, and by 1988 OFCCP had completed 5,474 reviews. Clearly, the emphasis was on productivity, but according to some career staff (now retired), the increased number of reviews and complaint investigations was achieved at the expense of quality and thoroughness.

For example, despite the number of reviews, no affected class cases (those where groups of workers were found to be under represented in the workforce) were reported. Also, the amount of back pay obtained for victims of discrimination declined from $1,296 million in 1983 to $299 million in 1985. Throughout the Reagan administration, the average annual amount of back pay was $3.9 million, compared with $16.2 million during the first three years of the Bush administration.

Other evidence of the performance of OFCCP during the Reagan years shows:

Number of debarments
FY 1981 to 1985—4
(Carter years, 1977 to 1980—13)

Requests for solicitor filings of complaints
FY 1980—173
FY 1985—25

Persons receiving back pay
FY 1980—4,336
FY 1986—499

Conciliation Agreements as percent of cases with violations
FY 1980—49 percent
FY 1985—33 percent

In summary, the leadership of the Reagan administration pursued a conscious, deliberate effort to weaken and undermine the federal government's program to protect equal job opportunity and affirmative action among government contractors. In sharp contrast to policies pursued by previous administrations, including two Republican presidents, the Reagan team sought to expunge affirmative action from national social policy. While not completely successful, their efforts produced a much smaller, and largely demoralized, staff that was unable to fulfill the OFCCP mission. As a result, much employment discrimination was permitted to go unchecked for almost a decade during the 1980s.

NOTE

This chapter is an expression of the author's view and *is not* an expression of U.S. Department of Labor policy.

BIBLIOGRAPHY

Anderson, Bernard E. "Black Employment in the Telephone Industry." In Phyllis A. Wallace, ed., *Equal Opportunity and the AT&T Case*. Cambridge, Mass.: MIT Press, 1974.

Becker, Gary. *The Economics of Discrimination*. Chicago: University of Chicago Press, 1956.

Bureau of National Affairs, *Affirmative Action Today: A Legal and Practical Analysis*. Washington, D.C.: BNA, 1986.

Bureau of National Affairs, *EEO Policies and Programs*. Personnel Policies Forum Survey no. 141.Washington, D.C.: BNA, 1986

Fernandez, John. *Survival in the Corporate Fishbowl: Making It into Middle and Upper Management*. Lexington, Mass.: Lexington Books, 1987.

Final Report of the Committee on Government Contracts, Executive Office of the President, May 1961.

Hill, Herbert. "Race, Ethnicity, and Organized Labor: The Opposition to Affirmative Action." *Journal of Intergroup Relations*, 31–82.

Johnson, Lyndon B. Commencement address, Howard University. Washington, D.C., June 5, 1965.

Jones, James E., Jr. "The Origins of Affirmative Action." *Iowa Law Review*, May 1985.

Korn/Ferry Executive Search, Inc. "Equal Opportunity in Corporate America," unpublished report privately distributed, New York, March 1986.

Larson, John A. *The Impact of the AT&T-EEO Consent Decree*. Philadelphia: Industrial Research Unit, University of Pennsylvania, 1979.

Leonard, Jonathan S. "The Impact of Affirmative Action on Employment." Paper commissioned for the Study Group on Affirmative Action, June 1988. *Local 28 Sheet Metal Workers* v *EEOC*, 41 FEP Cases 107 (July 2, 1986).

Loury, Glenn C. Comments on Affirmative Action. Paper presented before the 7th Annual Judicial Conference of the District of Columbia Circuit, May 19, 1986.

———. "Equal Opportunity: Reality, Achievable Goal, or Elusive Dream." Unpublished paper prepared for Symposium for Senior Corporate Officers on EEO, New York, December

11, 1985.

Madden, Janice F. *The Persistence of Pay Differentials*. Working paper. Department of Regional Studies, University of Pennsylvania, 1986.

Regents of the University of California v. *Bakke*, 438 U.S. 265, 288–289 (1978).

Smith, James P., and Finis R. Welch. *Closing the Gap: Forty Years of Economic Progress for Blacks*. Santa Monica, Calif.: Rand Corporation, 1986.

Sowell, Thomas. *Civil Rights: Rhetoric or Reality?* New York: Morrow, 1984.

U.S. Department of Labor, Employment Standards Administration, Employment Patterns of Minorities and Women in Federal Contractor and Noncontractor Establishments, 1974–1980: A Report of OFCCP. 1984.

U.S. House of Representatives, Committee on Education and Labor. *Final Report of the Advisory Group on Affirmative Action*. Washington, D.C., June 1987.

Wasserstrom, Richard. "A Justification of Preferential Treatment Programs." Conference report prepared for the Rockefeller Foundation. November 1983.

Wilson, William J. *The Declining Significance of Race*. Chicago: University of Chicago Press, 1978.

CHAPTER 5

Racial Differences in Employment Shares: New Evidence from the EEO-1 Files

William M. Rodgers III

INTRODUCTION

A resurgence has occurred in research that explores the ability of racial differences in access to suburban employment opportunities to explain the existence and persistence of racial differences in incomes. Proponents of this explanation, which is known as the "spatial mismatch hypothesis," argue that central city blacks experience lower relative wages and fewer employment opportunities due to high commuting costs and residential segregation. Numerous studies find that these structural impediments explain a portion of the observed racial differences in labor market outcomes. However, recent findings in Rodgers (1994b) demonstrate that during the 1980s, the dramatic erosion in minority wage and employment opportunities had little to do with racial and ethnic differences in access to suburban jobs, skills, family background, and neighborhood effects. Since this evidence came from the Current Population Survey, it can be considered only as indirect evidence. The results still cast serious doubt on the ability of "ghetto dispersal" and "gilded ghetto" initiatives to lead to significant reductions in the differences between black and white labor market outcomes.

Proponents of the job access explanation claim that the use of metropolitan residence to serve as a proxy for access to suburban jobs is quite crude. Access varies within central cities and suburbs, and thus, use of central city-suburb residence leads to estimated racial differences that are biased. This chapter responds to their concern. Using establishment data from the "Employer Information Report EEO-1" files, this study compares the race/ethnic-gender employment distributions of central city and suburban establishments. Typically, researchers use micro data from the Public Use Micro Data sets of the U.S. Census, and the National Longitudinal Survey of Youth, to study the impact that access to jobs has on racial differences in wages and employment. Researchers are now utilizing data collected from city-specific employer surveys. To my knowledge, they have not used the EEO-1 files to study the ability of firm location to explain racial differences in employment. Thus, analyzing employment shares by metropolitan location of the establishment provides a unique alternative. The obvious gain from using the EEO-1 files is the availability of large national samples. The drawback to using the files is the absence of the rich set of worker and employer information that many city-specific surveys contain.

The results for blacks and whites provide mild support for job access explanations. The share of black workers in central city establishments was three to four percentage points higher than the black share in suburban establishments. The share of white workers was largest in the suburbs; however, this advantage diminished during the 1990–1991 recession. Yet, compared with other predictor variables, metropolitan location of an establishment explains only 4 to 7 percent of the predicted variation in the black and white shares of employment.

The chief predictors of an establishment's share of black employment are census division location and occupation structure. Combined, these variables explain over 80 percent of the variation in the share of black employment. However, the fully specified model that contains additional information about federal contractor status and establishment type, explains only 25 percent of the variation in the share of black employment. Thus, employment practices within establishments play a key role in the allocation of blacks. A growing literature, led by Kirschenman and Neckerman (1991) and Moss and Tilly (1993), finds that employers view and treat blacks differently. This chapter also documents a modest rise in the segregation of black workers across firms.

The chapter provides a description of the experiences of Hispanics and Asians. The shares of both groups are largest in central city establishments; however, since 1990, the differences have diminished. I attribute this decline to the 1990–1991 recession, which had a more adverse impact on suburban areas. Census division location and occupational structure play the largest role in explaining the shares of employment, and the fully specified model can explain at most 25 percent of the variation in Hispanic and Asian shares. Segregation of Asians and Hispanics also increased from 1982 to 1992.

The next two sections describe the data and methodology used. These are followed by a section that presents a set of summary statistics and the regression results. The final section presents conclusions and offers an interpretation of the results.

THE DATA

The data for selected years come from the "Employer Information Report EEO-1" files. Each annual file provides the race/ethnic-gender distribution of employment within an establishment. The files typically account for between 40 and 50 percent of the Bureau of Labor Statistics employment, or approximately 34 to

42 million employees. The samples consist of private establishments that meet the following requirements. Establishments must have at least 100 employees. They may also have at least 50 employees, but then they must either have a federal contract or first-tier subcontract worth $50,000 or more, or act as depositories of federal funds in any amount, or act as issuing and paying agents for U.S. Savings Bonds and Notes. Prior to 1983, the minimum was 25 employees.

The major limitation that these filing requirements generate worsened during the 1980s. Table 5.1 illustrates that as a percentage of the Bureau of Labor Statistics total employment, the EEO-1 files coverage of employment fell in seven of the nine industries from 1980 to 1990. The decline in the ability to capture large segments of employment in the economy was due to the size of establishments that are required to file a report. The above restrictions clearly exclude small, single-establishment employers and multi-establishment employers whose entities have small workforces. The "Employer Information Report EEO-1" acknowledges this problem for construction, trade, services, and agricultural industries that have small single-establishment employers, as well as multi-establishment employers whose individual entities have small workforces. However, the industries that exhibit the largest decline in coverage are durable and nondurable manufacturing, and transportation. The fractions in durable and nondurable manufacturing fell from .77 to .69, and from .70 to .65, respectively. The fraction in transportation fell from .69 to .59.

The report's empirical analysis uses the establishment as the unit of analysis. Five types of establishment records exist. The first type is race/ethnic-gender reports for single establishments or stand-alone companies. The second type of record is the multi-establishment's consolidated report. This chapter contains the aggregate employment distribution of multi-establishments and all of their entities regardless of size. Headquarter reports constitute the third type of establishment information. The fourth type is the race/ethnic-gender distributions for the entities of the multi-establishment companies. Fifth is a set of special reports. To avoid double counting, the consolidated headquarter records are excluded from all empirical analysis.

METHODOLOGY

To determine the key predictors of a race/ethnic group's share of employment, I regress the log-odds ratio on indicator variables that denote the establishment's census division location, metropolitan location, establishment type, federal contractor status, industry affiliation, and occupational structure. The following description provides a more detailed explanation of the process used to describe the key predictors of a race/ethnic group's share of employment. Separate regressions are estimated for each race/ethnic group. The odds ratio for the rth race/ethnic group in the ith establishment in year t is:

$$E[\ln\left(\frac{P_i}{1-P_i}\right) | X_i] = X_i'\beta \ ,$$

where P_i is the ith establishment's share of employment for the rth race/ethnic group. In $[P_i/(1-P_i)]$ is the ith establishment's log-odds ratio, X_i is a k × I vector of predictor variables for the ith establishment, and β is a k x 1 vector of parameter. The notation $E[\ln(P/(1-P)|X]$ denotes the mean of the conditional distribution of the log-odds ratio given X. To correct for heteroscedasticity, the regressions are weighted by $(n_i/(P_i(1-P_i)))$, where n_i denotes the ith establishment's number of employees.

In order to describe the variation in the share of each race/ethnic group's employment, I regress the ith establishment's share of employment for the rth race/ethnic group, P_i, on the previously mentioned indicator variables.

The specification for metropolitan residence includes dummy variables for central city location and rural location, and a dummy variable that denotes whether the establishment's metropolitan location is unidentifiable. The excluded metropolitan group is suburban location. Thus, the coefficient of the central city dummy variable measures the difference in the share of the rth race/ethnic group's employment in central city and suburban establishments. An indicator variable that denotes whether an establishment has a federal contract is also included. Three indicator variables for establishment type were added. They denote whether the establishment is a stand-alone company or an entity of a multi-establishment company. Headquarter establishments are the excluded group.

The following industry dummy variables were added: agriculture; mining; construction; durable manufacturing; nondurable manufacturing; transportation; wholesale trade; retail trade; finance, insurance, and real estate; personal retail services; business-type services; entertainment; and health. Durable manufacturing is the excluded group. The occupational dummy variables are officials and managers, professionals, technicians, sales workers, office and clerical workers, craft workers, operatives, laborers, and service workers. Officials and managers are the excluded group. Finally, eight census division dummy variables were added. Establishments located in the South Atlantic Census Division comprise the excluded group.

Along with predicting and describing the variation in each race/ethnic group's share of employment, I am interested in determining whether racial segregation worsened during the 1980s. To do this, I constructed the S index of racial segregation. The index can be written as:

$$S = \frac{\sum_{i=1}^{I} T_i(p_i - p)^2}{Tp(1-p)} \ ,$$

where T denotes the total number of employees in all jobs, p denotes the fraction of the workforce that is of the race/ethnic group, and T_i and p_i are the values for the ith establishment. Values close to 0 indicate a high level of integration between establishments, and values close to 1 indicate a high level of segregation between establishments.

When one is restricted to establishment data, or, as in this study, use of micro data at the employee level is computationally unfeasible, the value of the S index can be used to calculate the variation "within establishment" component, which is the variance attributable to integration of establishments. Note that this does not necessarily mean that there will be integration within establishments, occupational segregation may still exist. See the Technical Appendix for a description of how to use the S index to calculate the variation "within establishment" component, even though we are constrained to using establishment data.

THE RESULTS

The Presence of Minorities in EEO-1 Establishments

Table 5.2 presents the results from a simple tabulation of the presence of various race/ethnic-gender groups in all establishments and headquarters. Panel A reveals that the presence of blacks grew slightly from 1979 to 1992, with the greatest gains during the 1983–1989 recovery. Black women experienced larger growth than black males. The growth was greater among noncontractors. However, compared with other race/ethnic-gender groups, blacks had the smallest increases. From 1979 to 1992, the presence of Asian males and females rose .13 in contractor establishments, and .10 and .12 in noncontractor establishments. These gains were distributed evenly across the 1980s in both contractors and noncontractors. The larger gains for Asians and Hispanics relative to blacks may represent a shift in employer preferences with regard to creating diverse work environments, or they may be due to the larger growth in each demographic group's population.

The most troubling result for minorities emerges when I analyze the effect of an increase in the minimum employment requirement. The parentheses contain the calculation of the presence of minorities under the old minimum of 25. Comparing the values against the fractions calculated under the new minimum requirement of 50 indicates that minorities are least represented in smaller firms. Excluding the smaller establishments raises the presence of minorities. This means that the smaller firms are less likely to have minorities as employees. The implication of this result is the need for a small establishment initiative to ensure that these firms are acting affirmatively.

Panel B of Table 5.2 contains calculations of the presence of minorities in headquarters of multi-establishments. During the 1980s, blacks, especially those in contractor establishments, experienced a decline in employment. What generated these results? The headquarter designation serves as a proxy for white-collar employment. A shift in employers' preferences with regard to filling minority slots may have occurred. Or, if outsourcing was great enough, many of the protection and cleaning services in which blacks are highly visible would no longer show up on establishments' headquarters report to the EEOC. This result clearly deserves further investigation.

The Share of Minority Employment in Establishments

Table 5.3 presents the share of employment by race/ethnic-gender group and contractor status. The most remarkable observation is the decline in the white male share in both contractors and noncontractors from 1979 to 1992. The decline was greatest during the 1983–1989 recovery. Who benefited from the decline in the white male share? The table indicates that the gains were distributed among all minorities and women, with women's shares rising the most. Table 5.4 presents the shares of headquarters. Again, white males experienced large declines in their share of employment during 1979–1992 period. The losses were distributed evenly between the early 1980s recession and the recovery. The headquarters data reveal a clear set of winners. The shares of white women, especially in noncontractors, exhibited the greatest increases. Asian and Hispanic women had smaller increases in their shares.

The remainder of this section presents shares of employment for the major industries in the sample. Table 5.5 contains the distribution of establishments by broad industry categories for 1979, 1983, 1989, and 1992. The choice of industries to highlight was based on the industry either having at least 10 percent of the sample's establishments or its growth in importance from 1979 to 1992. The manufacturing industries had percentages above 10 percent but showed a slight decline in importance. Over one-quarter of the establishments were in retail trade. Business-type services and health services showed remarkable growth. Business-type services more than doubled, while health services almost doubled. Tables 5.6 to 5.10 contain the race/ethnic-gender shares of employment for durable manufacturing, nondurable manufacturing, retail trade, business-type services, and health services.

For durable manufacturing (Table 5.6), the white and black male losses are offset by increases in the share of all women. The gains are spread out among each group. The key finding among nondurables (Table 5.7) is the decline in the share of white males and females in contractor establishments, and the tremendous gain by Hispanic males. Retail trade (Table 5.8) is the industry in which blacks make tremendous gains. The white shares, especially among noncontractors, fell dramatically. The white female share exhibits the sharpest decline. The share continued its downward spiral during the most recent recession. As a result, black and Hispanic shares exhibit dramatic increases. The reverse almost occurs in business services (Table 5.9). Both black and white male shares fall, but white women in contractors and noncontractors experience large gains. Black women do not benefit from these changes in business services. Health services (Table 5.10) is the industry in which the shares of black women rise.

The Determinants of the Share of Employment

Table 5.11 presents estimates from the log-odds ratio model. The analysis uses data for 1982, 1984, 1988, 1990, and 1992. The central city coefficients confirm the existence of spatial mismatch. The share of black workers in central city establishments is three to four percentage points higher than the share of black workers in suburban establishments. White suburban shares of employment are larger than central city shares; however, during the 1990–1991 recession, the differential exhibits a decline. The coefficients for Asians and Hispanics indicate that they, too, are concentrated in central city establishments; however, since 1990 this distinction has diminished. I attribute the decline in each race/ethnic group's share to the adverse impact of the 1990–1991 recession on suburban labor markets.

The results for establishment type suggest that black workers have lower likelihoods of being employed in the headquarters of multi-establishments. This result reflects the small share of black workers in white-collar jobs, which have a higher likelihood of being in an establishment's headquarters. As discussed earlier, this result could also reflect the outsourcing of protection and cleaning services that occurred during the 1980s. Hispanic workers tend to be located in smaller single-establishment companies. The regression coefficients for white workers clearly indicate that they are more likely to be found in the multi-establishments' headquarters.

The federal contract coefficients indicate that the presence of a contract provides greater opportunities for blacks and Asians. For whites and Hispanics, the presence of a federal contract lowers their probability of employment. All of the results are statistically significant.

Finally, the census division location, industry, and occupational variables reveal several interesting results. Due to space considerations, I report only the region of location coefficients. Tremendous regional variations in the shares exist. The white share of employment is greatest in the New England, Middle Atlantic, East North Central, West North Central, East South Central, and Mountain census divisions, and the importance rose during the second half of the 1980s. For blacks, the share of employment is greatest in the South Atlantic and East South Central census divisions. Hispanics and Asians are well represented in the Pacific census division. The share of white workers is greater in the high-wage service industries such as finance, insurance, and real estate. The shares of black, Hispanic, and Asian workers are greater in low-wage service industries. In terms of occupation, the share of white workers is greater in officials and managerial, and professional occupations, while the shares among minorities are greater in the blue-collar occupations.

Accounting for the Variation in the Share of Employment

How much of the variation in the race/ethnic shares do the labor demand, labor supply, and institutional measures presented in the previous section explain? To answer this question, I utilize the R^2's from regressions where the measures are incrementally added to the model. Table 5.12 presents the contribution of each labor demand, labor supply, and institutional measure. Several striking results emerge from the analysis. First, from 1982 to 1992, the ability of these proxies for labor demand, labor supply, and institutional measures to explain the variation in each race/ethnic group's share of employment rises for all groups except Asians. More important, after all measures have been added to the model, approximately 25 percent of the variation in each race/ethnic group's share of employment can be explained. Thus, a large portion of the variation in the share of each race/ethnic group's employment is explained by employer practices within establishments.

Surprisingly, the metropolitan location measures explain only 4 to 7 percent of the variation in the shares of white and black employment, and this contribution remained constant during the 1980s. Thus, in the aggregate, it is hard to believe that job access within central city and suburban areas plays a major role in the allocation of labor, and can explain the dramatic deterioration in the labor market opportunities of blacks during the 1980s. The chief predictors of the share of employment are census division location and an establishment's occupational structure. Division location explains over half of the variation in white, black, and Hispanic shares of employment, and 80 percent of the variation in the share of Asian employment. Occupational structure accounts for a third of the variation in the share of white employment, approximately one-fifth of the variation in the share of black and Hispanic employment, and only 4 to 6 percent of Asian employment.

To conclude this section, I present calculated S indices to describe the level of racial isolation that exists across establishments. The indices' values must be interpreted as the exposure of a particular race/ethnic group to the rest of the workforce. The indices for blacks, Hispanics, and Asians exhibit modest increases from 1982 to 1992. The index for blacks rises from .178 to .203. The Hispanic index rises from .265 to .284, and the Asian index grows from .091 to .124.

SUMMARY AND CONCLUSIONS

Holzer, Ihlanfeldt, and Sjoquist (1994), Kain (1992), Holzer (1991), and many others attribute the existence and persistence of black-white wage gaps and employment differences to spatial disadvantages that blacks face. This study and Rodgers (1994a) do not reject the importance of spatial constraints on black mobility during the 1980s; however, the results in this report strengthen my skepticism that spatial mismatch explains much of the 1980s erosion in black labor market outcomes. Using data from the "Employer Information Report EEO-1" files, I found that metropolitan location of establishments does matter, but probably very little. The share of black employment is greatest in central cities, and the share of white employment is greatest in suburban areas. However, the empirical findings indicate that these relationships remained constant as the relative labor market status of blacks eroded. Furthermore, the contribution of metropolitan location in explaining the variation in the share of employment only explains 5 to 6 percent of the total variation.

Researchers and policy makers continue to rely on the intuitive appeal of spatial explanations. As a result, public policy initiatives focus on lessening racial differences in access to suburban employment, such as "ghetto dispersal" or "gilded ghetto" policies. Researchers should focus on understanding the chief predictors of a race's share of employment: the establishment's census division location, occupational structure, and labor market practices within establishments. Compiling information on labor market practices is of paramount importance, and the rise in segregation across firms warrants the need for greater vigilance in the enforcement strategies of antidiscrimination laws. (See Table 5A1.)

TECHNICAL APPENDIX

The derivation draws heavily from Zoloth (1976). Let R_{ij} denote an indicator variable that equals 1 if the ith worker in the jth establishment is from the race/ethnic group of interest, and 0 otherwise. A hypothesis test for racial equality across establishments can be derived from analysis of variance. Denote the expected value of R_{ij} as p and the variance of R_{ij} can be decomposed as

$$\sum_{i=1}^{I}\sum_{j=1}^{J}(R_{ij}-p)^2 = \sum_{i=1}^{I}\sum_{j=1}^{J}(R_{ij}-p_i)^2 + \sum_{i}^{I}(p_i-p)^2 ,$$

where the first term on the right-hand side measures the within-establishment variation. Zoloth interprets this as the variance due to having integrated establishments. As I stated earlier, this does not preclude substantial within-establishment segregation. The second term can be interpreted as the variance due to segregated establishments.

Zoloth demonstrates that the equation (2) above can be rewritten as

$$\sum_{i=1}^{I}\sum_{j=1}^{J}(R_{ij}-p)^2 = Tp(1-p)(1-S) + Tp(1-p)S$$

where $Tp(1-p)$ denotes the total variance in the system. Thus, S can also be interpreted as the percent of the total variance due to segregation. The measure of the within-establishment variation can easily be solved for. Values of T and p are calculated from the data, where T denotes the sample size and p denotes the mean share of employment.

SUMMARY

This study concludes that racial and ethnic differences in access to suburban jobs fail to explain the dramatic erosion in black male and female wage and employment opportunities during the 1980s. Data from the "Employer Information Report EEO-1" files indicate that during the 1980s the share of black workers in central city establishments was three to four percentage points higher than the suburban share of black employment. Furthermore, the central city-suburb distinction explains only 4 to 7 percent of the variation in the black share of employment from 1982 to 1992. The chief predictors of an establishment's share of black employment are census division location and occupation structure. Combined, these variables explain over 80 percent of the predicted variation in the share of black employment. However, the fully specified model that contains additional information about federal contractor status and establishment type, explains only 25 percent of the variation in the share of black employment. This report also documents a rise in the segregation of black workers.

This chapter extends the analysis to Hispanics and Asians, ethnic groups that receive little attention from labor economists. The results indicate that prior to the 1990–1991 recession, both groups had *higher* employment shares in central city establishments. However, the economic downturn of the earlier 1990s removed this advantage. Census division location and occupational structure play the largest role in explaining the shares of employment, and the fully specified model can explain at most 25 percent of the variation in Hispanic and Asian shares. Segregation of Asians and Hispanics exhibited a modest increase from 1982 to 1992.

What are the implications of these results? The central city-suburb comparisons presented in this study increase doubt about the ability of policies based upon narrowing spatial disadvantages that minorities face to have significant effects on narrowing aggregate racial differences in employment-population ratios, unemployment rates, and hourly wages. The rise in segregation and the importance of practices within establishments warrant continued vigilance in the enforcement of antidiscrimination laws. Researchers should continue to focus on describing and understanding the regional allocation of labor, the occupational structures of establishments, and employer practices within establishments.

Table 5.1
Comparison of EEO-1 and BLS Employment (Thousands)

Industry	1980			1990		
	EEO-1	BLS	EEO-1 as fraction of BLS	EEO-1	BLS	EEO-1 as % of BLS
Private, nonagricultural	34,146	74,486	0.458	42,025	89,346	0.470
Mining	579	1,025	0.565	429	735	0.584
Construction	573	4,469	0.128	620	5,204	0.119
Durable manufacturing	9,386	12,215	0.768	7,667	11,122	0.689
Nondurable manufacturing	5,674	8,146	0.697	5,128	7,940	0.646
Transportation	3,510	5,056	0.694	3,432	5,839	0.588
Wholesale trade	1,422	5,281	0.269	1,295	6,361	0.204
Retail trade	4,718	15,292	0.309	5,460	19,788	0.276
Finance, insurance, and real estate	2,604	5,162	0.504	2,987	6,832	0.437
Services	5,683	17,741	0.320	8,948	26,505	0.338
Agriculture	142	NA	NA	140	NA	NA

Sources: U.S. Equal Employment Opportunity Commission, *Equal Employment Survey, 1980 and 1990;* U.S. Department of Labor, Bureau of Labor Statistics, *Employment and Earnings,* March 1980 and March 1990.

Table 5.2
The Presence of Minorities in Establishments

Panel A: All Establishments

Contractors	1979[1]	1983	1989	1992	1992-79	1992-89	1989-79	1989-83	1983-79
Black males	0.76(0.69)	0.75	0.77	0.78	0.02	0.01	0.01	0.02	-0.01
Black females	0.66(0.57)	0.67	0.70	0.70	0.04	0.00	0.04	0.03	0.01
Hispanic males	0.53(0.46)	0.54	0.58	0.60	0.07	0.02	0.05	0.04	0.01
Hispanic females	0.42(0.36)	0.44	0.50	0.51	0.09	0.01	0.08	0.06	0.02
Asian males	0.34(0.28)	0.38	0.43	0.47	0.13	0.04	0.09	0.05	0.04
Asian females	0.28(0.23)	0.33	0.39	0.41	0.13	0.02	0.11	0.06	0.05

Noncontractors	1979[1]	1983	1989	1992	1992-79	1992-89	1989-79	1989-83	1983-79
Black males	0.68(0.62)	0.69	0.72	0.72	0.04	0.00	0.04	0.03	0.01
Black females	0.61(0.55)	0.64	0.69	0.68	0.07	-0.01	0.08	0.05	0.03
Hispanic males	0.46(0.40)	0.48	0.52	0.55	0.09	0.03	0.06	0.04	0.02
Hispanic females	0.40(0.35)	0.45	0.49	0.53	0.13	0.04	0.09	0.04	0.05
Asian males	0.29(0.24)	0.32	0.36	0.39	0.10	0.03	0.07	0.04	0.03
Asian females	0.29(0.24)	0.32	0.38	0.41	0.12	0.03	0.09	0.06	0.03

Panel B: Headquarters

Contractors	1979	1983	1989	1992	1992-79	1992-89	1989-79	1989-83	1983-79
Black males	0.65	0.63	0.61	0.59	-0.06	-0.02	-0.04	-0.02	-0.02
Black females	0.65	0.65	0.63	0.62	-0.03	-0.01	-0.02	-0.02	0.00
Hispanic males	0.48	0.48	0.49	0.49	0.01	0.00	0.01	0.01	0.00
Hispanic females	0.46	0.49	0.48	0.50	0.04	0.02	0.02	-0.01	0.03
Asian males	0.39	0.42	0.45	0.46	0.07	0.01	0.06	0.03	0.03
Asian females	0.36	0.40	0.42	0.44	0.08	0.02	0.06	0.02	0.04

Noncontractors	1979	1983	1989	1992	1992-79	1992-89	1989-79	1989-83	1983-79
Black males	0.58	0.57	0.57	0.56	-0.02	-0.01	-0.01	0.00	-0.01
Black females	0.53	0.54	0.56	0.56	0.03	0.00	0.03	0.02	0.01
Hispanic males	0.41	0.42	0.43	0.45	0.04	0.02	0.02	0.01	0.01
Hispanic females	0.37	0.40	0.42	0.43	0.06	0.01	0.05	0.02	0.03
Asian males	0.28	0.32	0.35	0.37	0.09	0.02	0.07	0.03	0.04
Asian females	0.27	0.30	0.35	0.37	0.10	0.02	0.08	0.05	0.03

[1]Calculated using the entities of multi-establishments that have at least 50 employees. The calculations in parenthesis are calculated from samples that include entities of multi-establishments that have at least 25 employees. In 1983, the reporting requirements for multi-establishments changed from having to supply race/ethnic-gender distributions of employment for entities with at least 25 employees to entities with at least 50 employees.

Sources: Author's tabulations from the EEO-1 files.

Table 5.3
Share of Employment by Race/Ethnic Group and Gender, Selected Years and Changes

Panel A: Males

Contractors	1979	1983	1989	1992	1992-79	1992-89	1989-79	1989-83	1983-79
White	0.506	0.487	0.448	0.463	-0.043	0.015	-0.058	-0.039	-0.019
Black	0.059	0.055	0.059	0.060	0.001	0.001	0.000	0.004	-0.004
Asian	0.007	0.009	0.013	0.015	0.008	0.002	0.006	0.004	0.002
Hispanic	0.034	0.033	0.040	0.043	0.009	0.003	0.006	0.007	-0.001

Noncontractors	1979	1983	1989	1992	1992-79	1992-89	1989-79	1989-83	1983-79
White	0.418	0.396	0.375	0.361	-0.057	-0.014	-0.043	-0.021	-0.022
Black	0.052	0.047	0.055	0.052	0.000	-0.003	0.003	0.008	-0.005
Asian	0.006	0.007	0.010	0.011	0.005	0.001	0.004	0.003	0.001
Hispanic	0.035	0.036	0.041	0.047	0.012	0.006	0.006	0.005	0.001

Panel B: Females

Contractors	1979	1983	1989	1992	1992-79	1992-89	1989-79	1989-83	1983-79
White	0.321	0.335	0.337	0.316	-0.005	-0.021	0.016	0.002	0.014
Black	0.043	0.047	0.059	0.057	0.014	-0.002	0.016	0.012	0.004
Asian	0.005	0.007	0.011	0.012	0.007	0.001	0.006	0.004	0.002
Hispanic	0.020	0.022	0.027	0.027	0.007	0.000	0.007	0.005	0.002
Noncontractors	1979	1983	1989	1992	1992-79	1992-89	1989-79	1989-83	1983-79
White	0.400	0.420	0.408	0.414	0.014	0.006	0.008	-0.012	0.020
Black	0.054	0.055	0.066	0.064	0.010	-0.002	0.012	0.011	0.001
Asian	0.007	0.008	0.011	0.012	0.005	0.001	0.004	0.003	0.001
Hispanic	0.024	0.027	0.031	0.034	0.010	0.003	0.007	0.004	0.003

Note: The samples consist of private establishments that meet the following requirements: (1) Establishments with at least 100 employees, (2) Establishments with at least 50 employees that either have a federal contract or first-tier subcontract worth $50,000 or more, or act as depositories of federal funds in any amount, or act as issuing and paying agents for U.S. Savings Bonds and Notes.

Source: Author's tabulations from the EEO-1 files.

Table 5.4
Share of Employment in Headquarters

Panel A: Males

Contractors	1979	1983	1989	1992	1992-79	1992-89	1989-79	1989-83	1983-79
White	0.492	0.468	0.456	0.453	-0.039	-0.003	-0.036	-0.012	-0.024
Black	0.035	0.030	0.031	0.030	-0.005	-0.001	-0.004	0.001	-0.005
Asian	0.008	0.011	0.015	0.018	0.010	0.003	0.007	0.004	0.003
Hispanic	0.021	0.020	0.023	0.025	0.004	0.002	0.002	0.003	-0.001

Noncontractors	1979	1983	1989	1992	1992-79	1992-89	1989-79	1989-83	1983-79
White	0.487	0.471	0.444	0.439	-0.048	-0.005	-0.043	-0.027	-0.016
Black	0.040	0.035	0.034	0.033	-0.007	-0.001	-0.006	-0.001	-0.005
Asian	0.007	0.008	0.011	0.013	0.006	0.002	0.004	0.003	0.001
Hispanic	0.025	0.024	0.026	0.027	0.002	0.001	0.001	0.002	-0.001

Panel B: Females

Contractors	1979	1983	1989	1992	1992-79	1992-89	1989-79	1989-83	1983-79
White	0.380	0.403	0.395	0.393	0.013	-0.002	0.015	-0.008	0.023
Black	0.037	0.038	0.039	0.039	0.002	0.000	0.002	0.001	0.001
Asian	0.007	0.009	0.013	0.015	0.008	0.002	0.006	0.004	0.002
Hispanic	0.017	0.018	0.022	0.024	0.007	0.002	0.005	0.004	0.001
Noncontractors	1979	1983	1989	1992	1992-79	1992-89	1989-79	1989-83	1983-79
White	0.379	0.396	0.407	0.410	0.031	0.003	0.028	0.011	0.017
Black	0.034	0.036	0.040	0.038	0.004	-0.002	0.006	0.004	0.002
Asian	0.007	0.008	0.012	0.014	0.007	0.002	0.005	0.004	0.001
Hispanic	0.019	0.019	0.023	0.023	0.004	0.000	0.004	0.004	0.000

Note: The samples consist of the headquarters of private multi-establishments with at least 50 employees that either have a federal contract or first-tier subcontract worth $50,000 or more, or act as depositories of federal funds in any amount, or act as issuing and paying agents for U.S. Savings Bonds and Notes.

Source: Author's tabulations from the EEO-1 files.

Table 5.5
Distribution of Establishments by Industry (percent)

Industry	1979	1983	1989	1992
Agriculture	0.4	0.4	0.4	0.4
Mining	1.8	1.8	1.1	1.0
Construction	2.0	1.9	1.8	1.9
Durable manufacturing	15.7	16.8	14.1	14.1
Nondurable manufacturing	13.4	14.4	11.7	11.9
Transportation	9.4	9.5	8.0	8.6
Wholesale trade	6.9	5.3	4.3	4.8
Retail trade	28.1	23.8	25.3	27.2
Finance, insurance, and real estate	10.2	9.9	8.9	8.9
Personal retail services	3.9	4.7	5.0	4.1
Business-type services	4.0	5.0	12.7	9.3
Entertainment	0.5	0.4	0.4	0.6
Health	3.9	6.0	6.2	7.3
Total	100	100	100	100
Number of Establishments	168,012 (15,386)	124,156 (14,679)	151,959 (19,375)	159,291 (22,120)

Notes: Entries in parentheses are the number of establishments whose industry of affiliation was a missing value. The industry category listed as Services in Table 5.1 has been disaggregated into Personal Retail Services, Business-Type Services, Entertainment, and Health.

Source: Author's tabulations from EEO-1 files.

Table 5.6
Share of Employment in Durable Manufacturing

Panel A: Males

Contractors	1979	1983	1989	1992	1992-79	1992-89	1989-79	1989-83	1983-79
White	0.609	0.606	0.574	0.588	-0.021	0.014	-0.035	-0.032	-0.003
Black	0.068	0.058	0.058	0.056	-0.012	-0.002	-0.010	0.000	-0.010
Asian	0.008	0.011	0.019	0.022	0.014	0.003	0.011	0.008	0.003
Hispanic	0.045	0.041	0.048	0.049	0.004	0.001	0.003	0.007	-0.004

Noncontractors	1979	1983	1989	1992	1992-79	1992-89	1989-79	1989-83	1983-79
White	0.566	0.569	0.552	0.561	-0.005	0.009	-0.014	-0.017	0.003
Black	0.073	0.063	0.067	0.061	-0.012	-0.006	-0.006	0.004	-0.010
Asian	0.006	0.009	0.016	0.019	0.013	0.003	0.010	0.007	0.003
Hispanic	0.064	0.059	0.064	0.065	0.001	0.001	0.000	0.005	-0.005

Table 5.6 (continued)

Panel B: Females

Contractors	1979	1983	1989	1992	1992-79	1992-89	1989-79	1989-83	1983-79
White	0.218	0.226	0.233	0.226	0.008	-0.007	0.015	0.007	0.008
Black	0.027	0.028	0.031	0.029	0.002	-0.002	0.004	0.003	0.001
Asian	0.004	0.006	0.011	0.012	0.008	0.001	0.007	0.005	0.002
Hispanic	0.016	0.018	0.022	0.021	0.005	-0.001	0.006	0.004	0.002
Noncontractors	1979	1983	1989	1992	1992-79	1992-89	1989-79	1989-83	1983-79
White	0.233	0.244	0.235	0.229	-0.004	-0.006	0.002	-0.009	0.011
Black	0.027	0.206	0.028	0.025	-0.002	-0.003	0.001	-0.178	0.179
Asian	0.004	0.005	0.009	0.010	0.006	0.001	0.005	0.004	0.001
Hispanic	0.023	0.022	0.026	0.026	0.003	0.000	0.003	0.004	-0.001

Note: The samples consist of private durable manufacturing establishments that meet the following requirements: (1) establishments with at least 100 employees, (2) establishments with at least 50 employees that either have a federal contract or first-tier subcontract worth $50,000 or more, or act as depositories of federal funds in any amount, or act as issuing and paying agents for U.S. Savings Bonds and Notes.

Source: Author's tabulations from the EEO-1 files.

Table 5.7
Share of Employment in Nondurable Manufacturing

Panel A: Males

Contractors	1979	1983	1989	1992	1992-79	1992-89	1989-79	1989-83	1983-79
White	0.523	0.530	0.511	0.511	-0.012	0.000	-0.012	-0.019	0.007
Black	0.076	0.072	0.074	0.074	-0.002	0.000	-0.002	0.002	-0.004
Asian	0.006	0.007	0.010	0.012	0.006	0.002	0.004	0.003	0.001
Hispanic	0.040	0.039	0.049	0.052	0.012	0.003	0.009	0.010	-0.001

Noncontractors	1979	1983	1989	1992	1992-79	1992-89	1989-79	1989-83	1983-79
White	0.418	0.432	0.421	0.440	0.022	0.019	0.003	-0.011	0.014
Black	0.054	0.052	0.057	0.056	0.002	-0.001	0.003	0.005	-0.002
Asian	0.004	0.006	0.008	0.011	0.007	0.003	0.004	0.002	0.002
Hispanic	0.041	0.039	0.046	0.053	0.012	0.007	0.005	0.007	-0.002

Table 5.7 (continued)

Panel B: Females

Contractors	1979	1983	1989	1992	1992-79	1992-89	1989-79	1989-83	1983-79
White	0.273	0.265	0.265	0.259	-0.014	-0.006	-0.008	0.000	-0.008
Black	0.050	0.053	0.053	0.054	0.004	0.001	0.003	0.000	0.003
Asian	0.005	0.007	0.007	0.008	0.003	0.001	0.002	0.000	0.002
Hispanic	0.022	0.025	0.025	0.025	0.003	0.000	0.003	0.000	0.003
Noncontractors	1979	1983	1989	1992	1992-79	1992-89	1989-79	1989-83	1983-79
White	0.378	0.370	0.356	0.335	-0.043	-0.021	-0.022	-0.014	-0.008
Black	0.059	0.060	0.064	0.056	-0.003	-0.008	0.005	0.004	0.001
Asian	0.006	0.006	0.009	0.010	0.004	0.001	0.003	0.003	0.000
Hispanic	0.035	0.032	0.034	0.035	0.000	0.001	-0.001	0.002	-0.003

Notes: The samples consist of private nondurable manufacturing establishments that meet the following requirements: (1) establishments with at least 100 employees, (2) establishments with at least 50 employees that either have a federal contract or first-tier subcontract worth $50,000 or more, or act as depositories of federal funds in any amount, or act as issuing and paying agents for U.S. Savings Bonds and Notes.

Source: Author's tabulations from the EEO-1 files.

Table 5.8
Share of Employment in Retail Trade

Panel A: Males

Contractors	1979	1983	1989	1992	1992-79	1992-89	1989-79	1989-83	1983-79
White	0.348	0.340	0.314	0.336	-0.012	0.022	-0.034	-0.026	-0.008
Black	0.050	0.050	0.069	0.077	0.027	0.008	0.019	0.019	0.000
Asian	0.008	0.008	0.010	0.013	0.005	0.003	0.002	0.002	0.000
Hispanic	0.035	0.035	0.047	0.050	0.015	0.003	0.012	0.012	0.000
Noncontractors	1979	1983	1989	1992	1992-79	1992-89	1989-79	1989-83	1983-79
White	0.362	0.355	0.331	0.324	-0.038	-0.007	-0.031	-0.024	-0.007
Black	0.041	0.042	0.055	0.052	0.011	-0.003	0.014	0.013	0.001
Asian	0.006	0.007	0.008	0.009	0.003	0.001	0.002	0.001	0.001
Hispanic	0.025	0.032	0.040	0.050	0.025	0.010	0.015	0.008	0.007

Table 5.8 (continued)

Panel B: Females

Contractors	1979	1983	1989	1992	1992-79	1992-89	1989-79	1989-83	1983-79
White	0.482	0.469	0.430	0.384	-0.098	-0.046	-0.052	-0.039	-0.013
Black	0.053	0.058	0.079	0.080	0.027	0.001	0.026	0.021	0.005
Asian	0.007	0.008	0.010	0.013	0.006	0.003	0.003	0.002	0.001
Hispanic	0.026	0.028	0.036	0.038	0.012	0.002	0.010	0.008	0.002
Noncontractors	1979	1983	1989	1992	1992-79	1992-89	1989-79	1989-83	1983-79
White	0.488	0.481	0.455	0.454	-0.034	-0.001	-0.033	-0.026	-0.007
Black	0.048	0.047	0.066	0.061	0.013	-0.005	0.018	0.019	-0.001
Asian	0.006	0.006	0.009	0.010	0.004	0.001	0.003	0.003	0.000
Hispanic	0.020	0.027	0.032	0.036	0.016	0.004	0.012	0.005	0.007

Note: The samples consist of private retail trade establishments that meet the following requirements: (1) Establishments with at least 100 employees, (2) Establishments with at least 50 employees that either have a federal contract or first-tier subcontract worth $50,000 or more, or act as depositories of federal funds in any amount, or act as issuing and paying agents for U.S. Savings Bonds and Notes.

Source: Author's tabulations from EEO-1 files.

Table 5.9
Share of Employment in Business Services

Panel A: Males

Contractors	1979	1983	1989	1992	1992-79	1992-89	1989-79	1989-83	1983-79
White	0.508	0.510	0.470	0.488	-0.020	0.018	-0.038	-0.040	0.002
Black	0.079	0.074	0.065	0.058	-0.021	-0.007	-0.014	-0.009	-0.005
Asian	0.014	0.016	0.019	0.026	0.012	0.007	0.005	0.003	0.002
Hispanic	0.029	0.033	0.040	0.035	0.006	-0.005	0.011	0.007	0.004

Noncontractors	1979	1983	1989	1992	1992-79	1992-89	1989-79	1989-83	1983-79
White	0.392	0.385	0.389	0.384	-0.008	-0.005	-0.003	0.004	-0.007
Black	0.087	0.069	0.059	0.055	-0.032	-0.004	-0.028	-0.010	-0.018
Asian	0.008	0.009	0.013	0.017	0.009	0.004	0.005	0.004	0.001
Hispanic	0.035	0.032	0.040	0.041	0.006	0.001	0.005	0.008	-0.003

Table 5.9 (continued)

Panel B: Females

Contractors	1979	1983	1989	1992	1992-79	1992-89	1989-79	1989-83	1983-79
White	0.274	0.277	0.307	0.300	0.026	-0.007	0.033	0.030	0.003
Black	0.063	0.056	0.056	0.050	-0.013	-0.006	-0.007	0.000	-0.007
Asian	0.008	0.009	0.013	0.016	0.008	0.003	0.005	0.004	0.001
Hispanic	0.021	0.021	0.025	0.023	0.002	-0.002	0.004	0.004	0.000
Noncontractors	1979	1983	1989	1992	1992-79	1992-89	1989-79	1989-83	1983-79
White	0.371	0.393	0.393	0.395	0.024	0.002	0.022	0.000	0.022
Black	0.071	0.072	0.063	0.060	-0.011	-0.003	-0.008	-0.009	0.001
Asian	0.007	0.009	0.011	0.014	0.007	0.003	0.004	0.002	0.002
Hispanic	0.025	0.028	0.028	0.031	0.006	0.003	0.003	0.000	0.003

Note: The samples consist of private business service establishments that meet the following requirements: (1) establishments with at least 100 employees, (2) establishments with at least 50 employees that either have a federal contract or first-tier subcontract worth $50,000 or more, or act as depositories of federal funds in any amount, or act as issuing and paying agents for U.S. Savings Bonds and Notes.

Source: Author's tabulation from EEO-1 files.

Table 5.10
Share of Employment in Health Industry

Panel A: Males

Contractors	1979	1983	1989	1992	1992-79	1992-89	1989-79	1989-83	1983-79
White	0.138	0.130	0.122	0.131	-0.007	0.009	-0.016	-0.008	-0.008
Black	0.026	0.032	0.030	0.032	0.006	0.002	0.004	-0.002	0.006
Asian	0.007	0.007	0.007	0.010	0.003	0.093	0.000	0.000	0.000
Hispanic	0.015	0.013	0.016	0.017	0.002	0.001	0.001	0.003	-0.002

Noncontractors	1979	1983	1989	1992	1992-79	1992-89	1989-79	1989-83	1983-79
White	0.130	0.125	0.138	0.131	0.001	-0.007	0.008	0.013	-0.005
Black	0.026	0.024	0.029	0.028	0.002	-0.001	0.003	0.005	-0.002
Asian	0.005	0.005	0.006	0.007	0.002	0.001	0.001	0.001	0.000
Hispanic	0.011	0.012	0.014	0.013	0.002	-0.001	0.003	0.002	0.001

Table 5.10 (continued)

Panel B: Females

Contractors	1979	1983	1989	1992	1992-79	1992-89	1989-79	1989-83	1983-79
White	0.642	0.609	0.586	0.575	-0.067	-0.011	-0.056	-0.023	-0.033
Black	0.106	0.146	0.165	0.151	0.045	-0.014	0.059	0.019	0.040
Asian	0.021	0.021	0.024	0.029	0.008	0.005	0.003	0.003	0.000
Hispanic	0.039	0.037	0.045	0.048	0.009	0.003	0.006	0.008	-0.002
Noncontractors	1979	1983	1989	1992	1992-79	1992-89	1989-79	1989-83	1983-79
White	0.659	0.664	0.628	0.628	-0.031	0.000	-0.031	-0.036	0.005
Black	0.123	0.116	0.127	0.131	0.008	0.004	0.004	0.011	-0.007
Asian	0.016	0.017	0.021	0.023	0.007	0.002	0.005	0.004	0.001
Hispanic	0.027	0.031	0.033	0.034	0.007	0.001	0.006	0.002	0.004

Note: The samples consist of private health establishments that meet the following requirements: (1) establishments with at least 100 employees, (2) establishments with at least 50 employees that either have a federal contract or first-tier subcontract worth $50,000 or more, or act as depositories of federal funds in any amount, or act as issuing and paying agents for U.S. Savings Bonds and Notes.

Source: Author's tabulations from EEO-1 files.

Table 5.11A
Logit Estimates of the Determinants of the White Share of Establishment Employment

	1982		1984		1988		1990		1992	
	β	ΔP	β	ΔP	β	ΔP	β	ΔP	β	ΔP
Central city	-0.3940 (0.0071)	-0.0657	-0.4000 (0.0068)	-0.0684	-0.3153 (0.0067)	-0.0571	-0.1660 (0.0066)	-0.0298	-0.1569 (0.0065)	-0.0283
Federal contract	-0.0557 (0.0082)	-0.0084	-0.0427 (0.0081)	-0.0066	-0.0727 (0.0073)	-0.0123	-0.0581 (0.0069)	-0.0101	-0.0805 (0.0068)	-0.0142
Single establishment	-0.1265 (0.0135)	-0.0195	-0.1475 (0.0136)	-0.0234	-0.1596 (0.0131)	-0.0277	-0.1580 (0.0125)	-0.0283	-0.1795 (0.0125)	-0.0326
Entity of multi-establishment	-0.0585 (0.0116)	-0.0088	-0.0731 (0.0116)	-0.0113	-0.0603 (0.0111)	-0.0102	-0.0847 (0.0105)	-0.0149	-0.0932 (0.0101)	-0.0165
New England	1.1354 (0.0170)	0.1144	1.1080 (0.0165)	0.1162	0.9642 (0.0153)	0.1180	0.9650 (0.0149)	0.1230	0.9520 (0.0149)	0.1231
Middle Atlantic	0.6033 (0.0134)	0.0729	0.5838 (0.0132)	0.0731	0.4920 (0.0124)	0.0702	0.5783 (0.0121)	0.0834	0.6036 (0.0120)	0.0872
East North Central	0.7543 (0.0105)	0.0866	0.7783 (0.0104)	0.0913	0.7812 (0.0099)	0.1015	0.8028 (0.0094)	0.1078	0.7942 (0.0092)	0.1080
West North Central	1.3008 (0.0160)	0.1239	1.3186 (0.0158)	0.1288	1.3687 (0.0153)	0.1467	1.3455 (0.0144)	0.1516	1.3264 (0.0139)	0.1520
East South Central	0.3058 (0.0149)	0.0409	0.3194 (0.0148)	0.0437	0.3288 (0.0141)	0.0494	0.3085 (0.0135)	0.0484	0.3061 (0.0132)	0.0485
West South Central	-0.2780 (0.0112)	-0.0448	-0.2496 (0.0111)	-0.0409	-0.1700 (0.0109)	-0.0296	-0.1991 (0.0104)	-0.0361	-0.2287 (0.0101)	-0.0421
Mountain	0.3249 (0.0167)	0.0432	0.3579 (0.0165)	0.0484	0.4520 (0.0158)	0.0653	0.4109 (0.0146)	0.0625	0.4003 (0.0141)	0.0616
Pacific	-0.2935 (0.0105)	-0.0475	-0.2878 (0.0103)	-0.0476	-0.3457 (0.0097)	-0.0630	-0.3128 (0.0093)	-0.0583	-0.3603 (0.0092)	-0.0685
P	0.8196		0.8134		0.7900		0.7799		0.7774	
Xβ	1.5136		1.4725		1.3248		1.2652		1.2505	

Table 5.11B
Logit Estimates of the Determinants of the Black Share of Establishment Employment

	1982		1984		1988		1990		1992	
	β_k	ΔP_k	β_k	ΔP_k	β_k	ΔP_k	β_k	ΔP_k	β_k	ΔP_k
Central city	0.3818 (0.0076)	0.0409	0.3865 (0.0072)	0.0426	0.3527 (0.0069)	0.0421	0.2887 (0.0071)	0.0339	0.2783 (0.0070)	0.0319
Federal contract	0.0871 (0.0088)	0.0083	0.0653 (0.0086)	0.0063	0.0977 (0.0078)	0.0106	0.0942 (0.0074)	0.0103	0.1257 (0.0073)	0.0136
Single establishment	0.0608 (0.0145)	0.0057	0.0580 (0.0146)	0.0056	0.0889 (0.0140)	0.0096	0.0854 (0.0136)	0.0093	0.1031 (0.0136)	0.0111
Entity multi-establishment	0.1376 (0.0125)	0.0134	0.1602 (0.0125)	0.0162	0.1680 (0.0119)	0.0187	0.1948 (0.0113)	0.0221	0.2067 (0.0110)	0.0230
New England	-1.3993 (0.0185)	-0.0753	-1.3798 (0.0179)	-0.0770	-1.3080 (0.0167)	-0.0834	-1.3423 (0.0165)	-0.0855	-1.3215 (0.0165)	-0.0826
Middle Atlantic	-0.7099 (0.0136)	-0.0495	-0.7038 (0.0134)	-0.0506	-0.6515 (0.0126)	-0.0530	-0.7043 (0.0124)	-0.0567	-0.7389 (0.0124)	-0.0573
East North Central	-0.7707 (0.0106)	-0.0525	-0.7944 (0.0105)	-0.0551	-0.7979 (0.0099)	-0.0614	-0.8116 (0.0095)	-0.0628	-0.8136 (0.0094)	-0.0614
West North Central	-1.3584 (0.0170)	-0.0742	-1.3778 (0.0168)	-0.0770	-1.4102 (0.0162)	-0.0867	-1.4166 (0.0153)	-0.0878	-1.4358 (0.0149)	-0.0862
East South Central	-0.0115 (0.0143)	-0.0011	-0.0289 (0.0141)	-0.0027	-0.0212 (0.0134)	-0.0022	-0.0035 (0.0129)	-0.0004	0.0219 (0.0125)	0.0023
West South Central	-0.2386 (0.0118)	-0.0200	-0.2933 (0.0117)	-0.0248	-0.3920 (0.0114)	-0.0352	-0.3732 (0.0109)	-0.0341	-0.3518 (0.0107)	-0.0316
Mountain	-1.8441 (0.0231)	-0.0850	-1.8934 (0.0227)	-0.0885	-1.9760 (0.0216)	-0.1002	-1.9942 (0.0201)	-0.1016	-1.9868 (0.0194)	-0.0989
Pacific	-1.0709 (0.0124)	-0.0650	-1.1344 (0.0123)	-0.0693	-1.1790 (0.0115)	-0.0788	-1.2428 (0.0111)	-0.0820	-1.2601 (0.0110)	-0.0805
P	0.1028		0.1060		0.1185		0.1198		0.1166	
Xβ	-2.1665		-2.1323		-2.0067		-1.9943		-2.0246	

Table 5.11C
Logit Estimates of the Determinants of the Hispanic Share of Establishment Employment

	1982		1984		1988		1990		1992	
	β	ΔP	β	ΔP	β	ΔP	β	ΔP	β	ΔP
Central city	0.3502 (0.0098)	0.0226	0.3570 (0.0092)	0.0235	0.2299 (0.0086)	0.0157	-0.0064 (0.0085)	-0.0004	-0.0110 (0.0083)	-0.0008
Federal contract	-0.0317 (0.0112)	-0.0017	-0.0178 (0.0110)	-0.0010	-0.0209 (0.0097)	-0.0013	-0.0397 (0.0090)	-0.0026	-0.0661 (0.0088)	-0.0045
Single establishment	0.2197 (0.0182)	0.0134	0.2586 (0.0183)	0.0163	0.2205 (0.0172)	0.0150	0.2353 (0.0163)	0.0174	0.2664 (0.0162)	0.0208
Entity multi-establishment	-0.0486 (0.0160)	-0.0026	-0.0523 (0.0159)	-0.0029	-0.0787 (0.0149)	-0.0047	-0.0310 (0.0138)	-0.0020	-0.0004 (0.0133)	0.0000
New England	-0.4729 (0.0229)	-0.0213	-0.4416 (0.0223)	-0.0205	-0.2194 (0.0201)	-0.0123	-0.1755 (0.0192)	-0.0109	-0.2117 (0.0191)	-0.0135
Middle Atlantic	-0.3067 (0.0198)	-0.0148	-0.2416 (0.0194)	-0.0122	-0.0972 (0.0175)	-0.0057	-0.2144 (0.0167)	-0.0131	-0.2371 (0.0165)	-0.0150
East North Central	-0.5948 (0.0161)	-0.0254	-0.5696 (0.0159)	-0.0251	-0.5561 (0.0147)	-0.0271	-0.5080 (0.0137)	-0.0274	-0.4767 (0.0133)	-0.0272
West North Central	-1.2276 (0.0242)	-0.0408	-1.2314 (0.0239)	-0.0416	-1.2942 (0.0228)	-0.0471	-1.1026 (0.0211)	-0.0469	-1.0289 (0.0201)	-0.0471
East South Central	-2.7445 (0.0353)	-0.0547	-2.7454 (0.0349)	-0.0557	-2.5904 (0.0320)	-0.0608	-2.4119 (0.0298)	-0.0651	-2.3537 (0.0285)	-0.0678
West South Central	1.1484 (0.0156)	0.1056	1.1949 (0.0153)	0.1138	1.1562 (0.0144)	0.1175	1.1850 (0.0136)	0.1305	1.1898 (0.0132)	0.1361
Mountain	1.1336 (0.0194)	0.1036	1.1538 (0.0190)	0.1080	1.0761 (0.0178)	0.1058	1.1626 (0.0164)	0.1269	1.1128 (0.0158)	0.1235
Pacific	1.3860 (0.0138)	0.1409	1.4161 (0.0135)	0.1479	1.4657 (0.0123)	0.1685	1.3664 (0.0116)	0.1614	1.3800 (0.0114)	0.1696
P	0.0587		0.0598		0.0661		0.0721		0.0755	
Xβ	-2.7748		-2.7553		-2.6484		-2.5555		-2.5050	

Table 5.11D
Logit Estimates of the Determinants of the Asian Share of Establishment Employment

	1982 β	1982 ΔP₁	1984 β	1984 ΔP₁	1988 β	1988 ΔP₁	1990 β	1990 ΔP₁	1992 β	1992 ΔP₁
Central city	0.3006 (0.0085)	0.0053	0.2853 (0.0082)	0.0056	0.1348 (0.0078)	0.0031	-0.0792 (0.0076)	-0.0018	-0.0604 (0.0074)	-0.0015
Federal contract	0.1240 (0.0098)	0.0020	0.1023 (0.0099)	0.0018	0.0712 (0.0089)	0.0016	0.0774 (0.00820)	0.0019	0.0940 (0.0081)	0.0025
Single establishment	0.0550 (0.0153)	0.0009	0.1172 (0.0157)	0.0021	0.0819 (0.0149)	0.0018	0.1116 (0.0140)	0.0028	0.1098 (0.0140)	0.0030
Entity of multi-establishment	-0.0987 (0.0130)	-0.0014	-0.0991 (0.0133)	-0.0016	-0.1239 (0.0125)	-0.0025	-0.1025 (0.0115)	-0.0023	-0.1103 (0.0111)	-0.0027
New England	-0.3543 (0.0193)	-0.0046	-0.2728 (0.0191)	-0.0041	-0.1175 (0.0175)	-0.0024	-0.0717 (0.0165)	-0.0016	-0.1115 (0.0165)	-0.0027
Middle Atlantic	-0.1010 (0.0163)	-0.0015	-0.0930 (0.0164)	-0.0015	0.0016 (0.0151)	0.0000	-0.0698 (0.0142)	-0.0016	-0.0832 (0.0140)	-0.0020
East North Central	-0.2234 (0.0133)	-0.0031	-0.2921 (0.0135)	-0.0044	-0.3776 (0.0128)	-0.0068	-0.3973 (0.0119)	-0.0078	-0.4113 (0.0116)	-0.0087
West North Central	-0.4460 (0.0189)	-0.0055	-0.4670 (0.0192)	-0.0064	-0.5664 (0.0186)	-0.0093	-0.4665 (0.0172)	-0.0089	-0.4284 (0.0166)	-0.0090
East South Central	-1.0260 (0.0237)	-0.0099	-1.0961 (0.0243)	-0.0116	-1.2160 (0.0233)	-0.0152	-1.1323 (0.0219)	-0.0162	-1.1289 (0.0211)	-0.0177
West South Central	0.1569 (0.0153)	0.0026	0.1550 (0.0156)	0.0029	-0.0063 (0.0152)	-0.0001	-0.0429 (0.0143)	-0.0010	-0.1195 (0.0140)	-0.0029
Mountain	0.3057 (0.0201)	0.0054	0.2552 (0.0204)	0.0050	0.1427 (0.0195)	0.0033	0.1211 (0.0179)	0.0030	0.0662 (0.0174)	0.0018
Pacific	1.7076 (0.0114)	0.0646	1.6836 (0.0114)	0.0699	1.6443 (0.0106)	0.0817	1.5036 (0.0099)	0.0760	1.4624 (0.0098)	0.0782
P	0.0155		0.0175		0.0218		0.0241		0.0263	
Xβ	-4.1487		-4.0293		-3.8036		-3.6996		-3.6107	
N	124,627		125,832		142,223		154,894		158,230	

Notes: For a given year, the log-odds ratio of a race/ethnic group's employment in the ith establishment is regressed on dummy variables that denote the establishment's census division location, metropolitan location, type, federal contractor status, industry affiliation, and occupational structure. The central city dummy variable equals 1 if the establishment is located in a central city, and 0 elsewhere. Dummy variables for rural location and metropolitan location unidentifiable are also included, but not reported in the table. The excluded metropolitan dummy variable is the suburban dummy variable. The federal contract dummy variable equals 1 if the establishment has a federal contract, and 0 if the establishment is a noncontractor. The single-establishment dummy variable equals 1 if the establishment is a "stand-alone," and 0 otherwise. The multi-establishment dummy variable equals 1 if the establishment is an entity of a multi-establishment company. The excluded group is headquarters. The following industry dummy variables are added: agriculture; mining; construction; durable manufacturing; nondurable manufacturing; transportation; wholesale trade; retail trade; finance; insurance; and real estate; personal retail services; business type services; entertainment; and health. Durable manufacturing is the excluded group. The occupational dummy variables are officials and managers, professionals, technicians, sales workers, office and clerical workers, craft workers, operatives, laborers, and service workers. Officials and managers are the excluded group. The regressions are weighted using $(n_i/(p_i(1-p_i))^{.5}$, where n_i denotes the total number of employees in the ith establishment and p_i denotes the fraction of the ith establishments employees that are of a given race or ethnicity. The change in the probability of observing an individual of a particular racial or ethnic group associated with the kth dummy variable is $\Delta P_k = [1 + \exp(-X\beta - \beta_k)]^{-1} - P$, where $X\beta = \ln[p/(1-P)]$ and P equals the average share in the sample, and β_k is the logit coefficient for the kth variable. The number of establishments in 1982, 1984, 1988, 1990, and 1992 are 124,627, 125,832, 142,223, 154,894, and 158,230. Standard errors are in the parentheses.

Source: Author's calculations from EEO-1 files.

Table 5.12
Ability of Labor Demand, Labor Supply, and Institutional Measures to Explain Race/Ethnic Shares of Employment: As a Percent of R² from Regression with all variables.

	White					Black				
Predictor Variables	1982	1984	1988	1990	1992	1982	1984	1988	1990	1992
Regional location	0.566	0.560	0.548	0.526	0.523	0.633	0.641	0.636	0.633	0.639
Metropolitan location	0.056	0.063	0.036	0.055	0.054	0.063	0.065	0.053	0.057	0.052
Industry	0.080	0.075	0.065	0.059	0.094	0.068	0.060	0.049	0.052	0.078
Occupation structure	0.289	0.298	0.347	0.357	0.325	0.227	0.226	0.253	0.245	0.213
Establishment type	0.004	0.000	0.004	0.000	0.000	0.005	0.005	0.004	0.009	0.009
Federal contractor	0.004	0.004	0.000	0.004	0.004	0.005	0.005	0.004	0.004	0.009
R² from regression with all variables	0.249	0.252	0.248	0.272	0.277	0.207	0.217	0.225	0.229	0.230

	Hispanic					Asian				
Predictor variables	1982	1984	1988	1990	1992	1982	1984	1988	1990	1992
Regional location	0.718	0.726	0.716	0.651	0.631	0.825	0.849	0.875	0.853	0.836
Metropolitan location	0.009	0.009	0.004	0.024	0.023	0.022	0.016	0.000	0.034	0.037
Industry	0.073	0.076	0.062	0.076	0.104	0.082	0.080	0.066	0.060	0.067
Occupation structure	0.191	0.175	0.204	0.241	0.235	0.063	0.052	0.055	0.049	0.052
Establishment type	0.009	0.013	0.013	0.008	0.008	0.004	0.000	0.004	0.004	0.004
Federal contractor	0.000	0.000	0.000	0.000	0.000	0.004	0.004	0.000	0.000	0.004
R² from regression with all variables	0.220	0.223	0.225	0.249	0.260	0.268	0.251	0.256	0.265	0.269

Notes: Entries are calculated from the R²'s from regressions that add the measures indicated in each row. The variables are added to the regression in the order that they appear in the table. Regional location measures are dummy variables that denote whether the establishment is located in one of the nine census divisions. Metropolitan status denotes whether the establishment is located in a central city, suburb, rural area, or location is unidentified. Dummy variables for industry classification denote whether the establishment is in agriculture, mining, construction, durable manufacturing, nondurable manufacturing, transportation, wholesale trade, retail trade, personal retail services, business-type services, entertainment, health, or finance, insurance, and real estate. Occupation structure describes the allocation of the establishment's labor into officials and managers, professionals, technicians, sales workers, office and clerical workers, craft workers, operatives, laborers, and service workers. The establishment type dummy variables denote whether the establishment is a single establishment, the headquarters of a multi-establishment, or an entity of a multi-establishment company. The federal contract dummy variable captures differences in employment shares between contractors and noncontractors.

Source: Author's calculations from EEO-1 files.

Table 5.A1
Ability of Labor Demand, Labor Supply, and Institutional Measures to Explain Race/Ethnic Shares of Employment: R²s from Regressions

Predictor Variables	White					Black				
	1982	1984	1988	1990	1992	1982	1984	1988	1990	1992
1. Regional location	0.141	0.141	0.136	0.143	0.145	0.131	0.139	0.143	0.145	0.147
2. Metropolitan location	0.155	0.157	0.145	0.158	0.160	0.144	0.153	0.155	0.158	0.159
3. Industry	0.175	0.176	0.161	0.174	0.186	0.158	0.166	0.166	0.170	0.177
4. Occupation structure	0.247	0.251	0.247	0.271	0.276	0.205	0.215	0.223	0.226	0.226
5. Establishment type	0.248	0.251	0.248	0.271	0.276	0.206	0.216	0.224	0.228	0.228
6. Federal contractor	0.249	0.252	0.248	0.272	0.277	0.207	0.217	0.225	0.229	0.230

Predictor Variables	Hispanic					Asian				
	1982	1984	1988	1990	1992	1982	1984	1988	1990	1992
1. Regional location	0.158	0.162	0.161	0.162	0.164	0.221	0.213	0.224	0.226	0.225
2. Metropolitan location	0.16	0.164	0.162	0.168	0.170	0.227	0.217	0.224	0.235	0.235
3. Industry	0.176	0.181	0.176	0.187	0.197	0.249	0.237	0.241	0.251	0.253
4. Occupation structure	0.218	0.220	0.222	0.247	0.258	0.266	0.250	0.255	0.264	0.267
5. Establishment type	0.220	0.223	0.225	0.249	0.260	0.267	0.250	0.256	0.265	0.268
6. Federal contractor	0.220	0.223	0.225	0.249	0.260	0.268	0.251	0.256	0.265	0.269

Notes: Entries are the R²s from regressions that add the measures indicated in each row. The variables are added to the regression in the order that they appear in the table. Regional location measures are dummy variables that denote whether the establishment is located in one of the nine census divisions. Metropolitan status denotes whether the establishment is located in a central city, suburb, rural area, or location is unidentified. Dummy variables for industry classification denote whether the establishment is in agriculture, mining, construction, durable manufacturing, nondurable manufacturing, transportation, wholesale trade, retail trade, personal retail services, business-type services, entertainment, health, or finance, insurance, and real estate. Occupation structure describes the allocation of the establishment's labor into officials and managers, professionals, technicians, sales workers, office and clerical workers, craft workers, operatives, laborers, and service workers. The establishment type dummy variables denote whether the establishment is a single establishment, the headquarters of a multi-establishment, or an entity of a multi-establishment company. The federal contract dummy variable captures differences in employment shares between contractors and noncontractors.

Source: Author's calculations from EEO-1 files.

NOTE

I thank William Spriggs, M. V. Lee Badgett, Carol Romero, and Rhonda Williams, and staff members of the National Commission for Employment Policy for their helpful comments and suggestions during my employment there. I am indebted to the following from the U.S. Department of Labor: Annie Blackwell, Robert Gelerter, and Cynthia Deutermann, for access to the data, and William Bates, for data and technical assistance. I also thank Joe Nekere, Gloria Davis, and Jim Neil of the Equal Employment Opportunity Commission for providing the data files that contained the information on the metropolitan location of establishments. Katherine Armentrout provided expert research assistance. Finally, this paper benefited from comments received during the session titled "The Labor Market, Business, and Racial Response," at the National Conference on Civil Rights and Race Relations in the Post Reagan-Bush Era, Hubert H. Humphrey Institute of Public Affairs, University of Minnesota, October 17, 1994.

BIBLIOGRAPHY

Badgett, M. V., and Rhonda Williams, 1994. "The Changing Contours of Discrimination: Race, Gender, and Structural Economic Change." In *Understanding American Economic Decline*. Edited by Michael A. Berstein and David E. Adler. New York: Cambridge University Press.

Bound, John, and Richard B. Freeman, 1992. "What Went Wrong? The Erosion of Relative Earnings and Employment Among Young Black Men in the 1980's" *The Quarterly Journal of Economics* 107 (February): 201–232.

Ferguson, Ronald F., 1993. "New Evidence on the Growing Value of Skill and Consequences for Racial Disparity and Returns to Schooling." Unpublished paper, John F. Kennedy School of Government, Harvard University (September).

Holzer, Harry J., 1991. "The Spatial Mismatch Hypothesis: What Has the Evidence Shown?" Urban Studies 28: 105–122.

———, Keith R. Ihlanfeldt, and David L. Sjoquist, 1994. "Work, Search, and Travel Among White and Black Youth." *Journal of Urban Economics* 35: 320–345.

Kain, John F. 1992. "The Spatial Mismatch Hypothesis: Three Decades Later." *Housing Policy Debate* 3: 371–460.

Kirschenman, Joleen, and Kathryn M. Neckerman, 1991. "We'd Love to Hire Them, but . . . ': The Meaning of Race for Employers." In *The Urban Underclass*. Edited by Christopher Jencks and Paul E. Peterson. Washington, D. C.: Brookings Institution.

Moss, Philip, and Chris Tilly, 1993. "Raised Hurdles for Black Men: Evidence from Employer Interviews." Unpublished paper, Department of Policy and Planning, University of Massachusetts-Lowell (March).

Neal, Derek A., and William R. Johnson, 1994. "The Role of Pre-Market Factors in Black-White Wage Differences." Unpublished paper, University of Chicago and University of Virginia (April).

O'Neill, June, 1990. "The Role of Human Capital in Earnings Differences Between Black and White Men." *The Journal of Economic Perspectives* 4: 25–45.

Rodgers, William M. III, 1993. "Employment and Earnings of Young Males, 1979–1991." Ph.D. dissertation, Harvard University.

———, 1994a. "Male Central City-Suburb Earnings Gaps, 1979–1991." Unpublished paper, The College of William and Mary.

————, 1994b. "Recasting the Debate on Racial Differences in Labor Market Outcomes: Evidence for the 1980s." Report prepared for the National Commission for Employment Policy, U.S. Department of Labor.

Zoloth, Barbara S., 1976. "Alternative Measures of School Segregation." *Land Economics* 52: 278–93.

CHAPTER 6

Where the Jobs Went in the 1990–91 Downturn: Varying (Mis)Fortunes or Homogeneous Distress?

M. V. Lee Badgett

INTRODUCTION

Technically speaking, a recession is defined as a drop in the nation's output, measured as a decline in gross national product (GNP). For most people, however, the job loss and higher unemployment rates that accompany falling GNP characterize a recession. During the recession of the early 1990s, GNP began to increase before the labor market began to improve. The National Bureau of Economic Research dated the recession from July 1990 to March 1991; employment began falling in mid-1990 but did not bottom out until early 1992. Unemployment peaked in June 1992 at 7.7 percent. Since then, unemployment has fallen and employment has risen in response to higher overall output.

Even in a recession, though, good news is mixed with the bad. Some regions, industries, or occupations may bear very little of the brunt of a recession. In the same industry, some companies will be laying workers off and shutting down while other companies are expanding or opening new facilities (Dunne et al., 1989; Leonard, 1988). To ask "where the jobs went" in a recession has two meanings, then: Who was losing jobs and who was gaining jobs?

A job lost or gained really means that an individual lost or gained employment. But an individual's gender and racial/ethnic group can affect his or her economic outcome for a variety of reasons during a recession. Men and women are employed in very different industries and occupations. Men tend to be in more cyclically sensitive industries and occupations, making their unemployment rate rise more than women's in a recession (Goodman et al., 1993). Moreover, white workers' and minority workers' employment distributions differ by region, industry, and occupation, all of which means that some groups of workers will face more economic hardship than others during a recession. In addition, the effects of past discrimination may show up in recessions as workers with less seniority are laid off first. Discrimination may also take the form of landing jobs in poorer paying and possibly more volatile firms (Groshen, 1991). Finally, women and people of color still face direct labor market discrimination—such as an increased probability of layoff or discharge—which many economists believe worsens during recessions. (See Cross, 1990; and Turner et al., 1991 for the ongoing existence of discrimination. See Freeman, 1973; and Shulman, 1984 for the recession effect.)

The economic, social, and even political disruptions that accompany recessions make detailed studies of employment distribution by race and gender important. The effective targeting of counter cyclical policies, such as the extension of unemployment insurance benefits and other aid, depends on knowing where (and when) aid is most needed. Further, different employment impacts by race and/or gender may imply a need for increased equal employment opportunity (EEO) enforcement efforts during recessions to prevent particular groups from bearing a disproportionate burden.

In addition to being the first detailed study of employment during the 1990–1991 recession, this chapter uses an underutilized data set with several valuable characteristics. The data come from the "Employer Information Report EEO-1" that is required of many large private firms and gives the race and gender composition of employment within companies, or, more specifically, within "establishments," which are defined as separate plants or locations operated by a company. The Civil Rights Act of 1964 requires firms of 100 or more employees to file an EEO-1. Executive Order 11246 (which requires affirmative action of federal contractors) requires the same form from federal contractors with 50 or more employees that are either (1) prime contractors (or first-tier subcontractors) with a contract of at least $50,000; (2) depositories of government funds; or (3) issuers of U.S. Savings Bonds and Notes. (EEO-1 Instruction Booklet). In addition, if a firm has more than one establishment (or location), it must file a separate EEO-1 form for each establishment with 50 or more employees.

As a result, this chapter can trace the race-gender composition of employment *within an establishment* over time, a feature found in no other large-scale dataset. Five racial/ethnic groups are distinguished: white (not of Hispanic origin), black (not of Hispanic origin), Hispanic, Asian or Pacific Islander, and American Indian or Alaskan native. Employment is divided into nine occupational groupings (plus two trainee categories that will not be used in here). Other information from the EEO-1 form includes establishment location, industry, and contractor status. Thus both the unit of observation and the level of detail make the EEO-1 data set a valuable and unique source.

In this chapter, understanding where jobs went in the 1990–1991 recession will mean breaking out the separate effects of industry, occupation, region, firm, race, and gender on individuals' employment. It begins with an overview of the aggregate employment impact of the recession. The next section (which nontechnical readers may skip) describes the share-shift decomposition method used to account for the different possible influences on employment, where the unit of employment is measured as a race-gender group's share of total employment. The results from the decompositions are described in the Fourth section, and the final section draws conclusions and policy implications.

The chapter contains several major findings and recommendations:

- Women's share of employment for all racial and ethnic groups was helped by their distribution of employment across industries, as is usual in recessions.
- Aside from the employment shifts associated with being in particular regions, industries, or occupations during a recession, employment within individual establishments also was being redistributed. In other words, perhaps because of either discrimination or differential seniority, establishments disproportionately hired, laid off, or fired particular groups.
- African American men and women and white women were hurt by this within-establishment redistribution. White men, Hispanic men and women, and Asian American men and women improved their employment position through the within-establishment redistribution.
- Regardless of region or occupation, Asian American and Hispanic workers consistently increased their share of employment, mainly through their rising share of employment within establishments.
- African American men and women fared better in higher paying occupations than in lower paying occupations.
- Newly reporting establishments have very different distributions of employment by race and gender than do firms that disappear from the EEO-1 reports.
- These patterns could be the result of employers' greater attention to affirmative action efforts for Asian Americans or Hispanic workers. But this chapter suggests that black workers and white women are bearing some of the redistribution burden even though they have not achieved equality.
- The evidence in this chapter suggests that the categories of "minority" and "women" should be disaggregated in the enforcement process, particularly in the procedure used to target compliance reviews.

THE EMPLOYMENT EFFECTS OF THE EARLY 1990s' RECESSION

During the recession period, employment fell. Data from the Current Population Survey of households (CPS) show a loss of 1.3 million jobs from the second quarter of 1990 to the first quarter of 1991, a drop of 1.1 percent. According to the Current Employment Statistics (CES) survey (of nonfarm establishments), the number of employed people fell by 1.1 million, or 1.0 percent of payroll employment.

Ultimately, however, the fall in employment was more dramatic, since it continued through early 1992, after GNP began to increase and the official recession ended. Unfortunately, the timing of the EEO-1 survey does not quite fit the employment turning points. The EEO-1 data were collected from establishments during the first quarter of 1990 and the third quarter of 1992.[1] Thus Table 6.1 compares the change in employment from the three surveys for the period covered in the EEO-1 data, and all three surveys show falling employment. EEO-1 employment fell by 0.7 percent, employment in the CPS fell by 0.3 percent, and the CES establishment survey employment dropped 1.9 percent. EEO-1 employment is only about 40 percent of CES employment, and the employment loss among EEO-1 reporters is lower than among all private establishments. The difference stems from the fact that the EEO-1 requirements result in an under representation of small establishments and of establishments in the construction, trade, and service industries (EEOC, 1992), some of which are typically hard-hit by recessions.[2]

Within the large group of establishments filing an EEO-1, three important subgroups can be distinguished in each year. First, some establishments, called "survivors," filed in both years. Second, some establishments filed in only one year.[3] Those establishments filing only in 1990 faced some misfortune: they either shrank below the reporting threshold or went out of business.[4] Those filing only in 1992 were establishments that fared well during the recession: they either grew to exceed the reporting threshold or were new establishments. A third group of establishments, termed "industry changers," are those whose industry code changed between 1990 and 1992, with industry measured at a highly aggregated level. In some cases, the establishment might truly have changed its product, but many of the industry changes are likely to be coding errors.

Table 6.2 breaks down the EEO-1 employment into these three categories, the largest clearly being the survivors. Fortunately, the industry changers account for only about 5 percent of employment in both years. The overall employment loss resulted primarily from declining employment among surviving establishments. Overall, employment loss was mitigated by higher employment among establishments filing only in 1992 compared with those filing only in 1990. That is, those "lucky" establishments provided more employment than what was lost through the disappearance of the "unlucky" establishments that reported only in 1990.

As noted above, differences in employment distributions by industry, occupation, and region, and differences in treatment because of race, ethnicity, or gender, mean that the recession might have hurt some groups more than others. Table 6.3 demonstrates the variation in employment outcomes, with the significant employment losses coming in the Northeast and West; in mining, construction, manufacturing (durable goods), and personal services; and in managerial, sales, clerical, craft, and operative occupations.

Table 6.4, which compares employment levels and employment shares (of the total) for different groups with the CPS and the EEO-1 data, suggests that some of the factors highlighted by Table 6.3 led to divergent outcomes for different race-gender groups. In the CPS, only white workers lost jobs over the time period.[5] White workers' share loss of 0.3 percentage point was almost matched by Hispanic workers' gain of 0.2 percentage point, while black workers' share of employment did not change. In the EEO-1 data, white workers' and black workers' employment fell, while both employment and employment shares of other ethnic groups increased. Black women's and black men's share of employment fell (by 0.1 percentage points), as did white men's share (by 0.6 point). Despite a small decrease in employment, white women's share of jobs increased by 0.2 percentage point. Asian American men's and women's shares both rose by 0.1 point, as did Hispanic women's, and Hispanic men's share of employment rose by 0.2 percentage point.

The changes in shares, measured in tenths of a percentage point, seem small. But even a small change of share is large relative to the recession-induced increases in unemployment over this same time period. For instance, white men's falling share of employment in the EEO-1 file (which covers 40 percent of private employment) was equivalent to 17 percent of white men's overall increase in unemployment from 1990 to 1992.[6] Similarly, black women's and men's loss of share was equivalent to 12 percent of black women's higher unemployment and 15.5 percent of black men's. And for the smaller ethnic groups, a small change in overall share is large relative to the size of the group.

For most race-gender groups, the changing share of employment provides a convenient measure of how the recession affected the group in both relative and absolute terms. (White women are the exception; their share rose but their employment level fell slightly.) But as Table 6.3 indicates, changes at an aggregate level can hide important effects within industries, occupations, regions, and firms that might push shares in opposite directions, making a more detailed analysis necessary.

ISOLATING THE DIMENSIONS OF CHANGE

Asking "where the jobs went" involves identifying the industrial, occupational, regional, and firm locations for employment, as well as identifying the race and gender of who got those jobs. In this study, the "who" and the "where" are summarized in the share of employment of a race-gender group (overall or in an occupation) in the nation as a whole or in a particular region. This section presents the method for breaking changes in shares into more illuminating components. The nontechnical reader may wish to skip this discussion.

The most detailed dissection is possible for the surviving establishments, since they are observed at the beginning and at the trough of the employment recession. That permits distinguishing between the effect on a race-gender group of being in particular establishments and that of being in particular industries. The method used here depends on a basic accounting identity. The share of black women's employment, for instance, depends on their share of employment within individual establishments, the importance of those establishments within their industry, and their industry's importance within the overall economy.

More generally, a race-gender group **g**'s share of employment, S, can be expressed as follows:

$$S^g \equiv E^g/E_T \equiv \sum_e \sum_I (E^g_e/E_e) \cdot (E_e/E_i) \cdot (E_i/E_T),$$
$$ G \qquad\quad F \qquad\quad I$$

where E represents employment for race-gender group **g** in establishment **e** in industry **I**. The first term on the right-hand side—call it G—is the group's share of establishment employment. The second term, F, is the establishment's share of employment in that industry. The third term, I, is the industry's share of total employment.

Changes in S can be caused by changes in a group's share of employment within establishments, by changes in the size of establishments relative to the industry, by changes in the industry's importance in the economy, or by some combination of those changes. In addition, those effects may interact: a group's share might be falling in industries that are becoming more important overall, for example.

Splitting the share into the components in the equation above allows a decomposition of *the change in S over time* into each of the possible reasons for change identified above, including four interaction terms:

$$\Delta S^g \equiv \sum_e \sum_i (\Delta G \cdot F \cdot I + G \cdot \Delta F \cdot I + G \cdot F \cdot \Delta I + \Delta G \cdot \Delta F \cdot I + \Delta G \cdot F \cdot \Delta I + G \cdot \Delta F \cdot \Delta I + \Delta G \cdot \Delta F \cdot \Delta I),$$

$$\quad\quad\quad (1)\quad\quad (2)\quad\quad (3)\quad\quad\quad\quad (4)\,(5)\quad\quad\quad\quad (6)\quad\quad\quad (7)$$

where the delta (Δ) represents the change in the term from 1990 to 1992 (and subscripts are suppressed for conciseness). Term (1) represents how much the group's employment share would have changed if only the shares within establishments changed; term (2) gives the share change if only establishments' relative size had changed; and term (3) gives the group's share change if only the industry distribution of employment had changed. The interaction terms allow two of the main terms to vary. For instance, term (5) shows how much the share would have changed because a group's establishment shares were changing in expanding (or contracting) industries. When summed over all establishments and industries, the decomposition terms for each race-gender group will provide the net effect of each of the seven terms on the group's share of total employment.

To see the effects of other important determinants of employment share changes (region and occupation), the decomposition of share changes among employees in surviving establishments has three parts. First, national employment share changes for eight race-gender groups will be decomposed. (Decompositions are not performed for Native Americans, although their employment is included in all totals. The employment of Native Americans is quite small in the EEO-1 firms, and the shares for both men and women did not change between 1990 and 1992.) Second, similar decompositions are performed for each of the four census regions. And third, share changes for five occupational groups are decomposed at the national level.

Analyzing the surviving establishments covers most of those employed in both years. But because of the single-year filers and the industry changers, these decompositions will not explain all of each group's change in share of total employment. However, for ease of comparison with the share changes listed in Table 6.3, the decomposition terms are calculated with EEO-1 employment totals (both overall and by industry, E_T and E_i), including the single-year filers and the industry changers. The contributions from those two groups will be added back into the survivors' results to complete the picture of the impact of employment shifts.

DECOMPOSITION RESULTS

Decomposition of National Employment Changes

Table 6.5 presents the decomposition of changes in shares of employment (in surviving establishments) for eight race-gender groups. The first column reproduces the last column of Table 6.4, the change in the group's share of total employment. The fourth column, which is the sum of all the decomposition terms, gives the contribution of employment changes in surviving establishments to the overall change. For instance, the first row in Table 6.5 shows that white men's overall employment share dropped by 0.6 percentage point (column 1). Survivor establishments contributed a disproportionate share to that change overall: white men's employment loss in survivors would have meant one full percentage point drop in total employment share (column 4). Employment loss in survivors "over explains" white men's share loss overall because white men gained jobs with other firms. As will be further explained below, white men had a higher share of employment among those establishments reporting only in 1992 as compared with those reporting only in 1990.

White men's disproportionate employment loss in survivor establishments resulted primarily from the establishment effect (column 6) and the industry effect (column 7). In particular, white men were in establishments that lost more jobs than the typical establishment in the industry, and they were also in industries that did especially poorly relative to the rest of the economy. Each of those effects contributed 0.4 percentage point to white men's declining share of employment. The "group" effect in column 5 is positive, however, meaning that white men's share would actually have increased had only their share within establishments changed. That is, white men's share within establishments was increasing in enough establishments to push up their group share had the 1990 establishment sizes and industrial employment distribution remained unchanged by the recession. This suggests that white men were maintaining their share of jobs within establishments, although those establishments and industries shrank relative to the rest of the economy represented in the EEO-1 file.

The negative net effect of some of the interaction terms (between group share and establishment share in column 8 and between establishment share and industry share in column 10) suggests two additional influences on white men's employment. First, white men were increasing their share of employment in establishments with overall declining employment. Second, white men lost share because they were heavily employed in establishments that were either growing but in shrinking industries, or were shrinking within growing industries.

Comparing the recession's impact on white men with the impact on the other groups reveals some expected and unexpected patterns in the national data. The impact of the recession on the industrial distribution of employment had the expected effect. In general, the industrial shifts favored women and hurt men. The employment shares of white women, and to a lesser extent of black women, rose because of the industrial shifts. For women overall, concentration in the health services (which continued to grow during the recession) helped boost their shares of employment. Men's losses were concentrated in agriculture, mining, construction, and manufacturing industries. The negative impact is small for most groups of men, reducing their shares of employment by less than a tenth of a percentage point, but the drop for white men was large.

Also, the establishment effect in column 6, which captures the impact of changes in an establishment's size relative to its industry, is negative for all race-gender groups, reflecting that term's dependence on employment in *all* establishments in a particular industry, including single-year filers and industry changers. Since the survivor establishments account for almost all of the loss in employment (from Table 6.2), the net establishment effect among survivor establishments is negative for all groups. White women were located in especially unlucky establishments, particularly in retail trade and health services, reducing their employment share by 0.6 percentage point. Most of the interaction terms are quite small for all race-gender groups.

The group effect (column 3) uncovers an important change normally hidden in micro data: within establishments, employees of some race and gender groups were hired, laid off, and/or fired at disproportionate rates. White women, in particular, lost employment at unexpectedly high rates. If white women's share of employment within establishments were the only element changed (leaving relative establishment size and the overall industrial distribution the same as in 1990), their employment share would have fallen by 0.3 percentage point, or half of their share loss from survivor establishments. Two-thirds of that loss resulted from changes in federal contractor establishments. For black workers, the effect is smaller, at least partly because the number of black workers is smaller, but the direction is also negative, suggesting that black workers were more likely to lose jobs (or less likely to gain jobs) than some other groups. White men, Asian American men and women, and Hispanic men and women all increased their shares within establishments. Among white men, the within-establishment share effect was driven by increases in their share of employment within noncontractor establishments. Hispanic men and Asian American workers gained primarily in contractor establishments.

Why would some workers lose (or gain) more than other groups? Differences in regional or occupational distributions might explain some of this effect and will be explored below. Another reason might be that members of some race-gender groups have more seniority than others. Many employers offered this reason to explain why their employment losses hurt black workers more than others during this recession (Sharpe, 1993). Discriminatory layoff policies could also explain this pattern. Without detailed data on individual employees, it is difficult to distinguish the effects of seniority from the effects of discrimination.

Comparing the single-year filers and industry changers with the survivor establishments shows that the establishments filing only in 1992 were the best source of employment for white or black workers during the recession. Table 6.6 shows that the single-year filers, which can be roughly classified as the "unlucky" establishments filing only in 1990 and the "lucky" ones filing only in 1992, had workforces disproportionately made up of white, black, and Hispanic workers. White men and women were the big winners, gaining 0.6 and 0.9 percentage point in their employment shares, respectively. A separate decomposition of changes in the single-year filers (not shown here), similar in spirit and method to that presented earlier (but without the within-establishment effect), showed that virtually all of these share increases come from the change in the share of employment reported by single-year filers rather than from industry shifts, for example. The group of industry changers contributed little to the change in employment shares for any group.

While there is no way to know which of those establishments filing only in 1992 were new establishments, they were at least lucky relative to many other EEO-1 establishments, and that luck was passed along to white workers in particular. For new or expanding establishments, seniority would not be a factor in hiring, suggesting that discrimination in hiring among those establishments might have boosted white employees' shares.

Decomposition of Regional Employment Changes

Although white workers are distributed fairly evenly across different regions of the United States, the other race/ethnic groups tend to be clustered in particular regions. Table 6.7 presents the employment distribution by region, totaling all three kinds of establishments (survivors, one-year filers, and industry changers). Black men make up the largest fraction of the EEO-1 workforce in the South. Asian American and Hispanic workers are a larger proportion of the workforce in the West. If the within-establishment (group effect) gains for Asian American and Hispanic workers that were visible in the national data are driven by changes in the West, then seniority differences could be important factors explaining the loss for black workers and white women in the nation as a whole.

Table 6.3 showed that the Northeast and West suffered employment losses overall, while the Midwest and South saw small gains in EEO-1 employment between 1990 and 1992. Tables 6.8A–6.8D show the decompositions of employment share changes for survivor establishments in each region. Some common patterns emerge across regions. For instance, the recession's effect on the industry distribution of employment reduced men's shares of employment, as seen in the national decomposition. And overall, surviving establishments lost employment (and employment share) in all regions, making the net establishment effect (size relative to the industry) negative for all groups.

Some patterns emerge for race-gender group effects across regions as well (column 5). In each region, white women lost employment share in the surviving establishments, most strikingly in the West, losing a full percentage point relative to total Western employment. Black workers, both male and female, uniformly lost employment share across regions, with the effect being roughly equal in each region. And although Asian American and Hispanic workers did not always improve their relative position within each region, in no region was their employment share reduced among survivor establishments. (The sole exception was a slight drop for Hispanic men in the Northeast.) In general, white men's share of survivor employment fell, but only in the Northeast and South was their group effect positive. Their group term was zero in the Midwest and negative in the West.

White men were the only ones whose group effect changed sign across the four regions. The magnitude of the group effect varied across regions for other race-ethnic groups. For instance, the group effects were relatively small for all groups in the Midwest. The West was the site of the largest within-establishment (i.e. group effect) gains for Asian American and Hispanic workers, with Asian Americans increasing their employment shares within establishments enough to equal their increase in share within the region as a whole (in column 1). Thus the West saw the most dramatic shifts within establishments, as white workers and black workers disproportionately lost jobs within their establishments but Asian American and Hispanic workers held onto a disproportionate share of jobs. (Only Asian American men and women actually increased their employment *levels* within the West's survivor establishments.)

With the exceptions noted above, the national decomposition results are seen in their sign, if not their magnitude, in each region. Returning to the question of how to interpret the group effect, the regional differences suggest adding issues of labor supply to the seniority and discrimination hypotheses. Is the growing supply of Asian American and Hispanic workers the real reason for their higher shares? The decompositions suggest that explanation is unlikely to hold up. First, among those establishments with falling employment, a changing *external* labor supply would be irrelevant unless white workers leave areas with rapidly growing Asian or Hispanic (but not black) labor forces. Second, given the fact that employment was falling in the West, throwing white and black workers disproportionately into a potential applicant pool for employers, those establishments that increased employment would not be facing a dramatically different applicant pool over a two-year time period. And finally, but perhaps most importantly, the group effect patterns were fairly consistent across regions, generally favoring white men, and Asian American and Hispanic workers.

Adding back in the other two categories of establishments in Tables 6.9A–6.9D shows that white workers were favored by the employment share differences between 1990 and 1992 single-year filers (except in the Northeast, where white women were the main beneficiaries). Black workers had a disproportionate share of 1992 filers relative to 1990 filers in the South and Midwest. Hispanic and Asian American workers also benefitted from the increase in single-filer employment in 1992 in the West.

Decomposition by Occupational Groups

Another source of different outcomes during the recession is the occupational distribution. Table 6.3 shows that officials and managers, sales/office/clerical, and craft and operatives all experienced employment losses during the recession. Table 6.10 breaks down the employment distributions by broad occupational category. Women—regardless of race or ethnicity—are heavily concentrated in the sales, office, and clerical category, although Asian American women are less represented in that category than in the professional and technician group. White men are over represented among officials and managers, professionals and technicians, and crafts and operatives. Both black and Hispanic men are more heavily concentrated among the blue-collar occupations (crafts/operatives or laborers/services). Focus first on the occupations that lost employment during the recession. Table 6.11A shows that white men bore the brunt of the decline in managerial jobs both overall and in the survivor establishments, losing 1.3 percentage points. Those losses stemmed from a combination of several factors: declining shares within establishments (column 5), and interactions between the group and establishment effects (column 8) and between the establishment and industry effects (column 10). In other words, for instance, group shares were rose in shrinking establishments and/or group shares fell in growing establishments. White men's establishment effect (column 6) was positive, however, suggesting that white male managers were somewhat protected from the recession by being in the stronger establishments within industries (mainly among noncontractors).

White women gained in share of managerial jobs from 1990 to 1992 overall, about half of which came from the survivor establishments, despite being in establishments that fared poorly relative to the industry (column 6). White women gained 0.3 percentage point from the group effect and also were employed in managerial positions in relatively sheltered industries. Black workers and Asian American men also gained within establishments, and no other group lost share from within-establishment shifts, suggesting that the glass ceiling also served as a solid glass floor preventing downward mobility during this recession.

In Table 6.12A, we see that white women got a further boost from their higher concentration of among 1992 single-year filers as compared with 1990 single-year filers.[7] White men's gains from single-year filers were netted out by the loss among the industry changers, and the other groups were helped somewhat by increases among the industry changers.

Within the sales, office, and clerical category (Table 6.11C), white men lost the most within establishments and between establishments. Interactions mitigated their losses somewhat, since their share was increasing in growing establishments (growing relative to the industry) or was falling in shrinking establishments (column 8). White women, who are over represented in this category, sustained heavy losses mainly from being in establishments that were shrinking relative to their industries. Black women also suffered heavy losses in this category, almost solely from the establishment effect. Hispanic men and women picked up 0.1 percentage point within this category, mainly because of gains within establishments.

Among craft and operative workers (Table 6.11D), a group facing the greatest employment losses overall, not as much redistribution occurred among the survivor establishments (or even overall). White men's share remained steady overall, but underlying the steadiness was a redistribution of white men in these blue-collar jobs between establishments and industries. The positive group and establishment effects for white men showed they were favored somewhat within establishments and were better represented in the establishments maintaining their industry shares. However, the net effect of interactions between those two effects pulled white men's share back down to its original level. White women lost the most from within-establishment changes, and Asian American and Hispanic men gained employment share within the survivor establishments.

The other two categories saw employment increases despite the recession. Among professional and technical workers (Table 6.11B), white men lost 2 percentage points in their share of employment in this category (although their absolute employment levels dropped only slightly). Their losses stemmed from within-establishment loss of share, between-establishment losses, and interactions between the establishment and industry effects. Because employment rose in this category, some of white men's loss of share probably resulted from differential hiring rather than layoffs. White women benefitted greatly from their industrial distribution of employment: had only the relative size of their industries changed, white women's share of professional and technical jobs would have increased by 1.7 percentage points. But their employment was rising in establishments in shrinking industries and falling in growing industries, reducing the net change for white female professionals in the survivor establishments. Overall, women increased their shares in this occupational category during the recession. Black and Hispanic women as well as Asian American workers increased their shares of professional and technical employment, primarily because of rising proportions within establishments (column 5).

The other growing occupation, laborers and service workers (Table 6.11E), saw a redistribution overall away from white men and black workers and a similar redistribution among survivors, including away from white women. The decompositions show that this redistribution hides white men's increasing shares in establishments, which mitigated their loss of share from the establishment and industry effects. Black workers' share of the increased employment was held down by the establishment effect and, for black women, the group effect. Hispanic workers benefitted greatly from the redistribution within establishments, which could account for virtually all of Hispanic workers' share gains in this occupation.

In most cases, the single-year filers favored white workers (see Tables 6.12A–6.12E). But in the laborers and service category (Table 6.12E), black women and Hispanic workers also got a boost from the 1992 single-year filers. With only two exceptions, the sign of the employment change was the same among the survivor establishments as it was for employment shares as a whole. One exception was for white men in the sales, office, and clerical occupations. Their shares fell among survivors but rose overall. The second exception was a similar pattern for white women in the laborer and service worker category.

Occupational Breakdowns for the West

Finer details for examining the interactions between region and occupation are possible, at the risk of producing too many tables. As an example of how much redistribution can take place within regions or occupations, Tables 6.13 (A and B) and 6.14 (A and B) examine the two highest-paying occupational groups (officials and managers, professionals and technical employees) in the economically troubled but ethnically diverse West. White men's losses in the share of these jobs among survivor establishments (Table 6.13) were not matched by increased employment among the 1992 single-year filers (Table 6.14). As Table 6.13A shows, almost all of the other groups gained within establishments in the officials and managers category, with white women gaining the most. In Table 6.13B, the redistribution more clearly favored Asian American men and women. Almost all of their higher employment shares in this category in the West come from within-establishment gains.

CONCLUSIONS AND POLICY IMPLICATIONS

As expected, the different occupational, regional, and industrial distributions for the eight race-gender groups played varying roles in the groups' employment outcomes during the recession's downswing. The force of the recession was most obvious in the employment declines in the West and Northeast, but the effects on different groups within regions did not vary greatly.

The differential industrial impact of the recession clearly played a role in changing the overall distribution of employment. Much of white men's share losses resulted from their employment in establishments that fared poorly relative to their industries and in industries that lost jobs relative to the economy as a whole. Since the industry effect, at least, tends to be cyclical, white men are likely to regain some of their original share of employment as the economy recovers. Their stable or increasing shares within establishments during the recession also foretells a rising overall share: if seniority helped maintain white men's share, then recalls of laid-off workers might also favor the more senior white men. If discrimination accounted for establishments seeming to favor white men's employment, then newly hired or recalled workers might also be more likely to be white men, depending on the local labor supply.

The occupational decompositions reveal more divergence from the national patterns than do either the regional decompositions or the industry contributions. The improvement seen overall for Asian Americans came not so much because of their regional distribution but because they did particularly well in growing occupations. White men did not lose employment share uniformly, but they increased their share in two shrinking categories: sales-office-clerical and craft-operative.

Following individual establishments over the downswing reveals other important influences on groups' employment shares that are establishment-specific. One term of the decomposition, the establishment effect, measured the impact of changes in establishment size relative to the industry. In the survivor establishment decompositions, which is the only subgroup of establishments that allows such a comparison, those terms were almost always negative (because the base included the single-year filers and industry changers). The exceptions were only for white men in the official-manager and craft-operative categories, perhaps suggesting a form of past discrimination in which employers in more stable establishments favored white men (relative to the overall industrial average share for white men).

The other important factor that these data highlight is the within-establishment or group effect. Over the downswing, establishments lay off and rehire workers in ways that change the share of jobs among race-gender groups. This intraestablishment redistribution will also affect group shares at the aggregate level, as we have seen here. Overall, the rising share of jobs going to Hispanic and Asian American workers stems primarily from their increasing shares within survivor establishments, not simply from their concentration in rapidly expanding labor markets (either regional, industrial, or occupational). As noted above, Asian American workers gained employment share in growing occupations, and some of that growth in those occupations occurred within establishments, especially in the professional and technician occupations.

What are we to make of the within-establishment redistribution? One possibility is that white men's group effect represents the effects of layoffs by seniority that disproportionately hurt more recently hired black workers. But that explanation is less plausible for explaining the often positive group effect for Asian American and Hispanic workers across regions. Perhaps employers are responding to past discrimination against Asian Americans and Hispanics and are increasing their efforts to hire and retain those workers during a recession. If this is so, black workers (and in some cases, white women)—who are also common victims of past and present discrimination—are sharing in the employment cost along with white men.

With several minority groups competing for jobs under the affirmative action banner, an employer's hiring options become more complicated in one sense, but might allow an employer to discriminate against one among the several minority groups. For instance, black workers are a minority among minorities in the West, suggesting that their position might be weakened by lower collective competitive clout in the labor market, leading employers to push more of the recession's burden onto black workers (see, e.g., Shulman, 1984).

The (at least) implicit competition among minority groups for jobs and the groups' differential success that is rooted within establishments present one important policy implication for Office of Federal Contract Compliance Programs' (OFCCP) compliance review selection procedures. Currently, the OFCCP formally seeks out possible audit targets by using two statistical comparisons: one compares a contractor establishment's female and total minority employment with the female and minority composition of similar establishments in an MSA, and the other looks for concentrations of women and minorities within particular occupations in an establishment. Other factors are used to prioritize audits and to flag additional audits at the discretion of the District Office directors. Two of those other factors involve dimensions related to this study: "expansion of employment in an industry" and "decreasing significant reductions in employment that impact minorities or women" (U.S. Dept. Of Labor, 1992, p. 5).

The diversity of employment outcomes within the broad categories of "minorities" and, to a lesser extent "women," identified in this chapter suggests the need to revise the compliance review selection process by disaggregating the categories. Since the current audit flagging procedure requires both an underutilization in the external comparison and an over concentration in the internal comparison (U.S. Dept. Of Labor, 1992, p. 41), the disaggregation would need to be implemented for both comparisons. Given the large within-establishment changes noted within occupations in the West (Tables 6.13 and 6.14) for Asian American and Hispanic workers, some disaggregating targeting methods might be experimented with in that region, in particular.

A second implication involves the importance of noting the stage of the business cycle. The less important selection factors implicitly involve an intertemporal analysis, namely, *increases* or *decreases* in industry or local employment. This study confirms that both rising and falling employment can result in employment redistribution, finding that redistribution during a recession occurs in regions that show either net gains or net losses in employment during the recession. The especially hard-hit Northeast and West showed basically similar redistribution patterns across the race-gender groups. Specifically targeting regions hard-hit by the recession might not be necessary or useful from a pure distributional perspective, although some comparisons with redistribution in upswings would be needed to confirm this suspicion.

Some more specific targets in addition to changing industries can be identified as a result of this chapter's findings. First, newly reporting establishments (single-filers in 1992) appear to have different race-gender distributions than the establishments that drop out of the EEO-1 file, and those differences have a large impact on some groups' overall employment shares. To the extent that those new establishments enter the EEO-1 universe because of new federal contracts, current compliance review selection procedures might flag them for audits (U.S. Dept. Of Labor, 1992, pp. 4–5). If these establishments are newly formed rather than new contractors, however, starting off with higher concentrations of white and/or male workers than other establishments in similar industries and with similar occupational mixes should arouse suspicion. Second, the within-establishment group effect in the occupational decompositions, i.e. that which is unexplained by recession-induced between-industry and between-establishment employment shifts, suggests that a focus on particular occupations could be helpful for white women and African American men and women. Interestingly, the higher-wage occupations, official-managerial and professional-technician, do not show a negative group effect for women and minorities. Significant losses occurred in the blue-collar occupations, however, and in the craft-operative category—hardest hit in this recession—white men actually increased their share over the course of the recession. White men also increased their share of jobs in one traditionally female category, sales-office-clerical jobs, but this increase resulted mainly from shifts between single-year filers and not from the group effect.

Starting a new decade with a recession is an inauspicious beginning for the U.S. economy, and the differential consequences for the race-gender groups considered here suggest that the 1990s present some new challenges for policy makers and EEO enforcement agencies. Jobs were not uniformly lost, nor were they lost according to the race- and/or gender-blind forces of a recession, that is, affecting only certain regions, industries, and occupations. Approaching the topic at middecade, this study presents evidence that the growing diversity of the U.S. workforce means that greater attention—not less—should be paid to ensuring that all workers, regardless of race, ethnicity, or gender, have equal employment opportunities.

Table 6.1
Comparison of Employment Changes Across Survey

	1990 (Q1)	1992 (Q3)	Change	% Change
CES (estab., private)	91,605,000	89,879,000	-1,726,000	-1.9%
CPS all households	118,131,000	117,742,000	-389,000	-0.3%
CPS comparable	89,346,000	87,436,000	-1,910,000	-2.1%
EEO-1 (estab.)	36,063,000	35,797,000	-266,000	-0.7%

Table 6.2
Employment in EEO-1 Establishment Groups

	1990	1992	Change	% Change
Survivors	29,871,165	29,053,646	-817,519	-2.7%
Contract both years	17,545,636	16,920,332	-625,304	-3.6%
Contract in 1990	1,737,269	1,653,026	-84,243	-4.8%
Contract in 1992	983,955	954,469	29,486	-3.0%
No Contracts	9,604,305	9,525,819	78,486	-0.8%
One year filers				
1990 only	3,989,188			
1992 only		4,655,226		
Difference			666,038	16.7%
Industry Changers	2,202,956	2,088,605	-114,351	-5.2%
TOTAL	36,063,309	35,797,477	-265,832	-0.7%

Table 6.3
EEO-1 Employment by Region, Industry, and Occupation

	1990	1992	% Change
Region			
Northeast	7,849,844	7,540,444	-3.9%
Midwest	9,655,938	9,707,670	0.5%
South	12,008,141	12,093,253	0.7%
West	6,549,386	6,456,110	-1.4%
Industry			
Agriculture, fishing, forestry	140,114	138,341	-1.3%
Mining	429,031	363,026	-15.4%
Construction	620,188	538,971	-13.1%
Manufacturing, durable	7,666,688	7,052,492	-8.0%
Manufacturing, nondurable	5,127,874	5,223,445	1.9%
Transportation, utilities	3,430,972	3,485,435	1.6%

Wholesale trade	1,294,651	1,344,024	3.8%
Retail trade	5,460,199	5,425,445	-0.6%
FIRE	2,986,636	2,880,101	-3.6%
Business type service	2,675,605	3,052,383	13.1%
Personal, repair service	1,788,749	1,317,341	-26.4%
Recreation, entertainment	230,819	275,263	19.3%
Health services	4,211,783	4,728,210	12.3%
Occupation			
Officials and managers	4,108,072	3,980,430	-3.1%
Professionals and tech.	7,048,571	7,365,424	4.5%
Sales, office, clerical	9,606,808	9,357,307	-2.6%
Craft and operators	9,134,802	8,808,361	-3.6%
Laborers and service	6,165,056	6,285,955	2.0%

Table 6.4
Employment by Race-Gender Group

	Employment *			Employment Share		
	1990 (Q1)	1992 (Q3)	Change	1990 (Q1)	1992 (Q3)	Change
TOTAL	118,131,000	117,742,000	-389,000			
White	102,229,000	101,498,000	-731,000	86.5%	86.2%	-0.003
Black	12,030,000	12,037,000	7,000	10.2%	10.2%	0.000
Hispanic	8,774,000	8,984,000	210,000	7.4%	7.6%	0.002
EEO-1						
Total	36,063,309	35,797,477	-265,832			
White						
Women	12,617,223	12,594,964	-22,259	35.0%	35.2%	0.002
Men	15,289,410	14,967,462	-321,948	42.4%	41.8%	-0.006

118

Black						
Women	2,422,098	2,383,508	-38,590	6.7%	6.7%	-0.001
Men	2,158,301	2,103,262	-55,039	6.0%	59.0%	-0.001
Asian American						
Women	483,792	523,772	39,980	1.3%	1.5%	0.001
Men	511,994	551,675	551,675	1.4%	1.5%	0.001
Hispanic						
Women	1,014,711	1,048,038	33,327	2.8%	2.9%	0.001
Men	1,403,372	1,461,252	57,880	3.9%	4.1%	0.002
Native American						
Women	70,489	71,018	529	2.0%	2.0%	0.000
Men	91,919	92,526	607	3.0%	3.0%	0.000

* Current Population Survey.

Table 6.5
Decomposition of Changes in Employment Shares: National

	Total Share Change (All estabs.)	Survivor Share 1990	Estab. Only Share 1992	Change	Main Terms Group (G)	Estab. (F)	Industry (I)	Interaction Terms G & F	G & I	F & I	G, F, I
White men	-0.006	0.349	0.339	-0.010	0.001	-0.004	-0.004	-0.001	0.000	-0.001	0.000
White women	0.002	0.294	0.288	-0.006	-0.003	-0.006	0.007	-0.001	0.000	-0.002	0.000
Black men	-0.001	0.050	0.048	-0.002	-0.001	-0.001	0.000	0.001	0.000	0.000	0.000
Black women	-0.001	0.056	0.055	-0.001	-0.001	-0.002	0.001	0.001	0.000	0.000	0.000
Asian American men	0.001	0.011	0.012	0.001	0.001	0.000	0.000	0.000	0.000	0.000	0.000
Asian American women	0.001	0.011	0.012	0.001	0.001	0.000	0.000	0.000	0.000	0.000	0.000
Hispanic men	0.002	0.031	0.032	0.001	0.001	-0.001	0.000	0.001	0.000	0.000	0.000
Hispanic women	0.001	0.023	0.023	0.000	0.001	-0.001	0.000	0.000	0.000	0.000	0.000

Table 6.6
Shares of Total Employment in All Established Categories: National

	Survivors			One-Year Filers			Industry Changers			Total Share Change (all estabs.)
	1990	1992	Change	1990	1992	Change	1990	1992	Change	
White men	0.349	0.339	-0.010	0.046	0.052	0.006	0.029	0.027	-0.002	-0.006
White women	0.294	0.288	-0.006	0.037	0.046	0.009	0.019	0.018	-0.001	0.002
Black men	0.050	0.048	-0.002	0.007	0.008	0.001	0.003	0.003	0.000	-0.001
Black women	0.056	0.055	-0.001	0.008	0.009	0.001	0.003	0.003	0.000	-0.001
Asian American men	0.011	0.012	0.001	0.002	0.002	0.000	0.001	0.001	0.000	0.001
Asian American women	0.011	0.012	0.001	0.002	0.002	0.000	0.001	0.001	0.000	0.002
Hispanic men	0.031	0.032	0.001	0.005	0.007	0.001	0.002	0.002	0.000	0.002
Hispanic women	0.023	0.023	0.000	0.004	0.005	0.001	0.002	0.002	0.000	0.001

Table 6.7
EEO-1 Regional Employment Shares

	Northeast		South		Midwest		West	
	1990	1992	1990	1992	1990	1992	1990	1992
White men	0.429	0.425	0.402	0.398	0.475	0.465	0.382	0.377
White women	0.382	0.385	0.322	0.323	0.383	0.390	0.313	0.311
Black men	0.047	0.047	0.095	0.093	0.047	0.045	0.030	0.029
Black women	0.062	0.061	0.103	0.103	0.051	0.050	0.031	0.029
Asian Am. Men	0.013	0.015	0.007	0.008	0.007	0.008	0.039	0.041
Asian Am. Women	0.012	0.014	0.007	0.008	0.006	0.007	0.038	0.041
Hispanic men	0.029	0.029	0.034	0.036	0.017	0.019	0.093	0.096
Hispanic women	0.023	0.023	0.025	0.027	0.011	0.012	0.065	0.067

Table 6.8A
Decomposition of Changes in Employment Shares: Northeast

	Total Share Change (All estabs.)	Survivor Share 1990	Estab. Only Share 1992	Change	Main Terms			Interaction Terms			
					Group (G)	Estab. (F)	Industry (I)	G & F	G & I	F & I	G, F, I
White men	-0.005	0.349	0.345	-0.005	0.004	-0.001	-0.004	-0.002	0.000	-0.003	0.000
White women	0.003	0.320	0.319	-0.001	-0.003	-0.002	0.008	-0.001	0.000	-0.003	0.000
Black men	-0.001	0.039	0.037	-0.002	-0.001	-0.001	0.000	0.001	0.000	-0.001	0.000
Black women	-0.001	0.052	0.051	-0.002	-0.002	-0.001	0.002	0.001	0.000	-0.001	0.000
Asian Amer. men	0.001	0.010	0.011	0.001	0.001	0.000	0.000	0.000	0.000	0.000	0.000
Asian American women	0.002	0.010	0.011	0.001	0.001	0.000	0.000	0.000	0.000	0.000	0.000
Hispanic men	0.000	0.024	0.023	0.000	0.000	0.000	0.000	0.000	0.000	0.000	0.000
Hispanic women	0.000	0.019	0.019	0.000	0.000	0.000	0.000	0.000	0.000	0.000	0.000

Table 6.8B
Decomposition of Changes in Employment Shares: South

	Total Share Change (all estabs.)	Survivor Share 1990	Estab. Only Share 1992	Main Terms				Interaction Terms			
				Change	Group (G)	Estab. (F)	Industry (I)	G & F	G & I	F & I	G, F, I
White men	-0.004	0.327	0.318	-0.009	0.001	-0.004	-0.003	-0.001	0.000	-0.002	0.000
White women	0.000	0.269	0.262	-0.007	-0.003	-0.006	0.006	-0.002	0.000	-0.002	0.000
Black men	-0.002	0.078	0.076	-0.002	-0.001	-0.002	-0.001	0.001	0.000	-0.001	0.000
Black women	0.000	0.086	0.085	-0.001	-0.001	-0.003	0.002	0.001	0.000	-0.001	0.000
Asian Amer. Men	0.001	0.006	0.006	0.000	0.001	0.000	0.000	0.000	0.000	0.000	0.000
Asian American women	0.001	0.006	0.006	0.000	0.000	0.000	0.000	0.000	0.000	0.000	0.000
Hispanic men	0.002	0.026	0.028	0.001	0.001	0.000	0.000	0.001	0.000	0.000	0.000
Hispanic women	0.002	0.020	0.021	0.001	0.001	0.000	0.000	0.000	0.000	0.000	0.000

Table 6.8C
Decomposition of Changes in Employment Shares: Midwest

	Total Share Change (all estabs.)	Survivor Share 1990	Estab. Only Share 1992	Change	Main Terms			Interaction Terms			
					Group (G)	Estab. (F)	Industry (I)	G & F	G & I	F & I	G, F, I
White men	-0.010	0.401	0.389	-0.012	0.000	-0.005	-0.005	-0.001	0.000	-0.001	0.000
White women	0.007	0.329	0.324	-0.005	-0.002	-0.008	0.007	-0.001	0.000	-0.002	0.000
Black men	-0.001	0.039	0.038	-0.002	-0.001	-0.001	0.000	0.001	0.000	0.000	0.000
Black women	-0.001	0.044	0.042	-0.002	-0.001	-0.002	0.001	0.000	0.000	0.000	0.000
Asian Amer. men	0.001	0.006	0.006	0.001	0.001	0.000	0.000	0.000	0.000	0.000	0.000
Asian American women	0.001	0.005	0.006	0.001	0.001	0.000	0.000	0.000	0.000	0.000	0.000
Hispanic Men	0.002	0.014	0.015	0.001	0.001	0.000	0.000	0.000	0.000	0.000	0.000
Hispanic Women	0.001	0.009	0.009	0.000	0.001	0.000	0.000	0.000	0.000	0.000	0.000

Table 6.8D
Decomposition of Changes in Employment Shares: West

	Total Share Change (all estabs.)	Survivor Share 1990	Estab. Only Share 1992	Change	Main Terms			Interaction Terms				
					Group (G)	Estab (F)	Industry (I)	G & F	G & I	F & I	G, F, I
White men	-0.006	0.306	0.290	-0.015	-0.002	-0.007	-0.004	-0.002	0.000	-0.001	0.000
White women	-0.002	0.253	0.243	-0.010	-0.005	-0.007	0.006	-0.002	0.000	-0.001	0.000
Black men	-0.001	0.024	0.023	-0.002	-0.001	-0.001	0.000	0.001	0.000	0.000	0.000
Black women	-0.002	0.025	0.023	-0.002	-0.001	-0.001	0.000	0.000	0.000	0.000	0.000
Asian Amer. Men	0.002	0.030	0.032	0.002	0.002	-0.001	-0.001	0.000	0.000	0.000	0.000
Asian American women	0.003	0.030	0.033	0.001	0.003	-0.001	0.000	0.000	0.000	0.000	0.000
Hispanic men	0.004	0.074	0.074	0.000	0.003	-0.003	0.000	0.001	0.000	0.000	0.000
Hispanic women	0.002	0.053	0.053	0.000	0.001	-0.002	0.000	0.001	0.000	0.000	0.000

Table 6.9A
Shares of Total Employment in All Established Categories: Northeast

	Survivors			One-Year Filers			Industry Changers			Total Share Change (All Estabs.)
	1990	1992	Change	1990	1992	Change	1990	1992	Change	
White men	0.349	0.345	-0.005	0.050	0.050	0.000	0.030	0.030	0.000	-0.005
White women	0.320	0.319	-0.001	0.041	0.045	0.004	0.021	0.021	0.001	0.003
Black men	0.039	0.037	-0.002	0.006	0.007	0.000	0.002	0.003	0.000	-0.001
Black women	0.052	0.051	0.002	0.007	0.008	0.000	0.003	0.003	0.000	-0.001
Asian American men	0.010	0.011	0.001	0.002	0.002	0.000	0.001	0.002	0.000	0.001
Asian American women	0.010	0.011	0.001	0.001	0.002	0.000	0.001	0.001	0.000	0.002
Hispanic men	0.024	0.023	0.000	0.004	0.004	0.001	0.002	0.002	0.000	0.000
Hispanic women	0.019	0.019	0.000	0.003	0.003	0.000	0.001	0.001	0.000	0.000

Table 6.9B
Shares of Total Employment in All Established Categories: South

	Survivors			One-Year Filers			Industry Changers			Total Share Change (all estabs.)
	1990	1992	Change	1990	1992	Change	1990	1992	Change	
White men	0.327	0.318	-0.009	0.047	0.053	0.006	0.028	0.027	-0.001	-0.004
White women	0.269	0.262	-0.007	0.036	0.044	0.008	0.018	0.017	-0.001	0.000
Black men	0.078	0.076	-0.002	0.012	0.012	0.001	0.005	0.005	0.000	-0.002
Black women	0.086	0.085	-0.001	0.013	0.014	0.002	0.005	0.004	0.000	0.000
Asian American men	0.006	0.006	0.000	0.001	0.001	0.000	0.001	0.001	0.000	0.001
Asian American women	0.006	0.006	0.000	0.001	0.001	0.000	0.000	0.000	0.000	0.001
Hispanic men	0.026	0.028	0.001	0.005	0.006	0.001	0.002	0.002	0.000	0.002
Hispanic women	0.020	0.021	0.001	0.004	0.004	0.001	0.001	0.001	0.000	0.002

128

Table 6.9C
Shares of Total Employment in All Established Categories: Midwest

	Survivors			One-Year Filers			Industry Changers			Total Share Change (all estabs.)
	1990	1992	Change	1990	1992	Change	1990	1992	Change	
White men	0.401	0.389	-0.012	0.042	0.050	0.008	0.032	0.027	-0.006	-0.010
White women	0.329	0.324	-0.005	0.034	0.048	0.013	0.020	0.018	-0.001	0.007
Black men	0.039	0.038	-0.002	0.005	0.006	0.001	0.002	0.002	0.000	-0.001
Black women	0.044	0.042	-0.002	0.005	0.006	0.001	0.002	0.002	0.000	-0.001
Asian American men	0.006	0.006	0.001	0.001	0.001	0.000	0.001	0.001	0.000	0.001
Asian American women	0.005	0.006	0.001	0.001	0.001	0.000	0.000	0.000	0.000	0.001
Hispanic men	0.014	0.015	0.001	0.002	0.003	0.001	0.001	0.001	0.000	0.002
Hispanic women	0.009	0.009	0.000	0.001	0.002	0.001	0.001	0.001	0.000	0.001

Table 6.9D
Shares of Total Employment in All Established Categories: West

	Survivors			One-Year Filers			Industry Changers			Total Share Change (all estabs.)
	1990	1992	Change	1990	1992	Change	1990	1992	Change	
White men	0.306	0.290	-0.015	0.051	0.062	0.011	0.026	0.025	-0.001	-0.006
White women	0.253	0.243	-0.010	0.042	0.050	0.008	0.018	0.018	-0.001	-0.002
Black men	0.024	0.023	-0.002	0.004	0.005	0.001	0.002	0.002	0.000	-0.001
Black women	0.025	0.023	-0.002	0.004	0.004	0.000	0.001	0.001	0.000	-0.002
Asian American men	0.030	0.032	0.001	0.005	0.006	0.001	0.003	0.003	0.000	0.002
Asian American women	0.030	0.033	0.002	0.005	0.005	0.001	0.003	0.003	0.000	0.003
Hispanic men	0.074	0.074	0.000	0.013	0.017	0.003	0.006	0.006	0.000	0.004
Hispanic women	0.053	0.053	0.000	0.009	0.011	0.001	0.003	0.004	0.000	0.002

Table 6.10
EEO-1 Occupational Employment Shares

	Officials & Managers		Professionals & Tech.		Sales, Office, Clerical		Craft & Operatives		Laborers & Services	
	1990	1992	1990	1992	1990	1992	1990	1992	1990	1992
White men	0.656	0.643	0.459	0.439	0.213	0.217	0.586	0.587	0.318	0.314
White women	0.243	0.253	0.392	0.404	0.573	0.567	0.168	0.164	0.294	0.296
Black men	0.029	0.030	0.026	0.026	0.030	0.030	0.093	0.093	0.116	0.110
Black women	0.021	0.022	0.041	0.044	0.097	0.094	0.048	0.048	0.108	0.106
Asian Am. men	0.013	0.014	0.026	0.027	0.008	0.008	0.013	0.014	0.014	0.016
Asian Am. Women	0.006	0.006	0.021	0.024	0.016	0.017	0.008	0.009	0.013	0.015
Hispanic men	0.020	0.002	0.017	0.018	0.018	0.020	0.057	0.059	0.082	0.086
Hispanic women	0.009	0.009	0.013	0.015	0.041	0.043	0.021	0.021	0.048	0.051

Table 6.11A
Decomposition of Changes in Employment Shares: Officials and Managers

	Total Share Change (all estabs.)	Survivor Share 1990	Estab. Only Share 1992	Change	Main Terms			Interaction Terms			
					Group (G)	Estab. (F)	Industry (I)	G & F	G & I	F & I	G, F, I
White men	-0.013	0.528	0.515	-0.013	-0.006	0.003	0.001	-0.005	0.000	-0.005	0.000
White women	-0.009	0.198	0.203	0.005	0.003	-0.004	0.004	0.003	0.000	-0.003	0.000
Black men	0.001	0.024	0.024	0.000	0.001	0.000	0.000	0.001	0.000	0.000	0.000
Black women	0.001	0.018	0.018	0.000	0.001	-0.001	0.000	0.001	0.000	0.000	0.000
Asian Am. men	0.001	0.010	0.010	0.000	0.001	0.000	0.000	0.000	0.000	0.000	0.000
Asian Am. women	0.000	0.005	0.005	0.000	0.000	0.000	0.000	0.000	0.000	0.000	0.000
Hispanic men	0.002	0.015	0.015	0.000	0.000	0.000	0.000	0.000	0.000	0.000	0.000
Hispanic women	0.000	0.007	0.007	0.000	0.000	0.000	0.000	0.000	0.000	0.000+	0.000

Table 6.11B
Decomposition of Changes in Employment Shares: Professionals and Technicians

	Total Share Change (all estabs.)	Survivor Share 1990	Estab. Only Share 1992	Change	Main Terms			Interaction Terms			
					Group (G)	Estab. (F)	Industry (I)	G & F	G & I	F & I	G, F, I
White men	-0.020	0.362	0.342	-0.020	-0.004	-0.009	0.001	0.001	0.000	-0.008	0.000
White women	0.012	0.337	0.338	0.001	-0.001	-0.004	0.017	-0.002	0.000	-0.010	0.000
Black men	0.000	0.021	0.020	0.000	0.000	0.000	0.000	0.000	0.000	-0.001	0.000
Black women	0.002	0.036	0.037	0.001	0.001	0.001	0.001	0.000	0.000	-0.002	0.000
Asian Am. men	0.001	0.020	0.020	0.001	0.001	-0.001	0.000	0.000	0.000	-0.001	0.000
Asian Am. women	0.003	0.018	0.020	0.002	0.002	0.000	0.001	0.000	0.000	0.000	0.000
Hispanic men	0.000	0.014	0.014	0.000	0.001	0.000	0.000	0.000	0.000	0.000	0.000
Hispanic women	0.001	0.011	0.012	0.001	0.001	0.000	0.000	0.000	0.000	-0.001	0.000

Table 6.11C
Decomposition of Changes in Employment Shares: Sales, Office, Clerical

	Total Share Change (all estabs.)	Survivor Share 1990	Estab. Only Share 1992	Change	Main Terms			Interaction Terms			
					Group (G)	Estab. (F)	Industry (I)	G & F	G & I	F & I	G,F,I
White men	0.004	0.172	0.167	-0.005	-0.004	-0.007	0.000	0.007	0.000	-0.001	0.000
White women	-0.006	0.473	0.456	-0.017	-0.001	-0.009	0.004	-0.008	0.000	-0.002	0.000
Black men	0.000	0.024	0.023	-0.001	0.000	-0.002	0.000	0.001	0.000	0.000	0.000
Black women	-0.003	0.080	0.076	-0.004	0.000	-0.004	0.001	0.000	0.000	0.000	0.000
Asian Am. men	0.001	0.006	0.006	0.000	0.000	0.000	0.000	0.000	0.000	0.000	0.000
Asian Am. women	0.001	0.013	0.013	0.000	0.001	-0.001	0.000	0.000	0.000	0.000	0.000
Hispanic men	0.002	0.015	0.015	0.001	0.001	-0.001	0.000	0.001	0.000	0.000	0.000
Hispanic women	0.002	0.003	0.034	0.001	0.002	-0.001	0.000	0.000	0.000	0.000	0.000

Table 6.11D
Decomposition of Changes in Employment Shares: Crafts and Operatives

	Total Share Change (all estabs.)	Survivor Share 1990	Estab. Only Share 1992	Change	Main Terms			G & F	Interaction Terms		
					Group (G)	Estab. (F)	Industry (I)		G & I	F & I	G, F, I
White men	0.001	0.493	0.493	0.000	0.003	0.004	0.001	-0.007	0.000	-0.001	0.000
White women	-0.004	0.141	0.137	-0.004	-0.006	-0.003	0.001	0.004	0.000	0.000	0.000
Black men	0.000	0.079	0.079	0.000	0.000	0.000	0.000	0.000	0.000	0.000	0.000
Black women	0.000	0.041	0.041	0.000	-0.001	-0.001	0.000	0.002	0.000	0.000	0.000
Asian Am. men	0.001	0.010	0.011	0.001	0.001	0.000	0.000	0.000	0.000	0.000	0.000
Asian Am. women	0.000	0.007	0.007	0.000	0.000	0.000	0.000	0.000	0.000	0.000	0.000
Hispanic men	0.002	0.045	0.047	0.002	0.002	0.000	0.000	0.000	0.000	0.000	0.000
Hispanic women	-0.001	0.017	0.017	0.000	0.000	-0.001	0.000	0.001	0.000	0.000	0.000

Table 6.11E
Decomposition of Changes in Employment Shares: Laborers and Service

	Total Share Change (all estabs.)	Survivor Share 1990	Estab. Only Share 1992	Change	Main Terms			Interaction Terms			
					Group (G)	Estab. (F)	Industry (I)	G & F	G & I	F & I	G, F, I
White men	-0.004	0.253	0.244	-0.009	0.004	-0.003	-0.004	-0.005	0.000	-0.001	0.000
White women	0.002	0.243	0.232	-0.011	-0.008	-0.009	0.004	0.004	0.000	-0.001	0.000
Black men	-0.006	0.092	0.087	-0.006	-0.001	-0.003	0.000	-0.001	0.000	0.000	0.000
Black women	-0.002	0.089	0.085	-0.004	-0.003	-0.005	0.003	0.001	0.000	0.000	0.000
Asian Am. men	0.002	0.011	0.012	0.001	0.001	-0.001	0.000	0.000	0.000	0.000	0.000
Asian Am. women	0.001	0.011	0.012	0.001	0.001	-0.001	0.000	0.000	0.000	0.000	0.000
Hispanic men	0.004	0.063	0.064	0.001	0.004	-0.002	0.000	0.000	0.000	0.000	0.000
Hispanic women	0.003	0.038	0.039	0.001	0.002	-0.002	0.001	0.001	0.000	0.000	0.000

Table 6.12A

Shares of Total Employment in All Established Categories: Officials and Managers

	Survivors			One-Year Filers			Industry Changers			Total Share Change (all estabs.)
	1990	1992	Change	1990	1992	Change	1990	1992	Change	
White men	0.528	0.515	-0.013	0.075	0.078	0.003	0.052	0.049	-0.003	-0.013
White women	0.198	0.203	0.005	0.031	0.035	0.004	0.014	0.015	0.001	0.009
Black men	0.024	0.024	0.000	0.003	0.004	0.000	0.002	0.002	0.000	0.001
Black women	0.018	0.018	0.000	0.003	0.003	0.000	0.001	0.001	0.000	0.001
Asian American men	0.010	0.011	0.000	0.002	0.002	0.000	0.001	0.002	0.000	0.001
Asian American women	0.005	0.005	0.000	0.001	0.001	0.000	0.000	0.000	0.000	0.000
Hispanic men	0.015	0.016	0.000	0.003	0.003	0.000	0.001	0.001	0.000	0.002
Hispanic women	0.007	0.007	0.000	0.001	0.001	0.000	0.000	0.001	0.000	0.000

Table 6.12B
Shares of Total Employment in All Established Categories: Professionals and Technicians

	Survivors			One-Year Filers			Industry Changers			Total Share Change (all estabs.)
	1990	1992	Change	1990	1992	Change	1990	1992	Change	
White men	0.362	0.342	-0.020	0.050	0.053	0.003	0.047	0.044	-0.003	-0.020
White women	0.337	0.338	0.001	0.031	0.042	0.011	0.025	0.024	-0.001	0.012
Black men	0.021	0.020	0.000	0.003	0.003	0.001	0.002	0.002	0.000	0.000
Black women	0.036	0.037	0.001	0.003	0.005	0.002	0.002	0.002	0.000	0.002
Asian American men	0.020	0.020	0.001	0.003	0.003	0.001	0.004	0.004	0.000	0.001
Asian American women	0.018	0.020	0.002	0.002	0.002	0.001	0.002	0.002	0.000	0.003
Hispanic men	0.014	0.014	0.000	0.002	0.003	0.000	0.002	0.002	0.000	0.000
Hispanic women	0.001	0.012	0.001	0.001	0.002	0.000	0.001	0.001	0.000	0.001

Table 6.12C
Shares of Total Employment in All Established Categories: Sales, Office, Clerical

	Survivors			One-Year Filers			Industry Changers			Total Share Change (all estabs.)
	1990	1992	Change	1990	1992	Change	1990	1992	Change	
White men	0.172	0.167	-0.005	0.029	0.038	0.009	0.012	0.012	0.000	0.004
White women	0.473	0.456	-0.017	0.069	0.082	0.013	0.031	0.030	-0.001	-0.006
Black men	0.024	0.023	-0.001	0.004	0.005	0.001	0.001	0.020	0.000	0.000
Black women	0.080	0.076	-0.004	0.013	0.013	0.000	0.004	0.004	0.000	-0.003
Asian American men	0.006	0.006	0.000	0.001	0.001	0.000	0.000	0.000	0.000	0.001
Asian American women	0.013	0.013	0.000	0.002	0.002	0.000	0.001	0.001	0.000	0.001
Hispanic men	0.015	0.015	0.001	0.003	0.004	0.001	0.001	0.001	0.000	0.002
Hispanic women	0.033	0.034	0.001	0.006	0.007	0.001	0.002	0.002	0.000	0.002

Table 6.12D
Shares of Total Employment in All Established Categories: Crafts and Operatives

	Survivors			One-Year Filers			Industry Changers			Total Share Change (all estabs.)
	1990	1992	Change	1990	1992	Change	1990	1992	Change	
White men	0.493	0.493	0.000	0.063	0.065	0.001	0.030	0.029	-0.001	0.001
White women	0.141	0.137	-0.004	0.018	0.018	0.000	0.009	0.009	0.000	-0.004
Black men	0.079	0.079	0.000	0.010	0.010	0.000	0.004	0.004	0.000	0.000
Black women	0.041	0.041	0.000	0.005	0.005	0.000	0.002	0.002	0.000	0.000
Asian American men	0.010	0.011	0.001	0.002	0.002	0.000	0.001	0.001	0.000	0.001
Asian American women	0.007	0.007	0.000	0.001	0.001	0.000	0.001	0.001	0.001	0.000
Hispanic men	0.045	0.047	0.002	0.009	0.008	0.000	0.003	0.004	0.000	0.002
Hispanic women	0.017	0.017	0.000	0.003	0.003	-0.001	0.001	0.001	0.000	-0.001

Table 6.12E
Shares of Total Employment in All Established Categories: Laborers and Service

	Survivors			One-Year Filers			Industry Changers			Total Share Change (all estabs.)
	1990	1992	Change	1990	1992	Change	1990	1992	Change	
White men	0.253	0.244	-0.009	0.046	0.057	0.010	0.018	0.014	-0.005	-0.004
White women	0.243	0.232	-0.011	0.040	0.054	0.014	0.012	0.010	-0.002	0.002
Black men	0.092	0.087	-0.006	0.018	0.019	0.000	0.005	0.005	-0.001	-0.006
Black women	0.089	0.085	-0.004	0.015	0.018	0.003	0.004	0.004	-0.001	-0.002
Asian American men	0.011	0.012	0.001	0.002	0.003	0.001	0.001	0.001	0.000	0.002
Asian American women	0.011	0.012	0.001	0.002	0.002	0.000	0.001	0.001	0.000	0.001
Hispanic men	0.063	0.064	0.001	0.014	0.017	0.003	0.004	0.004	0.000	0.004
Hispanic women	0.038	0.039	0.001	0.008	0.010	0.002	0.002	0.002	0.000	0.003

Table 6.13A
Decomposition of Changes in Employment Shares—West: Officials and Managers

	Survivor Share 1990	Estab. Only Share 1992	Change	Main Terms			Interaction Terms			
				Group (G)	Estab. (F)	Industry (I)	G & F	G & I	F & I	G, F, I
White men	0.466	0.446	-0.020	-0.007	-0.005	0.001	-0.005	-0.001	-0.004	0.000
White women	0.197	0.200	0.003	0.003	-0.003	0.004	0.001	0.000	-0.002	0.000
Black men	0.016	0.016	0.000	0.001	-0.001	0.000	0.000	0.000	0.000	0.000
Black women	0.012	0.012	0.000	0.000	-0.001	0.000	0.000	0.000	0.000	0.000
Asian Am. men	0.025	0.026	0.001	0.001	0.000	0.000	0.000	0.000	0.000	0.000
Asian Am. women	0.013	0.014	0.001	0.001	0.000	0.000	0.000	0.000	0.000	0.000
Hispanic men	0.035	0.034	0.001	0.000	-0.002	0.000	0.001	0.000	0.000	0.000
Hispanic women	0.016	0.016	0.001	0.001	0.001	0.000	0.000	0.000	0.000	0.000

Table 6.13B
Decomposition of Changes in Employment Shares—West: Professionals and Technicians

	Survivor Share 1990	Estab. Only Share 1992	Change	Main Terms			Interaction Terms			
				Group (G)	Estab. (F)	Industry (I)	G & F	G & I	F & I	G, F, I
White men	0.357	0.334	-0.023	-0.006	-0.010	0.001	0.000	0.000	-0.008	0.000
White women	0.276	0.277	0.002	-0.002	-0.003	-0.019	-0.003	-0.001	-0.009	0.000
Black men	0.016	0.015	-0.001	0.000	-0.001	0.000	0.001	0.000	0.000	0.000
Black women	0.018	0.018	0.000	0.000	0.000	0.001	0.000	0.000	-0.001	0.000
Asian Am. men	0.045	0.046	0.001	0.003	-0.001	0.000	0.001	0.000	-0.001	0.000
Asian Am. women	0.038	0.044	0.005	0.004	-0.001	0.003	0.000	0.000	-0.001	0.000
Hispanic men	0.028	0.027	-0.001	0.001	-0.001	0.000	0.001	0.000	-0.001	0.000
Hispanic women	0.021	0.022	0.002	0.001	0.000	0.001	0.000	0.000	-0.001	0.000

Table 6.14A
Shares of Total Employment in All Established Categories—West: Officials and Managers

	Survivors			One-Year Filers			Industry Changers			Total Share Change (all estabs.)
	1990	1992	Change	1990	1992	Change	1990	1992	Change	
White men	0.466	0.446	-0.020	0.084	0.093	0.010	0.047	0.046	-0.001	-0.011
White women	0.197	0.200	0.003	0.039	0.042	0.004	0.016	0.016	0.000	0.007
Black men	0.016	0.016	0.000	0.003	0.003	0.000	0.001	0.001	0.000	0.001
Black women	0.016	0.012	-0.004	0.002	0.002	0.000	0.001	0.001	0.000	-0.004
Asian American men	0.025	0.026	0.001	0.005	0.005	0.000	0.003	0.003	0.000	0.002
Asian American women	0.013	0.014	0.001	0.002	0.003	0.000	0.001	0.001	0.000	0.001
Hispanic men	0.035	0.034	0.001	0.006	0.007	0.001	0.003	0.003	0.000	0.002
Hispanic women	0.016	0.016	0.001	0.003	0.004	0.000	0.001	0.001	0.000	0.001

Table 6.14B
Shares of Total Employment in All Established Categories—West: Professional and Technicians

	Survivors			One-Year Filers			Industry Changers			Total Share Change (all estabs)
	1990	1992	Change	1990	1992	Change	1990	1992	Change	
White men	0.357	0.334	-0.023	0.058	0.063	0.005	0.040	0.039	-0.001	-0.019
White women	0.276	0.277	0.002	0.035	0.042	0.007	0.023	0.023	0.000	0.009
Black men	0.016	0.015	-0.001	0.002	0.003	0.000	0.001	0.001	0.000	-0.001
Black women	0.018	0.018	0.000	0.003	0.003	0.000	0.001	0.001	0.000	0.001
Asian American men	0.045	0.046	0.001	0.007	0.008	0.000	0.006	0.006	0.000	0.001
Asian American women	0.038	0.044	0.005	0.005	0.006	0.001	0.003	0.004	0.000	0.007
Hispanic men	0.028	0.027	-0.001	0.004	0.005	0.001	0.003	0.003	0.000	0.000
Hispanic women	0.021	0.022	0.002	0.003	0.004	0.001	0.002	0.002	0.000	0.002

NOTES

This report was prepared while the author was employed at the National Commission for Employment Policy. She thanks William Spriggs, William M. Rodgers III, Carol Romero, and other Commission staff members for their helpful advice and conversations. She also thanks Annie Blackwell, Robert Gelerter, Cynthia Deutermann, and William Bates at the Office of Federal Contract Compliance Programs, U.S. Department of Labor.

1. Establishments may report employment from any pay period within the specified quarter.
2. In addition, multi-establishment companies required to file EEO-1 forms also file a "consolidated report" that includes their establishments that do not have to file separate EEO-1 forms. Unless otherwise specified, this study uses only employment in the individual establishments filing EEO-1 forms.
3. Establishments that changed ownership between 1990 and 1992 through mergers retained the same establishment number and would therefore be classified with the survivors.
4. Also, some establishments with employment between 50 and 100 may have lost federal contracts, bumping them out of the group required to file EEO-1 forms.
5. Because the size of the labor force continued to increase for all groups, the unemployment rate increased even though employment was rising for black and Hispanic workers. The unemployment rate for white workers rose from 4.5 percent to 6.6 percent, black workers' unemployment rate rose from 10.9 percent to 14.2 percent, and Hispanic workers' rate rose from 7.6 percent to 11.6 percent.
6. For instance, if white men had maintained their employment share at 42.4 percent, their employment would have been higher by 209,246 jobs. Over the 1990–1992 time period, white men's unemployment increased by 1,255,000. Thus, maintaining their share might have meant a much smaller increase in unemployment for white men.
7. Technically, in the occupational breakdowns, some of those classified as "not filing" may have filed but reported no 1990 or 1992 employment in a particular occupational category.

BIBLIOGRAPHY

Cross, Harry (with Genevieve Kenney, Jane Mell, and Wendy Zimmerman). 1990. *Employer Hiring Practices: Differential Treatment of Hispanic and Anglo Job Seekers*. Urban Institute Report 90–4. Washington, D.C.: Urban Institute Press.
Dunne, Timothy, Mark J. Roberts, and Larry Samuelson. 1989. "Plant Turnover and Gross Employment Flows in U.S. Manufacturing Sector." *Journal of Labor Economics* 7, no.1.
Freeman, Richard. 1973. "Changes in the Labor Market for Black Americans, 1948–72." *Brookings Papers on Economic Activity* 1.
Goodman, William, Stephen Antczak, and Laura Freeman. 1993. "Women and Jobs in Recessions: 1969–92." *Monthly Labor Review*, July.
Groshen, Erica L. 1991. "The Structure of the Female/Male Wage Differential: Is It Who You Are, What Your Do, or Where You Work?" *Journal of Human Resources* 26, no. 3: 457–472.
Leonard, Jonathan L. 1988. "Unemployment and Job Instability Across SMSA's." Unpublished draft for presentation at the Econometric Society Meeting, December.

Meisenheimer, Joseph R. II, Earl. F. Mellor, and Leo G. Rydzewski. 1992. "Job Market Slid in Early 1991, Then Struggled to Find Footing." *Monthly Labor Review*, February.

Nardone, Thomas, Diane Herz, Earl Mellor, and Steven Hipple. 1993. "1992: Job Market in the Doldrums." *Monthly Labor Review*, February

Sharpe, Rochelle. 1993. "In Latest Recession, Only Blacks Suffered Net Employment Loss." *Wall Street Journal*, Sept. 14.

Shulman, Steven. 1984. "Competition and Racial Discrimination: The Employment Effects of Reagan's Labor Market Policies." *Review of Radical Political Economics* 16.

Turner, Margery Austin, Michael Fix, and Raymond J. Struyk. 1991. *Opportunities Denied, Opportunities Diminished: Racial Discrimination in Hiring*. Urban Institute Report 91–9, Washington, D.C.: Urban Institute Press.

U.S. Department of Labor, Employment Standards Administration, Office of Federal Contract Compliance Programs. 1992. OFCCP Order no. ADM 92-1/SEL. Washington, D.C.: OFCCP.

CHAPTER 7

Foundation Connections to Black Workers and Labor Unions

Richard Magat

Compared with their engagement with other socioeconomic issues, foundations were late in addressing the issue of black workers and organized labor. That they did so at all is remarkable under the circumstances.[1] First of all, foundations were frightened away from controversy by a withering inquiry in 1914 by the U.S. Commission on Industrial Relations. The sharp criticism arose from the Rockefeller Foundation's role in the aftermath of a bloody mining strike in Colorado. For most foundations, there were no areas more controversial than unions and interracial issues. Second, Northern philanthropic educational efforts for Southern blacks tended either to promote the training of ministers and teachers, or to focus on the Negro as an agricultural worker. Virtually no attention was devoted to the economic status of blacks as industrial workers, much less on blacks in the labor movement. Finally, the predominant attitude of black leaders toward labor unions for at least a half-century after the Civil War was as suspicious as the attitude of white workers toward blacks was antagonistic.

FOUNDATION INTERESTS

Foundation programs involving unions have been minuscule relative to such major fields as education, the arts, and social and economic distress.[2] However, research attention to union-related issues by a few foundations was substantial in the 1920s. Although interest slackened in the next two decades, it picked up in the late 1950s and the 1960s, involving direct relations with unions as well as research. Since then, despite the decline of unions, foundations have become involved in an array of labor-related programs, ranging from union democracy to plant closings.

One strong motivation for foundation interest in organized labor, especially at the outset, was a desire for social control, including resistance to radicalism. In pursuit of this objective, many foundations have advocated reformist social change. Since financial panics and depressions could stir social unrest, foundations, along with business and political leaders, have also promoted economic stability.

Foundations that have dealt directly with unions have viewed them principally as a means, rather than an end in themselves. The Ford Foundation in the 1960s, for example, joined with the United Auto Workers and other unions to support community development corporations in Los Angeles following race riots.[3] Few foundation efforts have aimed at strengthening labor unions.

BLACKS AND UNIONS: HISTORICAL PERSPECTIVE

Labor organizations date back to the colonial period, including associations of black workers. The National Labor Union of the 1860s, the first national federation of trade unions, encouraged black workers to form their own counterpart unions within the framework of white-dominated federations. Thus a national convention of black workers was held in Washington in 1869, from which emerged the Colored National Labor Union. But it failed because attempts to unionize in Southern communities were often met with wholesale arrests, imprisonment, and lynching.[4]

Beginning with Reconstruction, blacks in the South were steadily eliminated from skilled and semiskilled occupations. When blacks began to move into industrial employment, they had to accept lower wages than whites; where unions existed, blacks were frequently enlisted as strikebreakers.

Blacks were finally welcomed into a labor union movement by the Knights of Labor, which was organized in 1869 and within a decade became the nation's largest labor union. The Knights' leader, William H. Sylvis, declared, "We are all one family of slaves together. The labor movement is a second Emancipation Proclamation."[5]

The Knights grew rapidly in the South, especially among blacks and farmers, with as many as 50,000 Southern workers. Local assemblies were racially segregated, but both black and white locals sent representatives to district and state assemblies. However, strikes initiated by the Knights in cotton mills and other Southern industries failed.

By the late 1880s most urban members had left the Knights of Labor. The American Federation of Labor was the greatest beneficiary of the groundwork laid by the Knights, and many AFL national unions originated in the South. In contrast to the building trades, waterfront unions organized black workers, usually in segregated locals, and introduced work sharing and coordinated bargaining. The failure of the railroad unions to organize the large number of black workers ironically made a large potential strikebreaking force available to antiunion employers.

For their part, black leaders viewed the labor movement with suspicion or hostility, or as irrelevant. For different reasons, these views were shared by figures as disparate as Booker T. Washington and Frederick Douglass. Douglass and other black Reconstruction leaders based Negro advancement almost wholly on political rights. They prevailed against the judgment of Wesley Howard, who told the 1869 convention, "The franchise without the organization of labor would be of little benefit."

It would be decades before black intellectuals like Ralph Bunche went so far as to predict that the whole problem of discrimination would be solved through an alliance of blacks and workers in industrial unions that would fight to bring social justice for all.

EARLY FOUNDATION ROLE

"Negro administrators of white philanthropy," as Harris and Spero labeled leaders of the Urban League and various committees of interracial cooperation, tried to lift trade-union barriers to black workers, but their principal appeal was to prominent trade-unions officials. Their appeal "makes no attempt to reach the white or black rank and file."[6]

The National Urban League was formed in 1906 at the instigation of William Baldwin, a railroad executive who was president of the Rockefeller-sponsored General Education Board. The League dedicated itself to "[Making] the Negro's position [in Northern cities] following the great migration of the last two years from the South one of helpfulness to the community rather than a menace."[7]

Beginning in 1918 and continuing for ten years, the Laura Spelman Rockefeller Memorial (LSRM) was the League's largest source of foundation funds, joined by the Altman Foundation and the Phelps Stokes Fund.

The Ludlow Massacre at Rockefeller's Colorado Fuel and Iron Company in 1914 marked an encounter between a foundation and a union with substantial numbers of black members. State militia killed ten workers and a child; eleven other children and two women suffocated to death when the tents in which they were living were torched. A majority of the company's 3,500 miners were foreign-born, but one-third of the American workers were black. Nationwide revulsion at the Ludlow violence prompted John D. Rockefeller, Jr., to hire a Canadian labor authority, W. L. Mackenzie King, to investigate the affair and devise plans for improved industrial relations. King was placed on the payroll of the Rockefeller Foundation, where he created The Division of Industrial Relations.[8] This connection was denounced by the U.S. Commission on Industrial Relations, which held hearings for two years. Stung by criticism, the Foundation closed the unit.[9]

Officers of two foundations, the Phelps Stokes Fund and the Jeanes Fund, were among the signers of a letter to the annual meeting of the AFL in 1918 that suggested more steps to advance the position of Negro workers. But until the mid-1930s, the practice of organized labor, with few exceptions, was one of outright exclusion—or segregation—of blacks. Entreaties to the AFL continued into the post-World War II period, most prominently by A. Philip Randolph, whose persistence won him a public rebuke by the AFL in 1963.

Northern philanthropies began to branch out to interracial activities in the 1920s. The rationale for interracial committees was that "solutions can be obtained through the cultivation of interracial goodwill." By and large, Bunche wrote, "this conception steers clear of the more ominous aspects of the problem, such as strife between black and white labor."[10]

The Laura Spelman Rockefeller Memorial sponsored conferences on "Negro problems" in New Haven (1927) and Washington (1928). The Social Sciences Research Council, largely foundation-funded, formulated a research plan for the Washington conference. One of its sections took up problems of racial discrimination by unions and employers.

RADICALS AND LIBERALS

One of the few foundations to deal directly and sympathetically with the labor movement was the Garland Fund, known officially as the American Fund for Public Service. Its board ranged from liberals to Communists and—unique among foundations then and since—it included several labor leaders. It was also alone in having a black board member, James Weldon Johnson. Johnson, a writer, diplomat, and intellectual, was the first black to head the NAACP.[11]

The Fund's credo expressed "opposition to economic oppression and the necessity for abolishing it. The labor movement is the only force capable of accomplishing this and establishing a new, free social order."

The Fund's first grant, $2,000, was made to the strike relief fund of District #2 of the United Mine Workers (UMW) in West Virginia. The UMW was the most racially integrated union in the country. Among other recipients were labor education schools, labor publications and the Federated Press, the Amalgamated Association of Street and Electric Railway Employees, and the American Federation of Teachers.

A. Philip Randolph obtained a loan and a grant from the Garland Fund for his magazine, *The Messenger*, which opposed "the capitalist exploitation of the workers especially the Negro."[12] The Brotherhood of Sleeping Car Porters, which Randolph founded, also obtained a Garland grant, as a challenge to the Pullman Company's Employee Representation Plan. Over six years, the plan had failed to remedy poor working conditions, Randolph said. The Pullman Company finally signed a contract with the Brotherhood in 1937, the first ever between a large company and a union with black workers.

The Garland Fund subsidized publication by the Vanguard Press of *Negro Labor in the United States*, by Charles H. Wesley, chairman of the history department of Howard University. Also with support from Garland, Vanguard published such works as Scott Nearing's *Black America*.

The AFL attacked the Fund as "Bolsheviks in sheep's clothing," the federal government kept it under surveillance, and it was cited extensively beginning in 1930 by the House Un-American Activities Committee. Having spent the bulk of its funds in the 1920s, the Fund formally dissolved in 1941.

Besides being weakened by external forces, concludes Gloria Garrett Samson, historian of the Fund, it suffered from back scratching within the board, scatteration, and an excess of research. Yet it "helped keep the idea of industrial unions alive, provided for institutions where militants could come together, and helped to educate a group that would become part of the CIO cadre of organizers and labor educators."[13]

Beginning in the mid-1930s, the Committee (later Congress) of Industrial Organizations (CIO) began massive organizing drives in the steel, auto, mining, packinghouse, and rubber industries, all of which employed large numbers of blacks. Although the CIO did not entirely break down discrimination, it marked a significant step forward for black workers by affording them, along with white workers, protection against arbitrary dismissals. CIO unions also forbade discriminatory clauses in their constitutions.

By World War II, even liberal philanthropists feared the radicalization of blacks through unions and other organizations. Thus, in a significant shift from a policy of racial accommodation to one encouraging racial integration, the Rosenwald Fund established the American Race Relations Council in the 1940s, in part from the concern of its president, Edward Embree, "that unless influential liberals acted quickly, a black proletarian movement would emerge and destroy the 'good will' that had been developing between the races."[14] Such radicalization included the labor movement, said Charles S. Johnson, a prominent black scholar, first research director of the Chicago Urban League, and one of Embree's advisors.

In *An American Dilemma*, Gunnar Myrdal declared that the white upper classes (from which foundation officials were largely drawn until the 1960s) "have probably to a large extent been dominated by a fear that lower class whites and blacks might come to terms and unite against them."[15]

DEPRESSION ERA RESEARCH

The Depression stimulated foundation-funded research on the status of blacks in the economy, including their role in labor unions. In 1929, the LSRM resolved to "delve more deeply" into studies of Negro life, including standards of living and conditions of women in Chicago industry. At the Russell Sage Foundation, Mary van Kleech launched a major study of labor. The effect on blacks of National Recovery Administration codes was examined in a Twentieth Century Fund study, *Labor and Government*; some codes carried exemptions that in effect established wage differentials between Negro and white workers. But it was the Julius Rosenwald Fund that led the way. It sponsored a conference on the economic status of the Negro in Washington. Using a secret $50,000 grant from the Rockefeller Foundation, the Fund established the Committee on Negroes in the Economic Reconstruction that commissioned three seminal scholarly studies on labor economics in the South: *The Collapse of Cotton Tenancy*, by Edward Embree, Will Alexander, and Charles Johnson (1935); *A Preface to Peasantry*, by Arthur Raper (1936); and *Black Workers and the New Unions*, by Horace Cayton and George Mitchell (1939).[16]

The National Negro League grew out of a 1935 conference in Washington, "Economic Conditions Among Negroes," which was supported by the Phelps

Stokes Fund and sponsored by the Joint Committee on National Recovery and Howard University. Its first meeting drew an extraordinary attendance of 5,000 men and women from 28 states. Lester Granger of the National, noted, "The League [demonstrated] the growing importance of labor leadership and the power of the labor movement. Delegates were present from 80 trade unions, as opposed to only 18 professional and educational groups."[17]

Anson Phelps Stokes, head of the Phelps Stokes Fund, helped establish the Committee on Negro Americans in Defense Industries in 1941. Its manifesto declared, "Negro Americans favor all suitable tests of fitness for any jobs, but . . . rightly oppose those based merely on race. Evidences are increasing of the exclusion of their skilled workers from certain defense industries and of the frequent refusal to admit qualified Negro students into training and apprenticeship programs."[18]

The towering work of the late Depression era was the Carnegie Corporation-funded *An American Dilemma: The Negro Problem and Modern Democracy*, by Gunnar Myrdal. Several commissioned studies of Negro labor were incorporated into the report.[19]

The Carnegie trustee who proposed the project, Newton D. Baker (a lawyer, former secretary of war, and former mayor of Cleveland), sought to expose the situation of the Negro as a national and urban problem rather than as an exclusively Southern one. Furthermore, Baker and Frederick Keppel, president of the Carnegie Foundation, sought to counter the prevailing view of Northern philanthropists that "education should prepare Negroes to remain in rural areas in the South, in largely agricultural occupations."[20]

In his study for Myrdal, Ralph Bunche remarked that the use of Negroes as scabs and strikebreakers "decimates the strength of labor unions and reduces the collective bargaining power of all workers. The strength of the working class is in its . . . ability to present a unified front to the bosses. Therefore, white and Negro workers must cast aside their traditional prejudices, lock arms and march shoulder to shoulder in the struggle for the liberation of the oppressed working masses."[21]

A 767-page manuscript that Paul Norgren prepared for the Myrdal study, "Negro Labor and Its Problems," dealt exhaustively with particular crafts and industries. "The bulk of the colored non-farm population in the South obtains its livelihood in segregated and non-segregated populations," he wrote. "Their wages were lower than in industries and occupations in which whites comprised the bulk of the labor force." They also faced a higher risk of accidents, disease, noise, and pollution than white workers, he reported.[22]

Norgren paid homage to the "detailed and penetrating" treatment of blacks in the craft union movement in Spero and Harris's *The Black Worker* (1931). Not only trade unions, but also unions in service occupations (e.g., hotels and restaurants) discriminated against Negroes, they reported, and in those jobs blacks' wages were lower than whites'.

CIO unions' policies toward Negro workers were much more liberal, Norgren concluded. However, the CIO "does not carry its egalitarianism to the point of demanding that they be given the same opportunities for promotion to better and more lucrative jobs." Still, he said, "the only real hope for the future lies in large-scale manufacturing."[23]

Myrdal stressed the centrality of unions, quoting James Weldon Johnson: "Organized labor holds the main gate of our industrial and economic corral; and on the day that it throws open that gate . . . there will be a crack in the wall of racial discrimination that will be heard round the world."[24]

ORGANIZING AGRICULTURE

Despite flagrant injustices, concerted action by black agricultural workers was late in coming. Myrdal cited as reasons elements of rural culture that made for inertia against organization, poverty, the low educational levels of rural workers, the tradition of paternalism and dependence inherent in the plantation system, a weak legal system, and antagonism between blacks and whites.

The predominantly black Southern Tenant Farmers Union (STFU) arose in Arkansas in 1934, triggered by the stringencies of the Agricultural Adjustment Act (AAA). The policies of the agency were discriminatory in their application, favoring larger farm and plantation owners. The AAA also provided incentives to substitute machinery for human labor. This, coupled with a sharp drop in cotton prices, further displaced black agricultural workers.

STFU's attempts to organize sharecroppers were met with terrorism and violence. A strike the STFU organized among cotton pickers in 1935 was defeated by harassment and intimidation.[25] Had the STFU been white only, it would still have been hated by planters and comparatively easy to crush by the time-honored method of replacing whites with unorganized blacks. By bringing whites and blacks together in one union, the STFU threw the planters into a frenzy of anger and fear.[26]

Most of the STFU's funds came from the Garland Fund and the Strikers Emergency Relief Committee, which had been set up in New York City by the League for Industrial Democracy in 1929. H. L. Mitchell, one of the founders of the STFU, "disliked having his union serve primarily as a pet for philanthropists."[27]

More efficacious than the limited philanthropic support of the STFU was pathbreaking research on the evils of the South's land tenure system, its over dependence on cotton, and the peon status of the Negro. Financed by the Rosenwald Fund and directed by its president, Edwin R. Embree, the study was conducted jointly by Dr. Will W. Alexander, director of the Commission on Interracial Cooperation, and Professor Charles S. Johnson of Fisk University. The resulting book, *Collapse of the Cotton Tenancy*, reported that there were 1.1 million white and 698,000 black tenant farmers, whom the authors called peasants, in the South. Only government relief prevented "wholesale" starvation and rioting among black and white farmers in the South, the report said.[28]

Although President Franklin Roosevelt, mindful of the political power of the South in Congress, declined to take a public stand on farm tenancy, he met privately with Rosenwald staff. Foundation personnel familiar with rural Southern conditions eventually did influence federal policy. Under pressure from liberals, Roosevelt in

1936 authorized the Committee on Farm Tenancy, staffed by Will Alexander and Charles Johnson (coauthors of the Rosenwald-funded study), and Edwin Nourse of the Brookings Institution. The Committee's report led to the establishment of the Farm Security Administration in 1937, with Alexander as its head.

With World War II, rapid farm mechanization, and the continued migration of black farmworkers, the STFU dwindled, was renamed the National Farm Labor Movement, and moved to California to conduct a grape workers' strike. "That marked the end of the agricultural union movement in the Deep South."[29]

UNION DEMOCRACY

Black workers along with white have been affected by direct foundation intervention in union affairs through support of "union democracy" movements—efforts by dissident union members to oust allegedly corrupt or ineffective officials.

Partisans argue that union reform movements provide models for exercise of grassroots democratic idealism, including racial integration. Union reform has given rise to such organizations as Miners for Democracy (MFD), Teamsters for a Democratic Union, and Steelworkers Fight Back. Serving the union democracy movement through research, technical assistance, and public information is the Association for Union Democracy, which has been supported by several foundations.

Unions in the Southern coalfields were largely integrated in the 1920s. Despite the UMW's liberal policies toward blacks, black workers charging union neglect in practice formed the rival National Miners' Union (NMU) in 1928. That union was active in strikes in Pennsylvania and Kentucky that failed. Although the NMU became inactive, it was credited with having stimulated black-white cooperation and interracial leadership. By the 1950s corruption had seeped into the UMW. Black union members in the South were active in insurgencies that were the basis for the MFD, which was organized in 1970, after Joseph "Jock" Yablonski, a dissident union member, and members of his family were murdered following his successful campaign against W. A. "Tony" Boyle for the presidency of the UMW. Two years later (1972), the 1969 election was overturned and an MFD slate won. MFD received support from the Field Foundation and the Stern Family Fund, but appeals to a dozen other foundations, including several self-styled "progressive" foundations, failed.[30]

MFD's activities included organizing the Black Lung Association (whose first president, Charles Brooks, was black) and disabled miners' and widows' groups. The militant president of the Disabled Miners & Widows of Southern West Virginia, Robert Payne, was a black.

THE CIVIL RIGHTS AGE

The civil rights movement unleashed a great flow of foundation funds for such mainstream black organizations as the NAACP and the Legal Defense Fund. To the extent that such grants were general purpose, as they often were, they enhanced these organizations' capacity to work on all fronts, including organized labor. For example, the NAACP joined black union members in appeals to government agencies and the courts to end discriminatory practices by employers and unions.

Addressing the AFL-CIO convention in 1961, Martin Luther King, Jr., observed, "Negroes are almost entirely a working people. There are pitifully few Negro millionaires and few Negro employers. Our needs are identical with labor's needs—decent wages, fair working conditions, livable housing, old-age security, health and welfare measures, conditions in which families can grow, have education for their children and respect in the community."[31]

Mitchell Sviridoff, a former labor official who became a vice president of the Ford Foundation, was anxious to strengthen connections between the labor movement and minority leaders. He noted, "Without George Meany's personal intervention there would have been no Title VII against discrimination in employment in the Civil Rights Act of 1964."[32]

But even after passage in the 1960s of Title VII and other legislation prohibiting discrimination in employment, union as well as company tactics resisted implementation. "The unions . . . dug in their heels to litigate against any revision of systematic practices which carried forward the effects to past discrimination. . . . The tragedy is that employment is the key to the attack upon the barriers of racial discrimination in other areas such as education and housing."[33]

Title VII of the Civil Rights Act of 1964 (against discrimination in employment) facilitated Foundation programs in minority employment and union representation. Labor historians differ on the degree to which organized labor treated blacks, even after Title VII and notwithstanding the CIO's reputation of racial even handedness. According to NAACP's Herbert Hill, former labor director of the NAACP, now on the faculty of the University of Wisconsin, the bill that organized labor supported was limited to future discriminatory practices and would have insulated establishing seniority systems, "thus preserving the racial *status quo* in employment for at least a generation." He also charges that organized labor failed to implement the statute and "repeatedly resisted the law once the federal courts began enforcement."[34] Robert Zieger, in his history of the CIO, writes that by the 1950s, "the CIO relegated African American workers to the margins."[35]

The environment for black workers in Henry Ford's auto plants was regarded as relatively progressive for the 1930s. The foundation that Ford established ignored the minority/union issue for some 20 years after his death. In the 1950s and early 1960s, the Ford Foundation supported many labor-related research projects. Grants were also made for university-level education for union leaders.

Then, over a ten-year period, the Ford Foundation carried out one of the most sustained foundation efforts to combat bias in the labor movement. A 1966 internal memorandum stated, "Labor unions are key to the success of equal employment efforts by both private employees and government administrators. Studies by economists . . . have held that employee resistance is the greatest single barrier to non-discriminatory hiring. Human relations education within the . . . labor movement is a need of such urgency that we have been promised the full support and assistance of AFL-CIO leadership in carrying it out."[36]

In a major three-year grant to the National Urban League in 1965, the Ford Foundation addressed obstacles to black participation in many blue-collar occupations as a result of restrictive labor union practices. The League set up the Labor Apprenticeship and Education Program, which conducted seminars with black community leaders and organized labor in several cities. It also ran outreach projects in which nearly 1,000 black apprentices were brought into the building and construction trades, and negotiated agreements with electrical industry unions and employers to recruit black journeymen.

Even more effective was the Ford Foundation-supported Joint Apprenticeship Program, sponsored by the Workers Defense League and the A. Philip Randolph Institute. It devised journeyman upgrading programs, and by thoroughly analyzing apprenticeship admission tests and providing minority applicants with rigorous tutorials, the program opened doors to many minority applicants.

Addressing the paucity of minority union leaders, the Ford Foundation in 1973 granted $100,000 to the A. Philip Randolph Institute for a national leadership training program. At the time only two small unions out of 114 affiliated with the AFL-CIO had a black president and there were only an estimated 25–30 black vice presidents, though 15 percent of total union members were black. Many of the several hundred union members who participated in the program won election to local and international union offices.

Ironically, the Ford Foundation in the late 1960s became embroiled in a dispute with the New York City teachers' union that had bitter racial overtones—a clash over the issue of decentralization of the public schools, which had been mandated by the state legislature. The Foundation made grants for three experimental school districts in which the Board of Education gave parent and community groups a greater participatory role. The union accused parents and community groups, composed mainly of minorities, of seizing power and firing and reassigning teachers without due process. The dispute led to a long teachers' strike and bitterness toward the Foundation.[37]

In contrast, foundations and the Chicago Teachers Union (CTU) cooperated in the 1990s in a sweeping school decentralization plan. The CTU, whose president and half of whose members were black, initially opposed the legislation that mandated a decentralized system in which elected councils in over 500 schools were given a major role in school governance. Since its passage, the CTU has collaborated in Foundation-supported implementation efforts.[38] A center to develop innovative teaching has received grants of more than $1 million from the John D. and Catherine T. MacArthur Foundation.

Among the organizational outgrowths of the civil rights movement, the A. Philip Randolph Institute (APRI), an organization of black trade unionists, is a key agency through which foundations have helped blacks, especially in the building trades and construction industries.

In Los Angeles in the mid-1990s, black bricklayers formed their own contracting cooperative because relatively few had been employed under a union agreement with 140 contractors. The effort was launched with grants of nearly $500,000 from six foundations after the head of the national bricklayers union called APRI's attention to the situation.

In part because of its dependence on the AFL-CIO, APRI was challenged by the establishment in 1972 of the Coalition of Black Trade Unionists, representing 37 unions. One of its founders, William Lucy, secretary-treasurer of the American Federation of State, County and Municipal Employees Union, said the Coalition would work within the trade union movement, where "before now there has been no forum for black militancy." Although the Coalition continues, it appears to have come to terms with APRI.

Southern Institutions

Nowhere has opposition to unionism been more bitter than in the South, and where labor organizing has involved black workers, resistance has been particularly intense. Struggling against such intransigence have been several Southern institutions assisted by foundations.

The leading training center for Southern labor throughout the Depression was the Highlander Folk School in Tennessee. Frequently harassed because it was racially integrated and perceived as radical, Highlander trained hundreds of labor leaders from throughout the South, and school staff members participated in organizing drives and strikes. However, support for the school from organized labor was halfhearted. Union contributions reached a high of $6600 in 1946 and then dropped sharply.[39] Highlander sought unsuccessfully to work with the AFL and cooperate with the Communists. Later it forged close ties with the CIO, but the relationship soured when the CIO demanded conformity to its anticommunist policies. Foundation support declined after World War II, then increased substantially when Highlander changed its focus to civil rights leadership training.

From 1946 to 1950 the Julius Rosenwald Fund provided the bulk of financing for the Georgia Workers Education Service. Programs were held on a desegregated basis, recalls its director, "which restricted its activities with a number of unions and earned it the enmity of others." When Rosenwald funds ran out, the Ella Lyman Cabot Trust supported the Atlanta Labor Education Association.

The Atlanta-based Southern Regional Council (SRC) was founded in 1944. It grew out of dissatisfaction among moderate blacks and liberal whites with the Commission on Interracial Cooperation, whose white leadership they accused of timidity and paternalism. In the late 1940s and early 1950s, the SRC took forthright stands on racial justice and then embraced the *Brown* decision. From almost the beginning the SRC attracted substantial foundation support, initially from the North, later from the South as well.[40]

George M. Mitchell, a former staff member of the CIO's Political Action

Committee, worked with unions in 11 Southern states when he headed the SRC from the mid-1950s to the mid-1960s. The SRC was assisted in this period by the Whitney, Field, and Ford Foundations. The SRC then employed Emory Via of the University of Wisconsin Workers School as a full-time labor consultant. "The rationale for picking me was straightforward," Via recalls. "It was rare to find a Southern white, of moderately good education, sympathetic and familiar with unions, who was 'right on race' and who had labor education skills."[41]

Before joining the SRC, Via had conducted one-month union staff training institutes in the South with support from the New World Foundation. "The programs were successful," he recalled, "in that they brought together 20 or so union staff persons across racial lines. They lived and studied together, sharpened basic union skills, and got a substantial dose of the issues facing a changing South—politically, economically, in race relations, in the labor movement, and civil rights."[42]

The staff of the national AFL-CIO cooperated with the SRC's efforts, according to Via. "They welcomed having a Southern voice, one not 'tainted' by simply being official policy, to reach out constructively to unions in the South. Unions in the South that were approachable were not always, by a long shot, those with the largest civil rights reputations at the national level."[43]

The Institute for Southern Studies in Durham, N.C., founded in 1970, is a low-profile but highly effective center, conducting strategic research for labor organizing. It also works with grassroots groups on issues ranging from race relations to health and the environment. The Field Foundation and the Stern Family Fund were early supporters of the Institute's union work, notably the long struggle of textile unions to organize the J. P. Stevens Company.

This work has also been assisted by the Public Welfare Foundation, the Ruth Mott Fund, and churches. Grants from Southern foundations go for such projects as health improvement rather than union organizing. "The notion that workers should have a grievance system is totally alien to such foundations," said Robert Hall, the Institute's director. "In our proposals to them we never use the word 'union.' It's OK to talk about grassroots efforts, health, and human suffering, but if something even suggests union-style organizing, they will tell us to put it differently." Support from the Mary Reynolds Babcock and Z. Smith Reynolds foundations for the Brown Lung Association and the Women's Center for Economic Alternatives, which is focused on services for workers in the poultry industry, one of the fastest-growing in the South, has been particularly valuable, Hall said.[44]

Southerners for Economic Justice (SEJ), based in Durham, N.C., began with funding from the Amalgamated Textile Workers and worked to build community support for, or at least neutralize community antagonism toward, labor organizing drives. It is now funded by foundations, church groups, and individuals. Although the SEJ's board includes union officials, Leah Wise, a former steelworker who is its director, is somewhat disenchanted with unions. "The North Carolina AFL-CIO, for example," she said, "feels threatened by organizing efforts by nonunion, community self-help organizations. The union's focus is on the legislature. They seem to be afraid that local efforts will fail."[45]

Where unions are weak or choose to ignore certain categories of workers, SEJ and similar organizations function like unions in many respects save collective bargaining. They act as a sounding board for, or themselves identify, worker grievances; conduct research on matters affecting workers' well-being, such as plant closings, racial discrimination, and health and environmental hazards; and lobby for legislative reforms, as in the aftermath of the fire in a North Carolina poultry plant that took 25 lives.

CURRENT AFFAIRS

Foundation funding for union-related activities in the 1980s and 1990s has tended to focus on foundation interests in a variety of fields outside union organizing per se, such as the environment, health care, immigration, and sexual harassment. One focus has been plant closings and industrial restructuring. The Midwest Center for Labor Research, established in 1982 (with funds from the Stern Family Fund) to fight plant closings in the steel industry, has received grants from nine additional foundations. Most of the unionized companies with which the Center deals have black workers.

Combining sophisticated research with technical assistance, the Center helps unions in their contract negotiations and facilitates purchase or transfer of companies so that they can remain in place. It also promotes employee ownership of plants and has engineered several company buyouts and transfer to local entrepreneurs of absentee-owned companies whose aging owners made no plans for succession.

Some foundations are helping organizations that resemble unions, but are structured differently, to improve the condition of black workers in rapidly expanding occupations—home care, for example. Thus, in the Bronx, the New York Community Trust recently made two grants to ensure that home care workers for the homebound elderly receive fair wages and benefits.

In 1994 William B. Gould was confirmed as head of the National Labor Relations Board. Gould, whose nomination was opposed by the National Association of Manufacturers and conservative groups, is a Stanford University law professor. In 1977, under a Ford Foundation grant, he wrote *Black Workers in White Unions: Job Discrimination in the United States*, in which he reached a gloomy conclusion: "A principal obstacle to a more progressive labor movement in the United States is its unwarranted self-satisfaction and smugness about organizing new categories of workers. The effect is to disregard the interests of those who need protection most—the significant number of the poor who are members of racial minorities."[46]

Notwithstanding declining union membership, is the outlook today more promising?[47] For one thing, the number of black union officials has increased, especially in public service unions, where membership is growing. For another, the AFL-CIO made an important commitment, institutionally and financially, in 1989 to a freestanding center—the Organizing Institute—dedicated to recruiting and training young labor organizers, especially among minority groups and graduates from working-class backgrounds.

John N. Sturdivant, a black who is national president of the American Federation of Government Employees, believes that although foundations are helpful to society, they "generally buttress the ideological interests of their sponsors." His union has jointly funded or collaboratively sponsored projects with foundations in occupational health research, safety, voter registration, and education. Foundation staff people know little about the labor movement, he has said, but collaboration could help both unions and foundations be more responsive.[48]

Within the foundation community, the last 20 years have seen a great increase in the number of blacks and other minorities on staffs.[49] But will black foundation officials differ from their white counterparts in their attitudes toward organized labor in general? Even among officials of foundations that have dealt with union-related matters in the last decade, a survey discloses wariness at worst, but more often distance or disinterest. Kirke Wilson of the Rosenberg Foundation, for example, remarked, "In the post civil-rights environment, trade unions and their leaders are too often either opponents of social change or outside the debate."[50]

It remains to be seen whether the new breed of foundation officials will differ from their more traditional colleagues in their attitudes toward organized labor. During the 1930s and 1940s, liberals and intellectuals, from whom foundation staffs are mainly drawn, allied themselves closely with organized labor, but disenchantment began to set in, as Maurice N. Neufeld demonstrated, "after the passage of time disclosed that labor unions suffered from the same natural shocks that all other human organizations are heir to." Most of the younger liberals and intellectuals had no personal knowledge of the labor movement, and in later years their excessive enthusiasm brought "its inevitable consequence, immoderate disillusionment."[51]

The present generation is no closer to the labor movement than their forebears a half-century ago, but at least as represented in the nation's foundations, they are more richly diverse. And within labor, new young recruits may bring changes in what Clark Kerr termed "the phenomenon of a great social institution remaining virtually unmoving on a plateau while society all around it keeps on growing and changing."[52]

NOTES

1. On labor, see Maurice F. Neufeld, Daniel J. Leab, and Dorothy Swanson, *American Working Class History: A Representative Bibliography* (New York: Bowker, 1983); on foundations, see Margaret Chandler Derrickson et al., *The Literature of the Nonprofit Sector: A Bibliography with Abstracts*, 3 vols. (New York: The Foundation Center, 1989–1991).

2. In 1993–1994, 156 labor-related grants, totaling $4.8 million, were made, representing only .08 percent of the 68,500 sampled grants that foundations made in all fields—a total of $5.6 billion. Tiny proportions hold for earlier years. *Labor Union-Related Grants by Foundations, 1984-1994*, DIALOG File 27 (New York: The Foundation Center).

3. Mitchell Gordon, "Organized Labor and Organized Communities: The Watts Labor Community Action Committee—A Prototype for Community Unions?" Project evaluation (August 1969), Ford Foundation Archives, New York City.

4. Philip Foner, "Black Workers," in *Encyclopedia of Southern Culture* (Chapel Hill: University of North Carolina Press, 1989), pp. 199–200.

5. *The Negro Almanac: A Reference Work on the African American* (Detroit: Gale Research, 1989) 5th ed., p. 555.

6. Sterling Spero and Abram Harris, *The Black Worker: The Negro and the Labor Movement* (New York: Columbia University Press, 1931), pp. 467, 34.

7. Laura Spelman Rockefeller Memorial (LSRM) Papers, series III, Box 99, Folder 1005, Rockefeller Archive Center, Pocantico Hills, N.Y.

8. Howard M. Gitelman, *Legacy of the Ludlow Massacre: A Chapter in American Industrial Relations* (Philadelphia: University of Pennsylvania Press, 1988), p. 5.

9. John Lankford, *Congress and the Foundations in the Twentieth Century* (River Falls: Wisconsin State University Press, 1964) and *The American Fund for Public Service: Charles Garland and Radical Philanthropy, 1922–1941.* (Westport, CT: Greenwood, 1966).

10. Ralph Bunche, "Conceptions and Ideologies of the Negro Problem" (March 1940), Microfilm #323, 173C, reels 1 and 2, Carnegie-Myrdal Papers, Schomburg Library, New York City.

11. For this account of the Garland Fund, I am indebted to the dissertation by Gloria Garrett Samson, "Toward a New Social Order: The American Fund for Public Service, Clearinghouse for Radicalism in the 1920s" (University of Rochester, 1987, vi). I also gratefully acknowledge her helpful comments on other aspects of my research.

12. Ibid., pp. 484–92.

13. Gloria Garrett Samson, "Toward a New Social Order—The American Fund for Public Service: Clearinghouse for Radicalism in the 1920s." (Ph.D. diss., University of Rochester, 1987), p. 492.

14. John H. Stanfield, *Philanthropy and Jim Crow in American Social Science* (Westport, Ct.: Greenwood Press, 1985), p. 108.

15. Gunnar Myrdal, [with the assistance of Richard Sterner and Arnold Rose], *An American Dilemma: The Negro Problem and Modern Democracy*, twentieth anniversary ed. (New York: Harper & Row, 1962), p. 118.

16. Stanfield, *Philanthropy and Jim Crow*, p. 128.

17. Lester Granger, "The National Negro Congress: An Interpretation," in *Opportunity* no. 14 (May 1939): pp. 151–153. Reprinted in Philip S. Foner and Ronald L. Lewis, eds., *Black Workers* (Philadelphia: Temple University Press, 1989).

18. Anson Phelps Stokes, "Negro Status and Race Relations in These United States," in *1911–1946: The Thirty-Five Year Report on the Phelps Stokes Fund* (New York: Phelps Stokes Fund, 1948), pp. 103, 105.

19. Although only one of some 30 specialized memoranda dealt directly with Negro labor—"Negro Labor and Its Problems," by Paul Norgren—several others examined the economic status of Negroes. They include "The Negro's Share in Income, Consumption, Housing and Public Assistance," by Richard Sterner; "The Programs, Ideologies, Tactics, and Achievements of Negro Betterment and Interracial Organizations," one of four papers by Ralph Bunche; "The Negro in Agriculture," by T. C. McCormick; and "The Negro in the American Economic System," by Ira DeA. Reid.

20. Ellen Condliffe Lagemann, *Private Power for the Public Good: A History of the Carnegie Foundation for the Advancement of Teaching* (Middletown, CT: Wesleyan University Press, 1983), pp. 123–24.

21. Bunche, "Conception and Ideologies."

22. Paul Norgren, "Negro Labor and Its Problems." pp. 4, 7, Microfilm #323, 173C, reel 10. Carnegie-Myrdal Papers, Schomburg Library, New York City.

23. Ibid., p. 398.

24. James Weldon Johnson, *What Now?* (New York: The Viking Press, 1974), 66.

25. August Meier and Elliott Rudwick, *From Plantation to Ghetto* (New York: Hill and Wang, 1966. 3d ed. 1976), p. 241.

26. Howard Kester, *Revolt Among the Sharecroppers* (New York: Arno Press, 1969 [1936]), p. 23.

27. Donald H. Grubbs, *Cry from the Cotton: The Southern Tenant Farmer and the New Deal* (Chapel Hill: University of North Carolina Press, 1971), p. 80.

28. "South's Land Evils Assailed in Report." *The New York Times*, Mar. 21, 1935.

29. Anthony P. Dunbar, *Against the Grain: Southern Radicals and Prophets, 1929–1959* (Charlottesville: University Press of Virginia, 1981), p. 256.

30. Miners for Democracy Collection, Boxes #15, 20, 24, 25, Reuther Labor Archives, Wayne State University, Detroit.

31. Bayard Rustin, "The Blacks and the Unions," *Harper's*, Apr. 1971, pp. 73–81.

32. Mitchell Sviridoff, oral History interview, Feb. 12, 1975, p. 5, Ford Foundation Archives, New York City.

33. William B. Gould, *Black Workers in White Unions: Job Discrimination in the United States* (Ithaca, NY: Cornell University Press, 1977), pp. 424, 429.

34. Hill to Magat, Sept. 10, 1996. See also Herbert Hill, *Black Workers, Organized Labor*, and" Title VII of the 1964 Civil Rights Act:: Legislative History and Litigation Record" in Herbert Hill and James E. Jones, Jr., *Race in America, The Struggle for Equality* (Madison: University of Wisconsin Press, 1993), pp. 269–70; and Herbert Hill, "The Problem of Race in American Labor History," *Reviews in American History*, v. 24, no. 2 (1996) pp. 109–188.

35. Robert H. Zieger. *The CIO 1935–1955* (Chapel Hill: University of North Carolina Press, 1995), p. 418. See also Bruce Nelson et al., "Robert Zieger's History of the CIO." *Labor History*, v. 37, no. 2 (1996), pp. 157–88.

36. Southern Regional Council Archives, Atlanta University Center Library, Series I, reel 24.

37. For contrasting views of the decentralization dispute, see Diane Ravitch, *The Great School Wars: New York City, 1805–1973* (New York: Basic Books, 1974), pp. 251–362; Mario Fantini, Marilyn Gittell, and Richard Magat, *Community Control and the Urban School* (New York: Praeger, 1970), pp. 77–172.

38. William S. McKersie, "Philanthropy's Paradox: Chicago School Reform," *Educational Evaluation and Policy Analysis* 15, no. 2 (Summer 1993): 109.

39. John M. Glen, *Highlander: No Ordinary School, 1932–1962* (Lexington: University Press of Kentucky, 1988), pp. 25, 118.

40. Anthony Newberry, "Southern Regional Council," in *Encyclopedia of Southern Culture* (Chapel Hill: University of North Carolina Press, 1989), pp. 425–26.

41. Emory F. Via to Richard Magat, May 5, 1994.

42. Emory F. Via to Richard Magat, Apr. 13, 1994.

43. Ibid.

44. Interview, Durham, N.C., Apr. 11, 1994.

45. Interview, Durham, N.C., Apr. 12, 1994.

46. Gould, *Black Workers*, p. 15.

47. Union membership declined 30 percent between 1975 and 1991, from 23.7 million to 16.5 million, according to the U.S. Department of Labor. During the same period, according to the Foundation Center, the number of foundations grew 52.5 percent, from 21,877 to 33,356, and assets increased 113.3 percent, from $1.2 billion to $2.26 billion (in 1967 constant dollars).

48. John N. Sturdivant to Richard Magat, July 27, 1993.

49. Black women are 11 percent of foundation program officers; black men, 7 percent. Despite gains, blacks are less likely than white males to be in top positions; one-third of white males in foundations are CEOs, compared with 7.8 percent of black males and 2.7 percent of black females. Lynn C. Burbridge, "Status of African Americans in Grant making Institutions" (Washington, D.C.: Association of Black Foundation Executives, April 1994), pp. vi, vii, 1.

50. Kirke Wilson to Richard Magat, Aug. 22, 1992.

51. Maurice F. Neufeld, "The Historical Relationship of Liberals and Intellectuals to Organized Labor in the United States," *Annals of the American Academy of Political and Social Sciences* 350 (November 1963): 115–29. Although earlier writers had examined deficiencies in the labor movement, including undemocratic governance and narrow goals, the criticism grew to a crescendo in the 1950s and 1960s. Among the critical Center for the Study of Democratic Institutions studies were *Unions and Union Leaders of Their Own Choosing*, by Clark Kerr, chancellor of the University of California and a leading labor economist; *The Decline of the Labor Movement and What Can Be Done About It* by Solomon Barkin, a veteran labor official; and *Old Before Its Time: Collective Bargaining at 28*, in which Paul Jacobs called collective bargaining obsolete.

52. Clark Kerr, *Unions and Union Leaders of Their Own Choosing* (New York: Fund for the Republic, 1957), p. 21.

CHAPTER 8

Diversity in the Workplace:
A Dialogue Among Corporate Executives

The moderator of this panel was Dr. Josie R. Johnson, Associate Vice President for Academic Affairs and Associate Provost at the University of Minnesota with responsibility for Minority Affairs. The complete panel consisted of V. Robert Hayles, Vice President of Human Resources & Diversity, The Pillsbury Company, Grand Metropolitan; Carolyn Irving, Manager of Work Force Diversity, Medtronic, Inc.; William Prock, Office of Civil Rights, Minneapolis; Steve Rothschild, director and founder, Twin Cities Rise, Inc.; and William R. Tamayo, Managing Attorney, Asian Law Caucus, San Francisco. The remarks contained herein are edited and abbreviated.

V. ROBERT HAYLES

I will illustrate the process [of diversity] in our organization. I preface this by saying that my belief regarding equal opportunity, affirmative action, and diversity is one of a medical perspective; a T.I.D. perspective, which says "take as indicated" —basically, take as needed; that all three are needed; and they need to be used appropriately and strategically. Sometimes one or another may not be the best approach, and I will tell a very brief story that I think characterizes this. The characters will remain anonymous.

There was a human resources director who came into an organization some years ago, and his boss came to him and said, "Okay, we need to move forward regarding diversity in this organization. Get your effort started. I understand you have a little experience in this area, so do what you think is most effective and begin." Another organization in this same company took a slightly different approach. The senior person in that organization said, "We're going to do this diversity stuff and we're serious and we're committed." And he began as follows: he went around the management table, and he said, "You—your representation levels are at 5 percent. At 18 months they will be at 10 percent. And just to help you get there, 10 percent of your bonus will be dependent upon whether or not you achieve these objectives. Do you understand?" The manager said yes.

Next manager: "Your representation level is 6 percent, I want you to move to 9 percent in 18 months, same deal regarding your bonus. Do you understand me?" The person went right around the table. In other words, there were clear, unambiguous goals, clear, unambiguous timetables. Do you believe those managers achieved those goals? Absolutely. Absolutely. They achieved those goals spectacularly. Representation went up in 18 months unbelievably. Now, that's Organization 2.

I'm going to come back to Organization 1 and tell a slightly different story. This particular human resource manager said to the senior people, "Now we have an affirmative action plan, but I'm not going to show it to you. Now what we're going to do is to engage in a process; a scientifically grounded, developmentally sequenced process of diversity education, diversity training, strategic planning, changes in practices, policies, and systems to reinforce what we wanted to achieve in this organization"—no hard goals, no hard timetable, but an emphasis on learning the skills to create a diverse workforce; an emphasis on acquiring the knowledge, exhibiting the right behaviors.

And key to this effort in the training program was a definition of diversity that was very, very clear. It was "all the ways in which we differ." It included such things as "If you live in Minnesota and do not fish. How many of you live in Minnesota? You know that if I walk down the street and ask for voter registration cards and fishing licenses, I will find more of which? Fishing licenses. We *are* in Minnesota." And so, that was a diversity issue as well as race and gender.

We began with that foundation, and with that foundation in place, we moved to establish a business case for diversity that was anecdotal and quantitative, where every manager was helped in an educational and developmental way to understand that diversity will enrich our business. Diversity will make us a higher performing organization. Every single person in the organization spent at least an hour examining the business case. Every single employee in the organization spent two or three hours experiencing the definition of diversity. Every single person, for at least an hour or two, talked about how diversity will be initiated in the organization. Again, no timetables, no goals—no hardness, in a sense.

Eighteen months later, what do you think happened with representation in this organization? It advanced a little, but not *nearly as much* as that first organization with those hard, concrete goals and timetables. Then both HR managers were called in by a higher executive. One was told, "Good job, keep up the good work." The other was told, "You know, you're going to be looking for another job here if you don't get it in gear." But each person was reasonably confident, and they continued their efforts.

How do you think the two organizations compared three and four years later? The organization with the hard targets and goals began to experience turnover. People of color left at twice the average rate. Women left at one and a half times the average rate. Their overall representation rate declined. What about that other organization with no hard targets, no goals, no timetables, but with a clear vision of diversity, a broad, inclusive definition and a developmentally sequenced process of training and education? Its representation continued to grow past the other organization. Five years later, representation continues to climb in that organization. Since then, the organization that took the hard target approach has revamped its effort and tried a new approach.

This is a true story, and I would be happy to share in private some names and specific numbers. But I'm sharing this story to say that we now know enough about diversity—the science of diversity—the techniques for helping people grow from a state of bias and racism to a state of more valuing and inclusiveness in a developmentally sequenced way. We know about how to change our policies, practices, and systems, and how to do it in an appropriately sequenced way to create more effective organizations where diversity is valued. It is in full compliance with the spirit of what we see in legislation as opposed to worrying about the letter of that legislation.

And so part of the message I want to leave with you today is that affirmative action is valuable, needed. But the managers in Organization 1 took what I call "pro-action" to add diversity where it was missing because it was valued and needed. They did not take pro-action out of fear of litigation, fear of lawsuit, or because of a hard target that had nothing to do with the performance of the organization.

We have today much better information to document the relationship between diversity and the stock price of a company; between diversity and being listed as a "most admired company" by *Fortune* magazine; between diversity and sales growth, profit growth, or performance in a down turning economy. With that kind of information, I believe we can motivate diversity with the carrot and less so with the stick. That comes from my personal belief that when you hurt someone to make them do what you want them to do, they will pay you back later. If I were to pull a weapon from this platform, and force all of you to engage in embarrassing and ridiculous behavior, and then later to sit down and take a nap, do you think I would be able to sleep safely? Probably not. You would pay me back. And while litigation and forced affirmative action are very effective—no doubt about it, they do create results—they also create backlash and resistance that can be avoided if done in a different way.

CAROLYN IRVING

I want to thank Dr. Hayles for his comments. He talked about the fact that we now know how to do this thing called diversity, and I have to say that Dr. Hayles has been one of the practitioners that has helped to make that so. I want to talk about the company that I work for in particular. You have heard from Dr. Hayles in general, and I want to tell you about our experience. To do that, I have to tell you a little bit about the company.

We are a 1.4 billion dollar medical device manufacturer. Our primary product is heart pacemakers, and we also make related cardiovascular products. We're an extremely successful company. We've seen increases in profitability over the last nine years, so things are going very well at Medtronic. We define diversity—or managing diversity—as a philosophy of valuing differences and the activity of creating a work setting where every employee has an opportunity for meaningful work and rewards. So there is a philosophy and there are actions.

We have done this in several different ways. We were very fortunate about five years ago to get a CEO who had come from an experience at Honeywell, where affirmative action really had been done very strongly. Honeywell went beyond the letter of the law and really tried to make advances, and did so quite successfully. At Medtronic, there was also support from our Human Resources Department, where this whole effort was delegated. At that time there wasn't an understanding that diversity was a topic that needed to be talked about at the highest levels of the organization—that it needed to be discussed as part of the overall business strategy—but it was seen as a very key human resources strategy. It in fact evolved in a couple of years to be one of three human resources thrusts: learning in the organization or continuing development of our employees, recognition and rewards for employees, and diversity.

At the time our CEO came on board, he met with different groups of employees. He met with women and minority employees to ask them, "What is it like to work here?" And they told him. He encouraged them at that time to form what we call employee resource groups. They are also called employee councils or affinity groups. To help the company understand ways in which we could make the environment and the experience of working at Medtronic a lot better, the Diversity Manager position was created, and I was hired into that position. I've been the only person that's been in that position. I am responsible for developing strategies along with other members of the organization, and then in consulting with management in our functional HR areas on implementing those changes. We established a council. Vision was communicated widely and continuously, sometimes to the dismay of our employees, who, as recently as last week, said, "When is this diversity thing going to go away?" And we are happy to say, "It's not."

We formed the employee resource groups. We did training, and I am happy to say that the training has not been a one-shot focus. We have had three different levels of training and a lot of reinforcing activities along the way. We've also looked at system changes in our Human Resources Department, changes in our practices, changes in our procedures and policies. We have now gotten to the point where we are including this discussion of diversity in our overall business strategy.

We market our products in 84 countries internationally, and our profitability in the future will be tied more and more to going into the developing economies. A lot of our expansion will be in Asia and Africa, the Middle East, Eastern Europe, and we understand that this is an issue that is alive not only here in the United States but that it impacts our ability to do business and to be successful internationally.

We also have some degree of measurement. Primarily, we use our EEO reports to track our progress and to set goals. We use biannual surveys to track employee attitudes and morale, and we also look at our turnover rates, which mirror the rates that Robert Hayles mentioned. What has worked in our organization is the top-level support from our CEO; also, having allies in other areas of the company. For instance, our Foundation Department, which was responsible for some of the funding here, has been a very good ally in forming the philosophy and strategy around how and where monies are given from the foundation. Our tying it in with our quality efforts at work has been very successful.

The employee resource groups have been very positive. One of the first groups that formed was our Women's Council. They did a survey, and there were three top areas that were identified as areas of concern: career development opportunities for women, pay equity, and inclusion and involvement. The things that have evolved from this study really have benefited the whole organization—all people, white males included.

Our Asian resource group has been very instrumental in working with our management to help provide contacts in some of the emerging markets to work as interpreters to help our business managers understand some of the business practices, especially in the medical industry in those countries. Our black employee resource group just recently—in fact, last week—brought in Dr. Benjamin Carson from Johns Hopkins University. We brought him here to speak to children in the community, to encourage them to excel. He also spoke with Medtronic management, and they were able to dialogue and share ideas about the work that he does and some of the products that we are developing.

There has been a very good synergy between what these groups want and what they want to see happen at the organization, and what the organization wants. There has been an increased focus on bringing minorities and women at all levels into key leadership positions at Medtronic. There has been greater involvement in communities of color as well.

Now, what are the continuing challenges in the work that we are doing? I believe that there is low accountability for the work that we are doing. Part of that has to do with the Medtronic culture, where influence is put at a premium. So, even though we have these strategies in place, and they're endorsed by management, it is key to have people who will go out and influence people really to get on board. That's valued a lot.

I believe that we can make a lot more progress with some types of directives, although I haven't been able to influence my management enough to take that course. There has been a backlash, predominantly white and predominantly male, but there has also been backlash from some of the other groups who might see that one group is getting more of the pie than another. There has been a competition for resources. We're a growing company, growing at 15 percent per year, so there is a real competition for resources in terms of time, money, and executive attention. I feel that there is a reluctance to step into a discomfort zone and really work on the tough issues, of which racism is one. A criticism that I hear from people is that by having a broad definition of diversity that includes all people, we dilute the effectiveness by not clearly focusing on one thing. I believe that we have to do both at the same time.

Another challenge is that this is a long-term change process and we are in an environment that values short-term orientation, so we have to really continue to talk about the process and the value of doing this work long-term in conjunction with our long-term business goals. We also have to produce some short-term results at the same time.

I continue to ask what's the motivation for people to get involved with this work personally. I like to talk about security and the ability to be valuable to the organization, to be able to manage in a diverse workforce, to have the opportunity for personal growth, and also to be a success in the marketplace.

WILLIAM TAMAYO

I firmly believe that the issue of diversity is rooted in the struggle against racism, and that's the principal starting point, but it has been expanded to include the diversity issues of women, the disabled, and so forth. But I think principally that is still our starting point. And with that, I think I would also like to use a quote that Professor Bill Hing from Stanford Law School often uses, which is, "It's no accident that the Statue of Liberty faces Europe and has her back to Asia and Latin America."

Now that is very important, because I think you have to bring that factor into the discussion of diversity, particularly the 1990s and we certainly feel it in California. We are involved in a global economy, with global migrations, as Carolyn Irving has mentioned. Some in the corporate sector are rationalizing that diversity is necessary in order to be able to engage in the global marketplace. You want to engage in international trade, investment, and business. You need people who are bilingual and bicultural. So, from a purely economic view, some corporations want to get into the diversity game rather than looking at it as a way to correct some past employment practices.

One of the other issues that we have to confront, as civil rights activists, is that we are dealing with the phenomenon of global migration. Last year the World Bank released a report stating that 100 million people have left their home countries basically searching for a better life or for work; 44 million people are refugees and about 24 million have left their countries. And the vast majority of refugees are from Africa—not from Asia, not from Latin America, but from Africa. Over the last four to five years, approximately 700,000 people have emigrated annually to the United States. About a half a million of those are primarily coming to reunite with families; others are coming as refugees or as workers.

If we want to do some projections, according to the State Department there are something like 3.6 million people registered for visas to emigrate to the United States on a permanent basis. That does not include people who are immediate relatives of U.S. citizens. Forty-eight percent will come from Asia, 41 percent from Latin American countries. We project that by the year 2000 Asians will be about 11 million of the U.S. population, Hispanics will be close to 30 million people. And that will largely be due to immigration. But despite the large numbers, while persons of Asian descent are 50 percent of the world's population, Asians are less than 3 percent of the U. S. population. And that's not a historical accident, given my starting quote about the Statue of Liberty.

Now what does that have to do with diversity in the workforce? The types of issues that we are litigating in the civil rights arena, particularly in employment discrimination, tend to come down to two areas: English-only laws and accent discrimination. By "English-only" we mean, basically, laws by employers that basically say nobody in the workforce can speak a language other than English. It's aimed, primarily, at many Filipino employees, Spanish-speaking employees, and Chinese-speaking employees who may be talking to each other on a purely personal basis. This is a nonbusiness-related discussion, and they are told they can only speak English.

Some of the justifications that employers are giving that have not been accepted by the courts are "Well, if managers don't understand what the employees are talking about, it breeds fear among the managers," or "Some of the other workers feel uncomfortable because you may be talking about them." This is kind of a sticky area, but it does reflect some of the hostilities or wariness about the new and emerging communities. And I would have to state that the Reagan and Bush administrations did contribute to some of the fears and latent xenophobia toward some of the new and emerging communities.

The EEOC guidelines covering English-only laws are fairly strong, though they basically say that if an employer has an English-only policy, we will presume it's a prima facie case of discrimination and the burden is back on the employer to justify why he or she needs to have an English-only policy, because the EEOC thinks it violates the rights of people who want to be able to speak or communicate in a language other than English. It is certainly a business-necessity defense, but the employer has to articulate that.

One of the more complicated areas that's coming up is the area of accent discrimination, which is when people are denied jobs, denied promotions, or their job conditions are changed because they don't speak "network English." They speak English with an accent. And everybody in this room speaks English with an accent.

We litigated a case recently where five Filipino security guards were removed from a job because one of them "had a communication problem." So the employer, using basically a racial criterion—national origin discrimination—removed all of the Filipino security guards from a federal building. Now all of these guys had been working anywhere from three to five years for the security company at federal buildings. Three of them had law degrees—college degrees. One of them had been a law clerk at the Supreme Court. He spoke English fluently but with a Filipino accent, and he wrote English very well. But we have a situation where you have people who speak English, not necessarily really as a second language, but have been speaking English from the time they were little kids or at least when they started school. And they will never lose that accent, because that's how they have learned English.

But now we are getting into a climate where people are starting to say, "Well, you have to speak English in a certain kind of way." What is that kind of way? I think that's still open for the courts, but I think you will be seeing more and more cases like this. The point being that I think for diversity managers, these are the issues of the '90s. These will be the issues of the next century as there is global migration and people are coming into this country.

I want to give you another case illustration while I just have another minute here. There is a case of a Filipino man in Hawaii who applied for a job as a clerk with the Department of Motor Vehicles. He scores the highest on the written examination, gets interviewed, and is ranked—he is considered qualified but ranked below two other people. And the reason that's given, particularly in Hawaii, is, "Well, we didn't understand his thick Filipino accent." Now, Mr. Furgante went to law school in the Philippines, speaks English fluently and grammatically, writes very well. But it's a question of what does the listener have to tolerate, or does the listener have to be a little more patient?

Now, interestingly enough, I think a lot of the people who will be affected by this will be people from Africa; from Nigeria, Zimbabwe, Kenya, Botswana, South Africa, where English is the medium of instruction, but they will come to the United States and they will be speaking it in a little different way. This somehow interacts with the racial dynamics. We are a little more tolerant of people who speak with a French accent, a British accent, an Australian accent. I have been on trips with people from Australia and New Zealand and I cannot understand them. It's one of those dynamics.

But I leave you with this: that I think the new diversity issues will be quite complicated. We need to know, though, that these new issues, although they are new areas, are still protected by Title VII of the Civil Rights Act of 1964. Title VII bars national origin discrimination. The courts are pretty clear that accent discrimination and English-only laws are covered by national origin discrimination. And so that getting into the job, in terms of diversity, is half the battle. Keeping your job and being promoted and not being fired is the other half. And I think we are going to have a real responsibility to try to address those during this next decade when you have a lot of changing demographics.

FROM THE AUDIENCE

As your companies are doing business overseas, [what] are your values? If you value diversity at a corporate level and you start to work with cultures who don't, for instance, value women in the same way as we do, are you adjusting how you do business in that country or are you holding onto your values here? And how do you do that?

ROBERT HAYLES

Within the Grand Met organization we are attempting to do our diversity work worldwide. We understand that different countries will be at different developmental stages regarding a specific issue such as gender. We are addressing the gender issue, believe it or not, in Germany, France, and the U.K., where it is very, very difficult. But we have a commitment from corporate to address that issue and we have started with the topmost senior 250 executives within Grand Metropolitan worldwide to go through intensive work around specific issues. The three issues we have chosen for the first wave are—after an introduction—work on race, which presents itself differently internationally, but is still fundamentally an issue of people of color; the issue of gender; and the issue of people with disabilities. These are the three that we have tackled on a worldwide basis. Moving to the intercultural differences is another piece that plays out in Europe.

CAROLYN IRVING

And I would concur that we are at a different stage in doing this work than Grand Met/Pillsbury, but it is our intention to do so also. Besides having values based on organizational values that we want to be in force everywhere in the world, we also see a lot of this impetus for change bubbling up from the people in the organizations. I have had people tell me that gender is not an issue and there is no harassment going on here. We did an employee survey, for instance, on harassment. We believe if there is one person experiencing harassment, that's too many. So we see the need to work on that.

FROM THE AUDIENCE

I think there were two omissions that I would like to hear the panel speak about. One is that we live not by the market alone, given the change in the structure of employment in which there is a broad range of middle jobs disappearing and there is a queuing on high-paying jobs and a lot of low-paying service jobs. It seems to me that structural barrier has to be faced before one says we can rely on the market alone to solve our problems, in view of the fact that we have a tremendous infrastructural rebuilding going on. And second, I don't believe that diversity is enough. No one talks about the fact that it's a question—in terms of a criterion—that there is a dominant-subordinate relationship in the process of experiencing the way people are allocated in an organization. Many minority groups get special markets but women get special areas. But I don't see too many cases where women supervise men, blacks supervise whites, Latinos and Asians supervise people opposite them in the mainstream. It seems to me that must be the criterion for a dramatic change in the corporate employment structure.

ROBERT HAYLES

In the best organizations we do some of that. After five hard years of work I can answer yes to your latter question. We do see some of that.

CAROLYN IRVING

And I would say that we have brought people into the organization or moved people around in the organization into key leadership positions. The whole process has to become natural, though, which gets into management training and into philosophies. And so there is still a lot of work, there but I think that's key.

The other thing I would like to add to your equation is this whole element of power in an organization and how it is used. I believe there needs to be a real fundamental structural change in the way that power is distributed, because without that change we can't accomplish some of the other goals that we have in organization, such as flattening the organization, such as having teams. If we still have that hierarchical power, we certainly can't have teams where power is distributed across networks. They just cannot exist together.

WILLIAM PROCK

I'd just like to comment on the market question. It was not my intention to suggest that the market solves all problems for all people. There's not a market system anywhere that does that. There are always people that fall through the cracks, and they have to be taken care of in other ways. My point was to say that we don't rely on the market system enough to take care of these problems, and I think if we can, it can work to our advantage, basically, because the world is changing. You are quite right there are high-skill jobs and there are low-skill jobs. There are lots of high-skill jobs being created in the service sector today that need to be filled, but there is a lack of skilled people in those jobs. And we can do a better job of matching people who are skilled with work that needs to be accomplished, and we are just not doing that appropriately enough.

WILLIAM TAMAYO

Just one thing: the question—does the market take care of it? I think it's pretty clear that it doesn't necessarily do that. I'll give you an example. In Silicon Valley there are a lot of young Asian engineers, some Asian Americans, some who had immigrated in the '70s and were hired as basically technical people at the starting computer companies. As these computer companies grew in the '70s and '80s, these same guys who had started with the companies kept hitting the glass ceiling. So they basically said, "I'm leaving." And they started their own companies, and they are the ones now engaged in a lot of the trade with Asia and the Pacific, leaving behind the companies that refused to promote them. The shortsightedness of those companies basically has prevented them from competing in the international marketplace. But would the market have taken care of it? Possibly, but I think the sad part is that although these guys came out better in the long run, the power trips within the companies and need for power and race control within those earlier corporations prevented them from seeing the long-range outcomes.

You asked a question about having women supervising men and blacks supervising whites, and you don't see very much of that. I think it's increasing, but I think the organizations that are making those moves owe those individuals the same degree of support that they gave their previous supervisors and managers. The individuals in those positions have to be given the same opportunity to succeed or fail as anybody else would. Too often we see a black woman put in a position as a supervisor over a crew and within five months she is out of a job because she wasn't being successful. Management allowed her employees to go around her and complain about her decisions, and they kept overriding those decisions. Women and minorities, when they are put in those positions—and it's happening more and more—need to be given the support that they deserve.

CHAPTER 9

A Local Conversation About Race

The moderator of this panel was Gary Gilson, Executive Director of the Minnesota News Council. The complete panel consisted of Bart Schneider, editor, Hungry Mind Review; *john powell, Professor, University of Minnesota Law School; Cathi Tactaquin, Research Associate, Applied Research Center, Oakland, California; Sheila Ards, Assistant Professor, Humphrey Institute of Public Affairs; and Mahmoud El-Kati, lecturer and writer on the African-American experience, Macalester College, St. Paul, Minnesota. The remarks contained herein are edited and abbreviated.*

BART SCHNEIDER

For those of you unfamiliar with the *Hungry Mind Review*, I just want to give a little bit of background about the magazine. It's now in its ninth year of publication, and it's published by the Hungry Mind Bookstore in St. Paul. In the last nine years it has become one of the major book review magazines in the country, existing almost entirely on the support of publishers' ads. The magazine has a print run of 50,000 copies an issue and is distributed free of charge to independent bookstores around the country. We don't distribute the magazines in chain bookstores. Each of our issues is a mix of book reviews and essays, and each issue is devoted to one particular theme. So when we decided to do the theme of "race" for our September 1994 issue, I wanted to set the stage for this issue by printing a questionnaire on race in the previous issue, so that we would get our readership thinking about race and hopefully talking about it amongst themselves. Last spring the staff of the *Hungry Mind Review* worked together for weeks to come up with a sequence of questions—questions that we felt were true to concerns—and we batted them around and sort of turned ourselves inside out, for weeks. When we thought we had a decent group of questions, we hosted a community meeting that included john powell. At that meeting it was pointed out to us that in subtle ways our questions were geared to a white audience. And after I understood the fallacy and the danger of that presumption, we re-worked some of the questions and sequencing with Elizabeth Burkes, an African-American professor at Macalester College, and that resulted in the questionnaire that we published.

We were overwhelmed by the responses—the reader responses—to this question-naire. In part, it was the sheer number of responses. Some days 10, 15, 20 of them came in the mail and you just peeled them open. I sat down almost immediately each day and read through them. It was one of the first things I did after the mail came. I was also very impressed by the intensity of the responses. People were filling them out, and you had the sense that they were spending two or three hours filling out these questionnaires, adding extra pieces of paper, contributing long personal accounts. It seemed to me that a lot of people had a lot to say.

One reason that I believe readers engaged so intensely with this questionnaire is that we sequenced it in such a way that people were able to take a retrospective look at how their views about race were formed. The first questions were *How was race explained to you as a child? Was it explained to you at all? What messages did your parents communicate to you about race issues?*

So by the time we got to the next question *How does that differ from the way you communicate to your children about race?*, many of the respondents said they relived their childhood, and some seemed absolutely startled by what they found. Right there on the page was an explosion of previously unexamined personal history.

Briefly, the two things that surprised me most about the mass of responses are these: I was surprised by how many insidious racist comments came through, and by the sophistication with which some of the respondents had built walls around themselves. Clearly, a quarter of the people who had filled out this questionnaire were like the guy who goes to the psychiatrist for the sole purpose of proving that he doesn't need to be there. But on the other hand, contrary to what our government leadership is telling us, I was surprised to see there are significant numbers of people out there of all races, of good faith, who do want to genuinely engage with the most difficult questions about race.

SHEILA ARDS

It was with great trepidation, with much anticipation, with fear of the unknown that I read the answers to the survey of the *Hungry Mind Review*. As I read the essays, I was struck by what appear to be shackles with which we have enslaved whites and blacks. These shackles define how we talk, how we walk, where we live, who our friends are, and who our friends are not. I am sure that the respondents to this survey on race are a biased sample to draw from in talking about issues surrounding race. These respondents have thought about the injustice of racism, the inequalities faced by people of color, and the inequity of our democracy.

I believe that these white respondents are not the average Americans who list their race as white. Yet I wonder about these respondents because of their perplexing answers. As children these respondents were taught to fear, to hate, and to stay away from those of a darker hue. They were taught that blacks were lazy and didn't want to work. They were taught that blacks were inferior and whites were superior. They were taught that people of color were to be tolerated, taken for granted, but not treated equally. They were taught these thoughts by their first teachers, mom and dad. Later these teachings were framed by the schools and the larger society. Yet these lessons that they were taught, they do not want to teach their own children. They want to teach that all men are created equal. They want to teach that people should be judged by the content of their character, not the color of their skin. They want to teach a new lesson, words to a different song. Yet as the Bible says, "Train up a child in the way he should go, and when he is old he will not depart," for these children learned their lessons well. They live in predominantly white neighborhoods. They have few, if any, black friends. They distrust affirmative action programs to accomplish their goals, and they live in fear. Their greatest fear surrounds personal violence. They fear being attacked because they are white; they fear crime-ridden neighborhoods—or code words for poor black areas. And they fear their own fear. They fear waking up and looking in their mirror and seeing reflections of their first teachers looking back at them. They fear that someday, sometime, somewhere, they will judge a person's actions or inaction by the color of his skin.

As I stated at the beginning, I wonder about these respondents and their answers to the survey. Why? Because if these individuals are the justice seekers, the equality bridgers, the hope upon which America's future social justice depends, then I am saddened, disheartened, and disappointed at how short a distance we have come. I am wearied by contemplating how far we have to go.

I am further convinced that America's policy toward dealing with the color problem by a group assimilation and cultural eradication is all wrong. For no matter how white I sound, how Western I dress, how many titles I have before and after my name, I am still a black woman in a white America. My accomplishments will be viewed as not enough; my scholarship as second-rate; and my years of working to become worthy as not worthy enough. My aspirations for equal treatment and social justice for me and for others seem to be lofty ideas that I should just blow away as one blows away dandelion fluff to the wind.

I was struck by the answers to the question "What is your race?" Because Germans, Scottish, Italians—people from the east to the west, north and south, Jews and gentiles alike—noted that they were white. But I wondered: Were they really saying that they were not black? I wonder about the whites who say that they rarely reflect upon being white, or that they only once in awhile think about race. Because when I wake up each morning and I drive through my neighborhood, I am conscious that my family is one of possibly two black families in a community of 3,000 families. Every day I think of my blackness, although our inalienable rights say that all men are created equal. I believe, from these responses, that we have a long road to tread before all men and women are treated as equals.

I am thankful for the opportunity to have read these surveys, because these surveys produced two productive outcomes. First, they allowed whites, predominantly, to reflect upon where they are in their thinking about race. But secondly—personally—it forced me to remember how America views me. They helped me to put into perspective the Saturdays, when I retreat into my jeans and sweatshirts, why the store clerks seem so unhelpful, disinterested, or sometimes even perturbed by my presence. I must remember that these clerks don't know—wouldn't dream, never could imagine—that on Mondays I dress in business suits, on Tuesdays and Thursdays I teach their sons and daughters in one of the greatest universities in America, or that I pay my account balances in full at the beginning of each month.

The answers to these surveys illuminate the need for rethinking our policies toward race and racial discrimination. Because when I think of Rodney King asking that simple yet profound question "Can't we all get along?" My answer is, sadly, "No. Because we don't know how."

How do we celebrate diversity without developing animosity? How do we value racial and cultural identity without denying our common ancestry? How do we learn not to live in fear without first not fearing to live? How do we learn that equality needs some measure of equity? How do we?

As I reflect on the surveys, I wonder just when Martin Luther King's dream will become a reality; when will brothers and sisters, Jews and gentiles, white children and black children be able to walk hand in hand and say and believe the words "My Country Tis of Thee, Sweet Land of Liberty." When will men and women be judged by the content of their character and not the color of their skin? It wasn't in Martin's time. Will it be in mine? Well, I wonder.

CATHI TACTAQUIN

It was difficult for me to summarize and formulate my thoughts about the responses in the questionnaires. What you saw in the *Hungry Mind Review* edition were just excerpts from the different responses. Each of us received about 200 copies—a big stack of handwritten responses to the questionnaire. As I was going through them, I was very sensitive to the fact that most of the respondents were white. Many lived in all-white neighborhoods. They were economically stable; appeared to be educated; many lived in Minnesota, others in the Northeast, and a sprinkling came from elsewhere around the country. Because of this, I read them with some caution.

I certainly found that many of the responses were reflective and seemed to be honest. Many people were hopeful, but as many were not. They were very cynical and frustrated, and, for the most part, gave no inkling that they knew how to get out of a very frustrating situation concerning race relations, to the extent that they understood the conflict.

And I saw many conflicting responses, if you were to read the response from a single person in its entirety. For example, in response to the question *"How important is race to your sense of self?"* the person said, "I have never consciously considered it." And yet also answered, "I've always stressed to our children that they treat and judge people or individuals regardless of race."

In response to the question concerning the ideal makeup of a neighborhood: "I have, by choice, always lived in all-white areas." The reason given was "to avoid hassles." And this was fairly typical of many of the respondents who would decry what they felt had come from their parents as fairly negative and prejudicial teachings and messages about race; claimed that they would never repeat that to their children; that they would teach their children to treat everyone equally—and yet, day by day, made choices that inevitably repeated a certain view of race for themselves.

Another response, again, that was typical and often coded in the messages was about the increasing lawlessness and violence by and among blacks and Hispanics, coupled with the quote, "'I was deprived' attitude has almost convinced me the situation will only worsen."

There were many such responses that typified people's perceptions of what was taking place among people of color as coming through the media; and that the media seemed to be the main venue. Since they were not living and working among people of color, they received these racial messages.

Another response: "I now live in an upper-middle-class suburb. I would not mind if all my neighbors were black, Hispanic, Asian, provided we all enjoyed a similar level of economic well-being."

Many, I think as Sheila Ards noted, expressed that their basic fear about race had to do with safety. Again, what they perceived as the violence and chaos among people of color is what they did not want brought into their communities.

There was, interestingly, considerable cynicism toward the melting pot concept, which I thought was interesting. There were some responses that said, "Yes, I still believe in the melting pot." A lot of people said, "Forget it, it doesn't work. That's really not what we're about."

Again, I found considerable uneasiness in how people understood why the distribution of wealth among whites, blacks, native Americans is nearly the same now as in 1866. So on the one hand, while there seemed to be some consciousness that there was unevenness among races, there seemed at the same time to be an incredible lack of historical and political sense of why that was really perpetuated. And I think in general that reflected a fairly low level of political consciousness in the United States, and especially on these questions of race.

I was concerned about the responses of those living in predominantly white neighborhoods and their preference to preserve their economic unity. I've seen in California how over 50 anti-immigrant organizations have arisen in the state from predominantly white, fairly educated, economically stable neighborhoods. These same people don't mind having immigrants as their nannies or their gardeners. But they don't want these immigrants moving into their neighborhoods. They don't want brown men standing on their street corners looking for jobs.

I wonder how people would respond to changes imposed on their neighborhoods, in the composition of their cities, of their streets. Juan Williams, last night, referred to an article which notes that the Latino population has surpassed that of blacks in several cities and may well become the shift in population that is recognized across the country in another 15 years. I wonder how many of the respondents would react to proponents of Proposition 187 in California, the anti-immigrant initiative, which appeals to people's fears of population changes. This is one of the pieces of literature from the official proponent campaign. "We are being invaded" (quote with picture). This is the message from the anti-immigrant groups, and this is the message from the governor of California, running for reelection. If you haven't been to California and haven't seen the campaign ads, the main one that he uses is an infrared video shot of people crossing the border near San Diego like little ants—they are clandestinely coming across the border and invading this country. These are the messages that have been very effective in predominantly white neighborhoods in California. And I wonder, as our population changes, and people realize that they don't have the choice about the neighborhood that they live in—as their neighborhoods and cities begin to change—how they are going to respond and will they respond in the same way a lot of people in California are responding?

This is an example of the kind of aggressive messages that have been thrown at communities. Anti-immigrant advocates in California have effectively gone after the traditionally white environmental movement, appealing to environmentalists that in order to preserve the environment in California, it's necessary to control population. And because immigrants are increasing the population, therefore we should control immigration.

There are many coded messages. Just to quote from this brochure: "Crowded cities, crowded freeways, crowded public transportation. The truth is there are just too many people in the state of California. Overpopulation is increasingly a problem made worse by the flood tide pouring over our borders. The deluge of illegal immigrants damages our physical environment and lowers the quality of life. Californians have the right and duty to defend the natural beauty and unique physical character of our state."

As for the implications of these responses in the survey, I can only echo what a number of others have stated in other general sessions in this conference, I think we do need to attempt to reframe our civil rights agenda within the context of this new global era in which our future in this country is very much tied to the future of our brothers and sisters around the world. Our economy has been and remains intertwined with economic life internationally. We're only 5 percent of the world's population, but we consume 30 percent of the world's resources. Our way of life is subsidized on the backs of those in less developed countries, often keeping those countries under-developed, impoverished, with displaced populations that are forced to migrate. We can't have an attitude that we have so many problems here that we can't worry about those in other countries. That's not going to work anymore.

Others have mentioned that there are over 100 million people in migration around the world. You would think we would be getting 25 percent. That's not the case. Nonetheless, this unprecedented flow of migrants that is a product of global economic restructuring and political realignment and chaos shows no sign of letup. This is the future.

Immigration and migration throughout regions in the United States is changing the ratio and cultural makeup of our population, and it is also increasing the multinational character of our neighborhoods and workplaces. Can our civil rights agenda include the fight to protect the rights of those who are not citizens? Or who may not have legal status? I think someone in an earlier session referred to this. And I see it as a question of whether our democracy can expand as it should, or will it continue to retract and constrict, which is what I believe has been happening?

We're not alone in grappling with the new issues posed for civil rights within a nation. Our situation is historically very complex. But I'm as shaken—and I do some international migrants' rights work and meet with people in other countries—I'm still shaken when I hear about the problems of racism felt by Kenyan women in Scotland; Algerians and other people from North Africa in France; any foreigner in Germany; Koreans in Japan; Turks in Romania; Filipinos in Saudi Arabia.

There's a new effort among African women in Europe to organize for the first time, because they are finding that they are experiencing the same patterns of racism and abuse in those countries that echo the patterns of racism in the United States. And they are looking toward the civil rights movement here for lessons and inspiration in how they take up that fight in other countries.

Because of this international phenomenon there are also efforts to set international rights standards that can be incorporated into civil law. And in the United States, I believe our civil rights work has the potential to help set high standards of rights protection, but we need to be more farsighted in incorporating this phenomenon in the global era. I think we need to examine ways in which we can popularly reach all communities. It bothers me that we have considerable portions of our population whose perceptions are shaped through messages sent by the media. The only way, I think, to counter that is through organizing—not just among institutions, but organizing as a movement that can reach beyond, and help reframe and shape and challenge those kinds of perceptions that are out there.

And while the center of that organizing has to be firmly anchored among communities of color, I think as a nation it is also our responsibility to reach into those predominantly white communities that still exist and work to reframe the agenda and thinking in those communities as well.

JOHN POWELL

In thinking about the questionnaire and some of our reactions to the questionnaire, like Cathi Tactaquin, I was struck by this range of responses. This range, in many ways, was quite diverse. On the other hand, it was also quite narrow. And I would like to talk a little bit about those ranges and some of the common threads. Again, most of the respondents to the questionnaire were white. There was, in many ways, an almost palpable unease with the whole discussion of race, notwithstanding, at the same time, a real desire—almost a burning desire—to have that discussion.

A number of the respondents talked about living in predominantly white neighborhoods. Some of them talked about living in these neighborhoods as if this was natural. Some talked about it as if it was unfortunate. But almost none of them talked about it in terms of racism.

Cornel West has said that we lack a conceptual framework to have a serious discussion about race. And this was very evident to me in terms of reading the responses. I think the responses were oftentimes quite heartrending. People were struggling to be honest. And I think they should be credited for that. I think part of the difficulty, at least in my reading of the responses, was that the lack of a conceptual framework to really talk about race was evident.

I would go further and say we not only lack a conceptual framework to have a serious discussion about race, we lack a conceptual framework to have a serious discussion about justice, and the two things are interrelated. In the questionnaires, when people talked about things like affirmative action, with a few noted exceptions, they talked about them in very thin terms: treat all individuals the same. "Why do we have to even look at race? I don't think of race. This country was founded upon the concept of equal opportunity."

Just stop for a minute in terms of the last response: "This country was founded upon the concept of equal opportunity." I teach over at the Law School, and I teach this concept of equal opportunity that this country was founded on. One of the courses I teach is Property, and there are a number of theories that support our approach in relationship to property. Let me just throw out two very quickly and refer back to this concept.

One is first possession—that property naturally belongs to the person who first possesses it. The second concept, which is equally powerful, is that property belongs to the person who mixes his or her labor with the property. After reaffirming these values, which are closely associated with a concept of equal opportunity, my students very quickly become familiar and comfortable with these concepts. And then I start talking about Native Americans and first possession. The students become very uncomfortable. Some of them, I think, start thinking that I'm some sort of angry person sent to make their lives uncomfortable.

But after we talk about first possession, we then move to the second concept of property, those who work the land, and then we start talking about slavery. And isn't it odd? In this country, which was founded on the concept of equal opportunity, the people who possessed the land and the people who worked the land have no land.

We have no conceptual framework to have this serious discussion about race. And, I would suggest, we have no conceptual framework to have a serious discussion about justice. And I think that the questions in the questionnaire reflected this lack. I think it's a challenge to all of us to think about this: What is a rich concept—a rich construct—of race and of justice that allows us to have a deeper conversation if we decide we want to talk at all?

There is also tremendous confusion about the concept of race itself. A number of people suggested that whites should not consider themselves a race; that whites, in fact, are not a race and that neither is anyone else. And we should just drop the term altogether and just be humans.

And the end of the questionnaire, the last question, was *What additional questions would you like to see asked?* And one of the questions was *What is race?* As you might imagine, this turns out to be a very complicated question. I don't know what the respondent had in mind when he or she put down *What is race?*, but I think part of the difficulty in having a serious discussion about race and about racism is that question itself. Unless we can ground in some way what we do mean by race, how can we then talk about racism? Are the two related? Are they strongly related or weakly related?

Let me just throw out to you a couple of examples of what I think is reflected in this confusion. In the last 30 to 40 to 50 years, there has been increasing scientific evidence that suggests the biological basis for race is simply false; that as biology, race does not exist; that race is at best a social construct. Well, some people have taken that to mean, "Well, I guess it doesn't exist. It's not biologic." But the confusion is thinking that only biological or scientific things exist and socially constructed things do not. My counter example to people is the Catholic Church. No one would say it was scientifically created, and it certainly was not biologically created, yet it is very real. And it affects a lot of people's lives in very profound ways, even those who are not Catholic. The confusion is thinking that if race is not biological, it must not exist at all.

To give you one more example, which may even be more powerful, there are some people—in fact millions, maybe even billions—who believe the self is socially constructed; that there is no biological or scientific foundation for a belief in a self. Many of these people call themselves Buddhists or Hindus. Yet few of us would say, therefore, "Let's not talk about a self, we need not have a self."

In terms of racism, it seems to me that many of those who answered the questionnaires, and indeed many people in our society, think of racism as simply an attitude. They really are talking about prejudice; we should not be prejudiced against each other.

The problem with focusing only on prejudice is that it fails to account for the economic, political, and structural forms that racism takes. In fact, I would suggest that a person need not be prejudiced, yet still be a white supremacist. In fact, I would suggest that many liberal Americans are struggling with prejudice, and yet continue to be white supremacists.

There's a song by an Irish songwriter, her name is Sinead O'Connor. Some of you may have heard of her. In this song she talks about the Irish potato famine. And she says the problem is there was no potato famine; that there was food in Ireland that was being taken out of Ireland to England at gunpoint. And she says the problem is that the pain remains but there's no remembrance. And unless we can have a remembrance, there can be no forgiving and no healing. When I heard that song, I thought: how appropriate for race relations in the United States. We have no remembrance, but we continue to have the pain. And the official stance of many in our society, including our president, is that we should continually forget. But can we forget until we first have a remembrance? However, it is difficult to have this remembrance, as the speaker suggested earlier. When you bring up these things, it sounds like an ugly, ugly truth. Something must be wrong with you.

Just to give you one example, I recently was talking to a friend and colleague, and I reminded him that our current living situation in terms of cities and suburbs was caused primarily by the federal government; that the federal government expressly created white suburbs and required that those suburbs be racially segregated. And it disinvested in cities where blacks lived. When I told this person this, his first response was, "Are you paranoid?" And then I said, "Well this was in writing. I didn't make it up, I'm just responding and quoting history." And he said, "But why would someone do that?" I said, "I don't know. They didn't think blacks and whites should go to school together. They didn't think blacks and whites should eat at the same lunch counter. They didn't think blacks and whites should go to the same hospital. I have no idea why they would think that blacks and whites should live in the same neighborhood."

We must remember. I think this questionnaire is very important. It gets us potentially not on the same page, but maybe in the same book. But if we are to really address this problem, it seems to me we must create a concept that allows us to really talk about race seriously and a conceptual framework that allows us to talk about justice.

CHAPTER 10

Hungry Mind Review Questionnaire

Betsy Hubbard, Kathleen Kalina, Rebecca Kelleher-Reeth, Dartrell Lipscomb, Reginald J. Mitchell, Sr., Michelle Revels

INTRODUCTION

The *Hungry Mind Review*, a national publication distributed through independent bookstores, challenged its readers in the summer of 1994 to think carefully about the issue of race. Readers were invited to participate in a survey regarding their views on race in preparation for an upcoming issue focusing on the subject. The survey consisted of 17 open-ended questions designed to elicit how the concept of race affects one's personal, political, and economic choices. As an incentive to complete the survey, the *Hungry Mind Review* offered a reduced-rate subscription to anyone who sent in a completed questionnaire.

The questionnaire tried to capture the complexity of emotions and behaviors surrounding the subject of race. The first six questions addressed the formation of individual and group racial identity. In this context, respondents were then asked to express their views on issues such as immigration policy, affirmative action, the melting pot theory, the ideology of ethnocentricity and its counterparts of Afro-centricity and Eurocentricity, and the economic inequity between whites, blacks, and Native Americans. The survey attempts to identify the relationship between the respondents' professed racial belief systems and how they develop their world outlook, spend their money, educate their children, choose their neighborhoods, and decide which public policies to support.

This chapter analyzes the 219 general readership survey responses. It examines (1) the messages people learned about race versus the messages they are teaching their own children; (2) if these messages affect how the respondents spend their resources, view their communities, and support a common yet controversial remedy for racial inequality; and (3) if there are inconsistencies between how readers respond to questions about race and how they organize their lives around this issue. Of the 17 questions on the original survey, six explored:

- What messages did your parents communicate to you about race?
- How does this differ from the way you communicate with your children about race?
- In what ways do you organize your identity and resources around race? How consciously does race affect your choice of where to live, shop, or send your children to school?
- For the first time, a majority of blacks and whites support the idea of integration, but ideas of what constitutes integration differ. What would be the ideal percentage breakdown for you between people of your race and of others in a neighborhood in which you lived? What is the actual percentage breakdown in your neighborhood? What would be the tipping point, the point at which the racial balance became uncomfortable enough to make you want to leave the neighborhood?
- Is affirmative action an appropriate way of redressing racial inequities in this country?
- What is your race?

METHODOLOGY

The respondents to the general readership surveys were self-selected. No one was required to either complete or return a questionnaire. An element of bias is intro-duced since it can be presumed that most of the readers who returned a response feel strongly about the issues it raises. As a result of this bias and because the general readership is not a randomly selected group, no accurate inferences can be made to the general population. However, the findings do provide some insight on how issues of race have affected this specific population.

In order to create a quantitative data set of the survey results, a preliminary reading of each questionnaire determined what variables could best describe the responses to each question. Exhaustive coding categories were created to encompass all of the responses to a given question. The challenge was to create a list of appro-priate variables while not losing the richness of the qualitative data. As a result, the variables are broadly defined. Nonetheless, care was taken to avoid forcing an answer into an inappropriate category. If an answer did not fit into any of the existing coding categories, a new variable was created to describe it. Three surveys were not coded at all because the respondents did not directly answer any of the questions.[1] (A detailed list of the variables chosen for each question is available in the appendix.)

To facilitate comparison of how the messages respondents received about race differed from the messages they were communicating to their own children, the same list of variables was used for questions 2 and 3. These variables were later collapsed into four mutually exclusive categories of "positive," "negative," "inconsistent," and "not an issue" in order to better measure the effects of these messages on the respondents.

After identifying the variables to be used for each question, the research group began to code each response by assigning it one or more or variables that best describ-ed the substance of the response. The respondents often communicated more than one idea in a single response. Consequently, one question can have more than one corres-ponding variable. This is known as a multiple-response data set. By utilizing the multiple-dichotomy method (where all corresponding variables are identified and marked with a 1 if present and 0 if absent), multiple responses to each question were recorded.

Coding is inherently a subjective process. To ensure consistency and reduce bias in the application of the coding system, the first 20–50 responses to each question were coded collectively in order to ensure that variables were interpreted in the same manner. At this point, two teams of two to three people worked together to code the remaining responses.[2] In every case, the coding was done during group meetings where any disagreements or questions would be brought before the entire group and resolved by consensus.

Once the surveys had been coded, the resulting quantitative data were entered into a database and imported into a statistical program (SPSS). From this point, there were two ways in which we looked at the data:

frequency distribution: For each question, a histogram or bar graph was created to display how often each response occurred. Data was also broken out according to the race of the respondents.

crosstabs: Crosstabulation is an analytical technique that shows the relationship between different variables. Crosstabs measure the tendency for two variables to covary, to occur simultaneously. Thus, they can be used to determine how many respondents with a specific characteristic also demonstrated another characteristic. For example, it was possible to identify how many of the respondents who were taught racial equality also live in integrated neighborhoods, or how many Native Americans were in favor of affirmative action. It is only a method of summarizing data and identifying patterns; crosstabs *cannot* identify causation.

A number of different types of crosstabs were run, using both elementary variables (defined as a single variable for a given question, such as "yes," "Asian," or "multicultural outlook") and multiple-dichotomy sets, which contained either all possible variables for a given question or a targeted subset of variables. Again, it is important not to overestimate the significance of the findings. Because the respondents individually chose to return the survey, the 219 survey responses do not constitute a random sample. Therefore, any inferences made, must be made with extreme caution.

ANALYSIS

The racial composition of the sample made it very difficult to draw comparisons between groups. The sample was approximately 80 percent white and contained a large amount of variation among the remaining 20 percent. Therefore, for comparative purposes, a nonwhite category encompasses those who identified themselves as belonging to racial groups other than white.

Figure 10.1
Race of Respondents

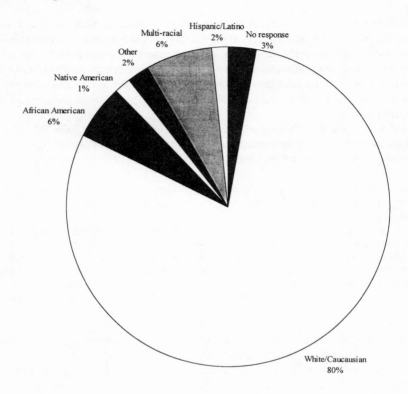

Initially question 5, "What is your race?," appeared to be the most straightforward question on the survey. However, it was soon apparent that the respondents had many different ideas of what constitutes race. Among the white respondents, many used various ethnic categories and nationalities in identifying their race. For instance, some typical responses were "Euro-American," "Anglo-Saxon," and "German-English American." Nine of the respondents, eight white and one Native American, identified their race as including their Jewish heritage. It is interesting to note that the third largest groups of respondents were African Americans and those who classified themselves as multiracial, a category not officially recognized by the United States census. The use of this category raises questions about the accuracy of the current racial classification in representing how people classify themselves. It also raises concerns about the legitimacy of defining groups of people according to racial distinctions that may in fact be very blurred. Several respondents objected to being asked to identify their race, on the grounds that race is a purely social construct with no biological validity. These respondents either gave no response or chose such answers as "human" or "two-legged."

This trend toward such an array of classifications underscores the difficulties in defining what constitutes "race." For our statistical purposes the respondents were grouped into nine different racial categories: White/Caucasian/Euro-American, Black/African American, Hispanic/Latino, Native American, Asian, Indian, Middle Eastern, Multiracial, and Jewish. We originally had three separate categories for Hispanic/Latino, but due to the small number of respondents we collapsed these into one category labeled Hispanic/Latino. (For a fuller appreciation of the variety of responses, refer to the full listing in the appendix.)

Figure 10.2
Messages Received vs. Messages Taught
What messages did your parents communicate to you about race?
How does this differ from the way you communicate to your children about race?

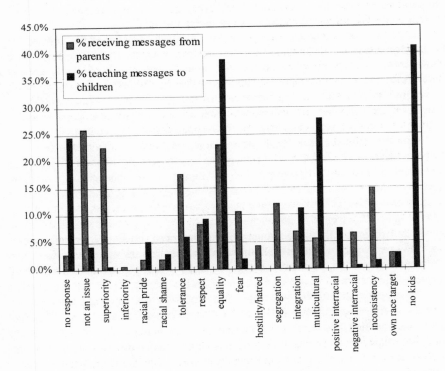

Question 2, concerning the messages respondents received from their parents regarding race, had a wide variety of answers, reflected by the 18 variables assigned to it. The three most common responses were that race was not an issue specifically discussed in their home, that all people were created equal, and that their own race was superior to other races. It is interesting to note that the seemingly opposite beliefs of equality and own-race superiority occurred with almost equal frequency. This would indicate the struggle for dominance of both an individual and a national racial belief system prior to the civil rights movement. In fact many respondents indicated receiving both negative and positive messages from their parents.

The next most common themes were those of tolerance and the inconsistency of messages sent by parents regarding race. It should be noted that while respondents were classified in several categories for each question, the respondents assigned to the tolerance and equality groupings tend to be two separate groups because these terms were interpreted as lying along a continuum, with tolerance being a less positive message than equality.

The same variables were used for question 3, concerning the messages that respondents stated they are communicating to their children regarding race. It should be noted that 89 respondents stated they did not have children, but the majority of these answered question 3 anyway. This may affect how their answers should be interpreted since these respondents are answering hypothetically.

The five most common answers given to question 3 were equality, multiculturalism, no response, integration, and respect. Respondents who stated they did not have children were less likely to include the values of equality, integration, and multiculturalism in their response. The majority of the "no response" answers were given by respondents who did not have children. Despite the often contradictory nature of the messages the respondents received, all of these responses, with the exception of the nonresponse category, can be classifed as positive in nature.

From the crosstabulation results of question 2 in comparison with question 3, it appears that respondents who received negative messages as children were more likely to communicate positive messages to their children. These respondents were twice as likely as the respondents who received positive messages as children to convey inconsistent messages. However, regardless of the messages received, the probability was at least 60 percent that the respondent would convey positive messages about race. This would suggest that a dramatic change has occurred among the generations in how people communicate about race. In addition to an increase in the communication of such positive messages as equality and respect, there is a marked decrease in the number of negative messages, such as fear and own race superiority.

The only exception to this was among the African-American respondents and the one Asian-American respondent. Half of the African Americans and the single Asian American reported they were taught that their own race would be the target of hostility and discrimination, and subsequently taught this message to their children. This was coded neither as a positive nor as a negative message since it may be view-ed as an attempt to prepare one's children for the harsh reality they may have to face.

Another significant comparison between questions 2 and 3 is the decrease in those indicating "not an issue" from what parents communicated to what respondents are communicating to their children. This seems to suggest a greater awareness of race as an issue and the importance (or social expectations) of communicating positive values to children regarding race.

Figure 10.3
Use of Resources

In what ways do you organize your identity and resources around race? How consciously does race affect your choice of where to live, shop or send your children to school?

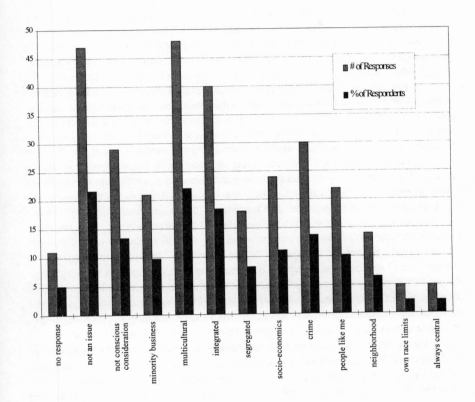

To facilitate comparisons between questions 2 and 3, the variables were collapsed into categories of positive, negative, inconsistent, and not an issue. Variables included in the positive category are racial pride, equality, respect, integration, multi-culturalism, positive view of interracial dating, and tolerance. The negative category includes racial superiority, racial inferiority, racial shame, hostility, hatred, segregation, and negative view of interracial dating. Respondents grouped into both of these categories were removed from them and placed in the inconsistent category, indicating the communication of both positive and negative messages. Respondents who stated that either they or their parents conveyed inconsistent message also were placed in the inconsistent category. These four mutually exclusive variables for questions 2 and 3 were used to analyze the effects of parents' and respondents' messages on the economic, social, and political behavior of the respondents as reflected in questions 7, 8, and 10.

Question 7 attempts to gauge social and economic behavior around the issue of race in contrast with the previous questions, which focused on the formation and delineation of the respondents' racial belief systems. The question asks how race affects where the respondent lives, shops, or sends his or her children to school. The most common responses to this question included "multicultural outlook and actions" (which were defined as a conscious effort on the respondent's part to interact with and learn the histories of other races), "not an issue," and "integration." Although many indicated that race was not a conscious consideration when they chose were to live, shop, or send their children to school, others were careful to specify that crime and safety issues were important determinants of their behavior. The "not an issue" variable was used to code those answers where (1) respondents indicated that they did not allow differences in racial composition of a neighborhood, school, or shopping area to determine how they made resource decisions; or (2) that due to the limited diversity in their area, they did not need to consider race when making their decisions.

Those who received negative and inconsistent messages as children were more likely to report that they consciously engaged in multicultural activity, whereas those who received positive messages were more likely to report that race was not an issue in their decision-making process. The prevalence of "multicultural outlook and actions" and "integration" indicates that the majority of respondents are very conscious of race and make specific efforts to be involved with people of other races. This may be a reflection of coding bias, since many of the respondents who indicated a multicultural outlook also indicated a positive view of integration. Overlapping of coded responses accounts for about one-third of each group.

The third largest group are those claiming that race really is not a conscious issue in decisions about shopping, schools, and so on. This finding may reflect the tendency of people to live in racially and economically segregated neighborhoods. Of the respondents, 28.7 percent identified an issue other than race as being central in their decision-making. These issues included crime, neighborhood quality, socio-economic status, and living with people who are similar to themselves in terms of education, professional status, and other qualities. This is particularly significant because the question did not ask the respondents to talk about any issues other than race. These responses raise the issue of whether socioeconomic class, crime, and neighborhood quality have become a new, and somehow more acceptable way, to express one's feelings about race.

In a significant portion of the questionnaires, issues such as crime and poor neighborhood quality were linked with the presence of particular nonwhite racial groups. The incidence of these responses appears to be affected by what messages the respondents received as children. "Not an issue" appears to double the probability of choosing a segregated neighborhood, with negative messages for question 2 being the next strongest predictor. However, in both of these cases the actual numbers were very small, limiting the accuracy of these predictions.

Negative messages also increase the likelihood of the respondents' reporting that socioeconomics was an important determinant of where they would choose to live, work, and shop. Those who received inconsistent messages were more likely to report the level of crime and the desire to "choose people like [themselves]" as the primary factors in their decisionmaking process. Respondents who reported positive messages were also more likely to state that crime rather than socioeconomic status was the major determinant.

Figure 10.4
Ideal vs. Actual Neighborhood Composition
What would be the ideal percentage breakdown for you between people of your race and others in a neighborhood in which you live? What is the actual percentage breakdown in your neighborhood?

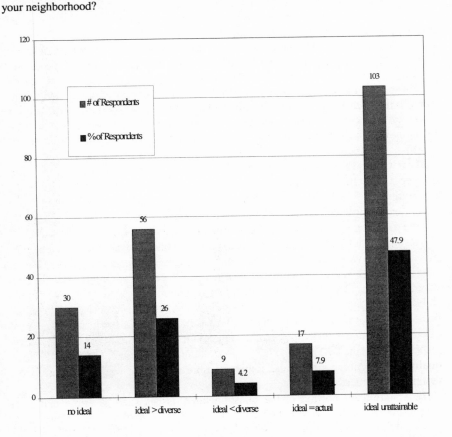

Question 8 attempts to measure how the respondent's definition of integration informed his or her choice of neighborhood. The question consisted of three parts: the respondents' ideal racial breakdown, how that breakdown compares with the actual racial breakdown of his or her neighborhood, and what would be the respondent's "tipping point" where the racial imbalance would make him or her uncomfortable enough to leave. We developed variables to correspond to the possible answers for each part of the question. Due to the prevalence of respondents citing an issue other than race being the determining factor for their "tipping point," we also developed variables under the heading "primary issue" to represent these responses.

Figure 10.5
Neighborhood Tipping Point
What would be the "tipping point," the point at which the racial balance became uncomfortable enough to make you want to leave the neighborhood?

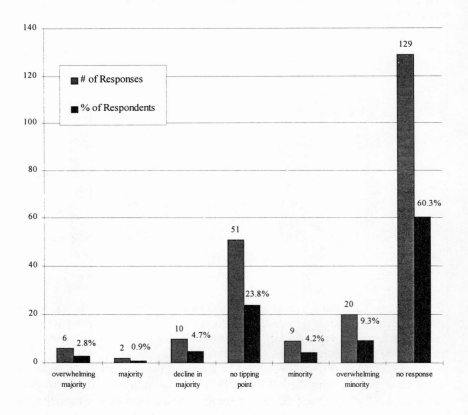

The most common responses to the first part of the question are "no response" and that the ideal neighborhood is more diverse than the actual neighborhood. The next most frequent response was that they did not have an ideal neighborhood. For the second part of the question, the most frequent answers were "no response," "no

Figure 10.6
Affirmative Action
Is affirmative action an appropriate way of redressing racial inequalities in this country?

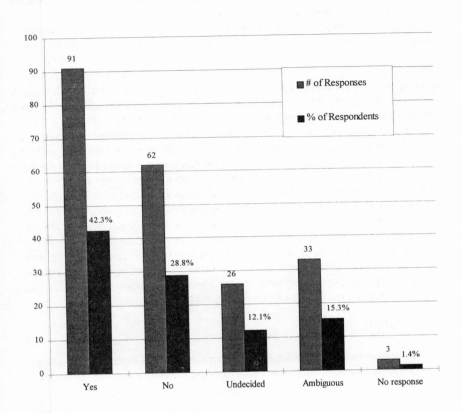

tipping point," and that "overwhelming own-race minority" would be the tipping point. For the third part of the question, the most frequent answers were "no response" and that "comfort level," and then the incidence of crime, were the primary issues determining when the respondent would leave a neighborhood.

It is also interesting that regardless of the types of messages the respondents received or were teaching their children, the most frequent answer to all parts of the question was "no response." However, those who received negative messages and those who did not discuss race were more likely to respond to the question. This appeared to be the most difficult question for the respondents to answer. For those who did answer, the only variation in choosing the three most frequent primary issues was for those who received inconsistent messages. Their most frequent response was "crime" instead of "comfort level."

These responses indicate that racially diverse neighborhoods are an ideal goal for many. However, due to the high level of crime and violence, lack of access to good public schools and hospitals, poor neighborhood quality, and low socioeconomic status associated with communities of color, most of the respondents feel that they are unable to live in their ideal neighborhood.

Question 10 evaluates how the respondent's racial belief system influences support for affirmative action, a controversial policy put forth as a remedy for racial inequality. The respondents usually gave lengthy answers explaining their positions. To present this information in a useful fashion, we classified the answers into five categories: yes, no, undecided, ambiguous (which means yes, but with quali-fications), and no response. 42 percent of the sample answered yes, approximately 29 percent answered no, and 15 percent answered yes but with qualifications.

Those who received positive, negative, and inconsistent messages were almost equally likely to support affirmative action. However, there was a difference in their level of opposition. Respondents who received positive messages had the lowest probability of opposition, with those who reported that race "was not an issue" following close behind. The group with the greatest likelihood of opposition was those who received inconsistent messages as a child. Both nonwhite and white respondents were approximately equally likely to support affirmative action; however, whites were more likely to oppose affirmative action than nonwhites, while nonwhites were more likely to express qualified support for affirmative action. Non-whites were more likely to express the view that affirmative action should not be the only way to address racial inequality, while white respondents were more likely to question its fundamental fairness as a remedy for racial inequality.

CONCLUSION

The examination of the questionnaires returned by 219 members of the general readership of the *Hungry Mind Review* illustrates the complex nature of "race" in our society. Issues of race, including even its definition, defy simplification.

The analysis reveals a prevalence of positive values concerning race. The detailed and lengthy responses returned to the *Hungry Mind Review* would indicate this was an issue of great concern to the respondents and that they were eager to discuss the issue. Many of them thanked the magazine for providing a forum to investigate and crystallize their views. This suggests the need for more public forums where people can explore their feelings about the role of race in their lives.

The examination also revealed the tendency for respondents to associate negatives, such as violent crime, loud music, neighborhood deterioration, and low socio-economic status, with people of color. This association occurred regardless of the messages the respondents taught or were trying to convey to their children.

The questions we would target for future research are the following:

- Question 4: What are your most basic fears about race?

- Question 14: What does the old concept of America as the melting pot mean to you?

• Question 11: Should whites in America think of themselves as a race?

Surveys such as this are a useful tool for helping policy makers understand Americans' perceptions of race issues' effect on their daily lives and decision-making processes. If remedies for racial inequality are to be effective, they must be designed with an awareness of current public thinking on the highly charged issue of race. Without this understanding, it will be difficult for policy makers to win public approval for their proposed remedies. As a result, proposals that may be effective and cost-efficient will be defeated before they have a chance to be tested.

APPENDIX

Questionnaire on Race, *Hungry Mind Review*, no. 30

Following is a list of simple and not-quite-so-simple questions on the subject of race in America. Of course, nothing about race is truly simple. We found that out as our staff tried to put together this group of questions. Our next issue, Fall 1994, will focus on the theme of race, and we want to begin a dialogue on the subject in advance of that issue. We will be very grateful to readers who take time to examine their views on race. We'll print a selection of readers' responses in our Fall Issue. We will send a copy of the Fall Issue to anyone who sends back a completed questionnaire, and will offer a $5/year subscription to all participants.

1. How was race explained to you as a child? Was it explained to you at all?

2. What messages did your parents communicate to you about race issues?

3. How does this differ from the way you communicate with your children about race?

4. What are your most basic fears about race?

5. What is your race?

6. How important is race to your sense of self?

7. In what ways do you organize your identity and resources around race? How consciously does race affect your choice of where to live, shop, or send your children to school?

8. For the first time, a majority of blacks and whites support the idea of integration, but the ideas of what constitutes integration differ. What would be the ideal percentage breakdown for you between people of your race and of others in a neighborhood in which you lived? What is the actual percentage breakdown in your neighborhood? What would be the "tipping point," the point at which the racial balance became uncomfortable enough to make you want to leave the neighborhood?

9. How do you account for the fact that the distribution of wealth among whites, blacks, and Native Americans is nearly the same now as it was in 1866, as slavery formally came to an end?

10. Is affirmative action an appropriate way of redressing racial inequities in this country?

Coding System

QUESTION 2:	**What messages did your parents communicate to you about race?**
QUESTION 3:	**How does this differ from the way you communicate with your children about race?**

2.1/3.1	no response: no answer/not applicable
2.2/3.2	nothing/not an explicit issue: didn't discuss; wasn't acknowledged or recognized as an issue; wasn't ever addressed
2.3/3.3	own-race superiority: supremacy; belief that other races are inferior; negative racial stereotypes
2.4/3.4	own-race inferiority: belief that race is inferior to others
2.5/3.5	racial pride: pride in one's heritage, history, traditions or accomplishments of one's race
2.6/3.6	racial shame: shame in one's heritage; ashamed of what your race represents or has done to others; taught not to acknowledge one's background; overt liberal guilt
2.7/3.7	tolerance: polite treatment of others; "separate but equal attitude"—accept differences but don't necessarily embrace them; don't be openly racist/appear racist
2.8/3.8	respect: uses the word "respect" to describe teachings; demonstrated respect but no interest in further interaction
2.9/3.9	equality: belief that all people are created equal or the same and should be treated equally
2.10/3.10	fear: mentions any type of fear; fear of other race or general fear associated with racial stereotypes
2.11/3.11	hostility/hatred: extremely negative comments or remarks conveying anger and/or explicit dislike of other races
2.12/3.12	segregation: belief that races should be kept separate; unease about interaction with other races
2.13/3.13	integration: belief that races should interact; evidence of interaction; good to have diverse friends; respect differences
2.14/3.14	multicultural outlook or actions: conscious effort to interact with other races, to learn and teach about contributions and histories of other races; convey diversity; activism; embrace differences
2.15/3.15	positive view of interracial relationships: involved in or approve of interracial relationships
2.16/3.16	negative view of interracial relationships: disapproval of interracial relationships
2.17/3.17	inconsistency: respondent indicated inconsistencies between what he or she was told and what he or she observed (i.e., between words and actions) or received different messages from different people (for example, mother and father)
2.18/3.18	own race target of racism/discrimination: society has already determined proper place or position; won't be able to advance or be given fair opportunities
3.19	no children

QUESTION 5: race of respondent

5.1	no response
5.2	White/Caucasian/European ancestry/Euro-American: all respondents who described

themselves as of European ancestry (for example, "Irish/Scotch/French") were considered to be white

5.3	Black/African American
5.4	Hispanic/Latino (white)
5.5	Hispanic/Latino (black)
5.6	Native American
5.7	Asian/Asian American
5.8	Indian (from India)
5.9	Middle Eastern
5.10	Mixed/multiracial/biracial: this included not only respondents who classified themselves as biracial or multiracial, but also those who would fall in more than one category ("Indian/Black"); these respondents were listed only in this "mixed" category
5.11	Jewish: each respondent also indicated another racial identity (such as "white")
5.12	Hispanic/Latino: Hispanic respondents who did not specify whether they were white or black were coded separately.

QUESTION 7: **In what ways do you organize your identity and resources around race? How consciously does race affect your choice of where to live, shop, or send your children to school?**

7.1	no response
7.2	not an issue: race doesn't affect decisions (either because respondent doesn't allow it to or because there is not enough racial diversity in area to make it an issue)
7.3	not a conscious consideration: don't think about race when making decisions; hard to tell if it may have an impact
7.4	consciously support minority businesses: make an effort to support businesses owned by minorities (or shop at ethnic markets, eat foreign foods, seek out foreign/minority art and artists, etc.)
7.5	multicultural outlook or actions: conscious effort to interact withother races, to learn and teach about contributions and histories of other races; belief in multicultural education/integrated schools
7.6	chose or considering integrated community: wanted racial diversity
7.7	chose or considering segregated community: wanted to live and/or shop where own race predominates
7.8	socioeconomic issues are central: class levels, property values, etc. more important
7.9	crime is central issue: crime, violence, fear or safety mentioned as criterion; chose neighborhood based on safety issues; would live anywhere as long as it was safe; etc.
7.10	chose people like me: wanted to live in neighborhood or be friends with people who share same characteristics; for example: quiet, professional, educated, concerned about property, etc.
7.11	neighborhood quality/amenities are central issue: more concerned about neighborhood schools/institutions/amenities or overall sense of community
7.12	limitations due to own race: own race restricts where you can go or how you can spend your money
7.13	race always central: always a consideration when making decisions of any type

QUESTION 8: **ideal percentage breakdown in neighborhood, actual percentage breakdown, tipping point**

ideal/actual racial breakdown:
8.1   no ideal/don't care
8.2   ideal more diverse than actual
8.3   ideal less diverse than actual
8.4   ideal = actual
8.5   ideal unattainable
8.51   no response

tipping point:
8.6   overwhelming own-race majority
8.7   own-race majority
8.17   decline in own-race majority
8.8   no tipping point
8.9   own-race minority
8.10   overwhelmingly own-race minority
8.101   no response

primary issue:
8.11   crime/safety/fear
8.12   amenities: access to good schools, hospitals, public institutions
8.13   comfort level: "as long as I was comfortable" or "there are people like me who share
         the same values and/or make good neighbors," etc.
8.14   socioeconomic issues
8.15   neighborhood quality
8.15   no response
8.16   response to question 8 not applicable; doesn't clearly address any of the question's
         central issues

QUESTION 10: support affirmative action?

10.1   Yes
10.2   No
10.3   Undecided
10.4   Ambiguous (a conditional support; "Yes, but . . .")
10.5   No response

NOTES

  1. The three respondents used more creative means to make their points or convey their
thinking. One respondent—a storyteller—wrote a story to describe her struggle with issues
of race. Another answered the questionnaire by regarding race as a verb: racing cars, running
races, etc. The third employed a stream-of-consciousness style that made the survey very
difficult to code accurately with our methodology. Thus, these three surveys were never
included as "valid" cases.

  2. The exception was question 10, concerning the respondent's views on affirmative
action. For this question all 219 answers were coded by the same two-person team.

CHAPTER 11

"Don't Throw Trash in the Well From Which You Must Drink": Black Demagogues, the Media, and the Pollution of Racial Discourse

Richard M. Benjamin

The famous American saying that "talk is cheap" is no longer just an insight; it is more like reality.

In this current age, where political posturing increasingly passes itself off as intellectual debate—conservatives categorize all progressive political thinking, no matter how complex, into the every-bogeyman category called "political correctness," while leftist critics dismiss as "parochial," "fanatical," or "provincial" any idea resistant to their rigid, self-referential world view—talk is cheap. Political and social utterances in America increasingly lack the value of logic, rigorous thinking, or even experience upon which to scaffold themselves. That is why David Duke can deny that he's a racist, insisting that he has forsaken his Nazi past in favor of wholesome Christian values; Oliver North can claim in his 1994 senatorial campaign that only he, not his opponent, has the moral authority to join the very institution he was convicted of lying to and obstructing; candidate Bill Clinton can confess that as a youngster he put a joint to his lips, but didn't really inhale. Truth and intelligence are no longer the standards against which "leaders" measure their words. Instead it's plausibility. In this era of permissive (and cheap) language, it follows, racial discourse is just as vulnerable to the political distortions, willful misinformation, intellectual deflation, and moral blind spots that pollutes the political discourse at large.

Indeed, discussions of race taking place today are poisoned. For one thing, recent discussions of race and civil rights in certain black quarters have taken a turn toward the negative. Propaganda disseminated by black activists, particularly Islamic and Christian fundamentalists, has as its missions, for example, criticizing Jews and discrediting the gay rights movement. Certain black leaders have restructured the movement from being humane, empathetic, and visionary to being paranoid, ethnically antagonistic, and reactionary.

The media's discussion of race has been just as disappointing. So has their portrayal of blacks. With few exceptions, the media have studiously avoided exploring the complex issues affecting black Americans and race relations, opting instead to use stereotypes, generalizations, and other methods of journalistic shorthand. In so doing, the media have done civil rights in general, and black Americans in particular, a disservice. For a people who can no longer afford to take any steps backward, then, what are the logical flaws and social implications behind the current prominence of black demagoguery and racism in the media?

This chapter will analyze post-Bush civil rights rhetoric as spoken by black demagogues, examining the anti-Semitism they advocate. Second, it will analyze how the homophobia of particular black ideologies undermines the national civil rights conversation. Recently, civil rights dialogue in the media and in the Clinton administration have concerned gays and lesbians. Therefore, examining the relationship between blacks and gays—and the relationship between their respective civil rights pronouncements—is especially important. Lastly, this chapter will unpack the sophisticated racism in the liberal media's portrayal of blacks, paying close attention to the *New York Times*'s coverage of the black underclass. I've talked about the Jews so the power structure, the whole Jewish controlled media, has set out to destroy me. On this altar I'm being slaughtered, my family is being slaughtered, a whole community is being slaughtered! But we don't bow down! We won't give up. *A luta continua!* The struggle continues.[1]

They're the bloodsuckers of the black nation and the black community.... You see everybody always talkin' about Hitler exterminating 6 million Jews. That's right. But don't nobody ever ask what did they do to Hitler. What did they do to them folks? They went in there, in Germany, the way they do everywhere they go, and they supplanted, they usurped, they turned around and a German, in his own country, would almost have to go to a Jew to get money. They had undermined the very fabric of the society. Now he was an arrogant, no good evil bastard, Hitler, no question about it. He was wickedly great. Yes, he was.[2]

By definition, a demagogue is an orator or political leader who gains power and popularity by arousing the emotions, passions, and prejudices of the people. The verb "to demagogue" means that one manipulates or distorts a political issue with emotionalism or prejudice. An ideologue, by contrast, is a person who zealously advocates an ideology, which is often independent of mass sentiments. The rise of anti-Semitism in black demagoguery presents two problems: it fuels the always already latent anti-Semitism within many African Americans, and it seriously impairs black progress, politically and morally.

The latent anti-Semitism harbored by many African Americans that demagoguery exacerbates has several sources. According to a survey conducted by the Louis Harris Organization, more than half of the responding blacks agreed with the following statement: "When it comes to choosing between people and money, Jews will choose money."[3] Thus, like a percentage of their white gentile counterparts, blacks perceive Jews to be greedy. So part of black anti-Semitism results from the same old die-hard stereotype of the greedy Jew.

Another source of black anti-Semitism concerns the notion of oppression. While

African Americans properly understand the financial and political power of Jews in this country, they are also constantly reminded of Jewish people's ubiquitous persecution. The opening of the Holocaust Museum in Washington, D.C., and the critical acclaim of Steven Spielberg's blockbuster movie, *Schindler's List*, made certain that the historical persecution of Jews penetrated the American consciousness. Thus, for African Americans to reconcile the discrepancy between Jewish people's obvious power and the media's emphasis on Jewish people's vulnerability requires a constant footnote to the imagination. How can power be persecuted? Blacks see their own oppression as authentic, but Jewish people's oppression, past or present, as gratuitous at best and concocted at worst. Put another way, black folks are sick of hearing about the Holocaust.

"I say to all Jewish people and all white people, don't compare me to your wicked killers," said Malik Zulu Shabazz, a student activist at Howard University Law School. "I sympathize with the suffering of all people, but stop pushing your Holocaust down my throat when the Black Holocaust is the worst Holocaust that humanity has ever seen." [4] And, blacks are not the only people tired of the Holocaust; so are some Jews. Given the mass ethnic slaughtering in Rwanda and the political exterminations in Haiti, it is irresponsible for any person, black or Jewish, to be "tired" of the Holocaust and the lessons it taught. But Shabbazz's statement is particularly worrisome because it exemplifies a growing ethnic competitiveness that is the mantra of contemporary black demagogues. It is not sufficient for them to blame Jews for black woes; they must also win the discrimination Olympics by dismissing the significance of Jewish people's past persecution and current political concerns.

Alas, blacks have concerns of their own. Black America is in crisis—the crisis is so obvious that the statistics which prove it are now a cliché, a point of common knowledge. At the "elite" level, there is also a crisis of thought. The political strategies that won blacks the vote and the intellectual assumptions that detonated the Black Power movement are now impotent in a society radically transformed by technology, the media, crack, the demise of America's urban manufacturing economy, and a growing pluralism fueled by immigration. No black intellectual has articulated an adequate critical vision for waging tomorrow's battles. Like all good propaganda, the rise of intolerant black demagoguery addresses a real set of emotions, suspicions, and political anger that blacks need to have addressed.

According to an ABC/CNN poll—it comes as no surprise—70 percent of blacks agreed that Louis Farrakhan "says things the country should hear" and 63 percent agreed that Farrakhan "speaks the truth." [5] Clearly the black demagogues are doing their jobs: to verbalize the frustrations of the people. When Leonard Jeffries proclaims that "we don't bow down [to the Jews]," he appeals to a sense of emotionalism and black pride that, unfortunately, does nothing to change the political realities haunting his young black audience. Therefore, many young African Americans, properly seduced, are oblivious to the anti-Semitic implications of the demagogue's message. They think that if you dismiss the emotionalism, you've dismissed the cause. In fact, the cause, black progress, becomes confused with the emotion itself, anti-Semitism, such that the reactionary hatred of others is willfully transformed into a progressive political act. But again, no one's socioeconomic status or moral well-being necessarily improves.

Black demagogues such as Khalid Muhammad use their dogma to pry personal wealth, fame, and power from the people. "There was power to be had, and even wealth and fame, in mining this vein of grievance, and plumbing the depths of suspicion and paranoia. It was a temptation difficult to resist, and one that many street-level leaders, politicians, radio talk show hosts, and even clergy freely indulged."[6] This passage recalls the self-aggrandizing impetus of many black demagogues.

Last, a Leonard Jeffries, or a Muhammad, makes the political climate safe for future demagoguery to work against black people. Of course, demagoguery against blacks already works, quite productively. But Farrakhan et al. make matters worse by establishing a symmetry of crackpot ideas that Americans use to justify the other extreme of demagogic racism. "Yes, Pat Buchanan is bad," people can then say, "but look at Farrakhan." Pat Buchanan's and David Duke's demagogic jihad against blacks, the poor, and gays would look even more ridiculous and paranoid had there not been a Farrakhan to counterweight its hatred by sustaining a climate ripe for blame mongering. Indeed, for many white Americans, the display of black racism provides a reassuring confirmation for the necessity of their own.

Such a climate is poisonous for the future. In an increasingly pluralistic country—the number of Latinos and Asians will increase through immigration and predictably steady birthrates—a nationalistic, ethnically antagonistic political disposition where tolerance is the exception and not the rule will not serve black Americans well. I do not suggest that blacks leave unexamined their relationship to other ethnic groups, whites not least among them. I do suggest that blacks examine their political situation more rigorously, more honestly, and even more optimistically, no matter how much their present circumstances may call for suspicion or fatalism. For reasons of political expediency, popular encouragement, and even personal gain, black (anti-Semitic) the public, and the media have been too willing to allow the demagogues' voices of irrationality and doom to dominate racial discourse.

"Beloved, she my daughter. She mine. See. She come back to me of her own free will and I don't have to explain a thing."[7] For black Americans the concept of belonging is important. Having suffered the middle passage, thousands of African Americans—for two centuries—belonged to white slave owners. For a people bereft of basic humanity, it was essential to turn "belonging" on its head, giving it the positive inference of family. Blacks belonged to family, the land, the community, each other. The homophobic rhetoric of black demagogues also boils down to a question of belonging. Black demagogues do not want gays to belong—to the mainstream, to the black family, or even to the military.

In the main, there are four reasons why black demagogues and their followers do not want gays to belong.

First, to the apostles of black nationalism, and all the machismo it engenders, homosexuality is an act of treason. Many Afrocentric critics point out that the emasculation of the black male can be traced to the days of slavery, when the masculinity of blacks was under constant assault. Homosexuality, it is reasoned, betrays black men by continuing this historical pattern of black emasculation. More to the point, homosexuality betrays the notion of blackness altogether, because it is something that bourgeois white men indulge in. And once AIDS, "a gay white disease," publicly afflicted several famous black men—Max Robinson, Arthur Ashe, Magic Johnson—black (hetero)masculinity came under intense media scrutiny and feverish public speculation followed, giving black ideologies a virulent new rash of homophobic anxieties: "Not us." Given the interrelationship between black nationalism, masculinity, and homophobia, it comes as little surprise that Morehouse College, a black all-male college in Atlanta, canceled a forum on AIDS in February of 1993, after students denounced homosexuality.[8]

Next, just as many black ideologies resent the power of Jews, they also resent the efficacy of the gay rights movement and the perceived power of gays. They feel that political elites are pushing the gay agenda down their throats.

While Congress, the media, and academics you never heard of continually debate the issue of gays in the military, we will again endure the punishing blows of the political elite as they wield their powerful tools of leverage in preparation for the next round of reshaping American politics. This time the issue involves the rights of homosexuals on the surface. Homosexual choice and civil rights are but a few of many language decoys designed to instruct us on how we must think on this issue.[9]

Next, black ideologies maintain that homosexuality is one of many contemporary threats to the black family and black family values. They say that the "deviant" sexual preference is the most recent of many social pathologies to endanger the black family. This claim has particular resonance, given the crisis of the black family: over 60 percent of black children are raised in single-parent homes.

Last, black ideologies are deeply vexed by gay attempts to liken the gay rights movement to the black civil rights movement, and to liken their plight to that of blacks.

One wonders how homosexuals could have the audacity to compare their situation to that of African Americans. They have never been denied the right to vote. They have always had equal protection under the law. They have always had recourse through the judicial system. They have always had freedom of movement. They may disguise their homosexuality; blacks have no such option.[10]

This comment exemplifies blacks' possessiveness of civil rights discourse: Who has the right to co-opt civil rights rhetoric? Who has the right to engineer the freedom train?

But certain black ideologies do not stop short of distancing the black cause from the gay rights movement. Like their turf-conscious demagogic brethren, they clamor to deny gay people "minority status."

Like many groups who lump their agenda under the premise of civil rights, what homosexuals are really asking the American people to approve is special rights based on a behavior . . . they should not be extended special rights. Should homosexuality attain a special status, we will open a Pandora's box in which any group of people engaging in questionable behavior could petition the government for special protection.[11]

Black ideologies contradict themselves on the issue of homosexuality. On the one hand, they portray it as a perverse alternative lifestyle belonging to urban decadent whites. Because gays are white, well-educated, and well-off, they argue, gay rights have nothing to do with blacks' civil rights. Moreover, "privileged" gays deserve no special rights.

On the other hand, black ideologies say that homosexuality threatens the black family and the already vulnerable masculinity of black men. Here is the contradiction: if homosexuality is the province of decadent white men seeking to "highjack the freedom train," how could this outside "perversion" possibly threaten the black family? How can something outside the black house threaten to implode it? This contradiction exists because black ideologies consciously define homosexuality in opposing ways. They emphasize the whiteness of homosexuality in order to vilify it. Also, by underlining the whiteness of homosexuality, the political concerns—and very existence—of gay and lesbian African Americans is glossed over. In whitewashing homosexuality, black ideologies seek to silence a group of people who can and will articulate the similarities between racial and sexual oppressions, an analogy black conservatives are loath to acknowledge.[12] But black ideologies must also acknowledge the existence of gay and lesbian black people in order to exaggerate their "destructive" threat to the black family.

The fact is that homosexuality is neither white nor decadent nor liberated.

Opponents of equal rights for gay and lesbian citizens have spread stereotypes and exploited public misunderstanding about the problem of job discrimination. These stereotypes are used to divert attention from the real problem of discrimination and to oppose equal protection under the law. The truth is that sexual orientation does not correlate to income, education, or any other class related characteristic. Gay and lesbian citizens are found in every type of workplace and every type of community.[13]

An independent economic study conducted by the University of Maryland at College Park found that gay and lesbian Americans earn less than their heterosexual counterparts of similar age, education, training, occupation, residence, and marital status.[14] The study refutes the image of gays as an affluent minority who greedily clamor for undeserved special rights. Contrary to what black ideologies claim, federal civil rights laws do not protect Americans from being fired, refused work, paid less, or otherwise treated unfairly in the job market because of their sexual orientation. The other difference between gays and straights, besides income levels, is the daily battle that gays face against residential and psychological discrimination.

In effect, persecution is also psychological and emotive, and cannot be tracked by economic indices alone; as a result, how can black ideologies deny the existence of homophobia or dismiss the similarity between homophobia and racism? For straight black ideologies to determine that "gays are mostly white and educated, and thus not an oppressed minority," is like historians determining that blacks prospered under slavery. Both conclusions are misinformed, no matter how logical they appear on paper. Because of the elusive, but no less real, nature of persecution, neither majority is in any position to deny the oppression of the other minority. The ability of gay people to step in the closet and conceal their identity is not some advantage that they hold over blacks—it's an act of survival.

In the national civil rights dialogue, many black ideologies furtively claim that in theory they support "equal opportunity" for all Americans, but in fact they do not support "the gay agenda" or "special rights." In reality, black ideologies deceptively interchange the concept of "basic right" with that of "special interest." As a black person famously said about Southern segregationists, "You can't change people's hearts, but you can change the law." So it goes with homosexuality; attitudes are ironclad, but laws can be challenged. But black ideologies act as if it were their hearts at stake, and not the law. Black ideologies are defending their culture, their religious beliefs, and their "privileged" status as the most oppressed minority as if it were these phenomena that gays seek to change. But this is not the case; the gay movement cares more about the lack of federal antidiscrimination laws than about corrupting black culture. In misrepresenting the objectives of the gay agenda, black ideologies shift the debate to more favorable turf; as it was for white Southerners in the 1950s, so it is far more persuasive for black ideologies to be more resistant about their hearts than about the law.

Gays and lesbians occupy the center of the civil rights struggle and media attention in the post-Bush era. As a result, they constitute a potent potential ally for blacks in what will always be a continuing political struggle for "minorities" to ensure that America delivers on its democratic promises. And black America needs allies more than it needs absolution. For the benefit of ultimate racial progress—assuming such an ideal exists—blacks cannot afford to redefine "civil rights" to refer to a hierarchy of benefactors and a social order where one group is essentially privileged over another. In black racial discourse, legal discrimination should be rejected all around, without exemption clauses directed at gays.

Media coverage of race in this country is anathema to blacks' advancement because it is too negative but not critical enough. In the post-Reagan/Bush era, the overwhelming coverage of African Americans has concerned what I call "black pathology," or black people's criminality and "misbehavior."

And, of course, post-Reagan/Bush media coverage of African Americans has focused on Michael Jackson, O. J. Simpson, and their respective personal pathologies, which are now metaphors for larger public pathologies: child abuse and spousal abuse, respectively. The media offered voluminous reports on the O. J. Simpson trial and the role of race (read: "reverse discrimination") in securing the defendant's acquittal. During the trial, *Time* magazine darkened Mr. Simpson's face on its front cover with out alerting the public to this deliberate misrepresentation of Mr. Simpson and his race. The magazine later apologized for its breach of journalistic ethics. Obsessed with Mr. Simpson's blackness, other magazines offered similar journalistic and design gimmicks to emphasize the race issue, without properly addressing the issue in the text—form subverting content. Similarly, on its September 1995 front cover, *Wired* magazine showed a graphically altered picture of O. J. Simpson with blue eyes and blond hair; this issue recalled the sensationalistic tactics of *Time's* cover. Ironically, the issue's feature story lamented "the collapse of civil life in the digital age." Insisting that "objectivity is obsolete" vis-à-vis racial issues, the feature story contributed to the collapse of "civil discourse" that it took pains to decry.

Post-Bush media coverage has also comprised frequent reports on the violence suffered and perpetrated by inner city youth, most recently the death of an 11-year-old Chicago drug trafficker named "Yummie," who killed a little girl, then was executed by his own gang members.

The coverage of the inner city, particularly the reporting on youth, is the most perniciously racist. It is this topic of media reporting on which I will focus. More-over, I will focus on the coverage presented by the *New York Times*. Why focus on the *New York Times*? First, the *Times* has the largest circulation of any metropolitan daily. Next, it sets the standard for "urban" coverage and is emblematic of other "quality" metropolitan dailies. Though other newspapers cover their particular metro beats far better than the *Times* covers its own, the *Times* excels at covering urban issues as they play on the national stage. Next, the *Times* is the Establishment's newspaper of choice—the Wall Street elites, political elites, media elites, and cultural elites: the white people who move, but mostly shake (down), America.

The *Times* often runs human interest stories about the down and out in the Big Apple. From April 8, 1993, to April 15, 1993, for example, it ran a ten-part series called "Children of the Shadows." In September of 1994, it ran a three-part series about Harlem called "Another America: Life on 129th Street." Poignant photographs and dramatic headlines accompany these series; and once the readers' attention is seized, the reporters hold it with vivid and descriptive narration, a reporting technique known as literary journalism. Editors place these stories on the front page, mixed with the other "news." The problem is that the value-laden, highly interpretive human interest stories are not labeled "news analysis" or "commentary," nor do they appear in the "Living Section" or any other feature section. Situated as they are, they pass for "objective news."

The first article in the Harlem series, "On a Harlem Block, Hope Is Swallowed by Decay," sets the tone for the series. The three articles depict the lives of the black people who live on 129th Street, on the block between Malcolm X. Boulevard and Fifth Avenue. Their block comes to symbolize the inner city: "It is a block in the other America, the America of the black underclass. It is a place—and it could be in Chicago, Miami, or Los Angeles—with its own values, rules, and economy . . . generations live and die on this block, a world apart." The first article also functions like a play's prologue and introduces us to the inhabitants of 129th Street: drug dealers, alcoholic parents, welfare mothers, and so on.[15]

The second article in the series, "Harlem Family Battles Burdens of the Past," focuses on Vikki, a longtime veteran of the block.

It was an exquisitely bad day in a time of long, bad days. The washing machine broke and the food stamps ran out. Despite scores of phone calls, the welfare case worker could not promise Vikki the bigger apartment she needed to care for the three cousins she was raising and the baby she was expecting. In a gloomy apartment in Harlem, Vikki, 26, has been waging a lonely campaign to keep it together. Once a key figure in a local drug operation, she is unemployed, diabetic, and overweight.[16]

The series ends with a third climactic article called "A Drug Dealer's Rapid Rise and Ugly Fall." The article narrates the life of Mel, a 19-year-old former drug dealer now confined to a wheelchair by a bullet lodged in his spine. He

recalls looking up and seeing fire falling from the sky as the fourth bullet hit him. He felt his chest burning. He fell to the ground and remembers people screaming as he felt his body swelling. Another bullet hit him in the head. . . . As they wheeled him to the emergency room, Mel said he begged the people in white hovering over him: "Please don't let me die. Please don't let me die." Later on, when the doctors told him he would never walk again, he wished he had died.[17]

Many other metropolitan dailies have published similar features, their reporters relishing the rich material the ghetto provides: ruthless drug dealers, welfare mothers, derelict fathers, crime sprees, and other black pathologies.[18] Despite its domination by white liberals, or perhaps because of it, the national print media will shroud their coverage of urban youth in a vague sense of regret—what I call passive concern—in a way that assuages their own liberal guilt without the burden of offering a critical class-conscious analysis of the government policies that perpetuate urban misery. In short, lost in the print media's swamp of maudlin human interest stories is a tough analysis of President Clinton's urban policy agenda, or lack thereof.

Indeed, covering the inner city by way of human interest stories is the dessert without the meat and potatoes. (And it is a tart dessert at that, imbued with literary cynicism and condescension.) Questioning the economic and political policies that sustain the ghetto requires journalists to undertake a rigorous class-conscious examination of power in this nation, jeopardizing their vast network of contacts within the political establishment; writing human interest stories, by contrast, requires only that they have a remote pity for blacks. A double standard emerges: white journalists condescend toward their black urban subjects, defending the practice as "literary journalism," while they instinctively kiss up to power and call it "objectivity."

The relationship between urban literary infotainment and objective reporting is never settled. Where the former ends, and the latter begins, no one can be sure. Reporters paint as grim, as pathologized, and as dramatic a picture of the inner city as possible, such that the readers are duly entertained. In the readers' minds, racial inequality becomes titillating; class hierarchies, arousing. Conceptualizing the metaphoric distance from the black street to the gilded suite—looking down at panoramic New York—is an exhilarating experience to the privileged *Times* reader. In depictions of urban blacks, serious newspapers like the *Times* relegate blacks to the role that white people traditionally have liked to see them play: the entertainer.

While making a spectacle of the black underclass, this genre of urban infotainment serves another purpose: to flatter the egos of upper-class readers. In a dialectic confirmation of their identity, *Times* readers have their success rubber-stamped, their privilege reaffirmed by bearing witness to the antithesis of themselves, their alter egos, the haunted and haunting projection of "misbehaving" blacks. Readers are the intelligent, successful, and deserving benefactors of a functioning democracy because they are not the heroin-injecting, crack-smoking, gun-toting, foul-mouthed, beer- and welfare-consuming idle Negro who peers at them from the printed page. In fact, in dialectically reaffirming the identity of the white upper middle class, the print media don't have a more subtle or persuasive way to assure these folks of what they are, other than to show them what they are not.

Why would the *Times* care about its readers' egos and justifying their success? For one thing, to validate its readers' prestige is to validate its own prestige. Also, the *Times* has an incestuous relationship with power; its staff is not just a bunch of journalists. Its op-ed writers are members of Congress, eminent professors, members of the Clinton administration, established media "pundits"; even *Times* correspondents are sometimes prominent professionals in other fields, such as law, business, or policy administration, who expect to reenter government, the private sector, or think tanks. Therefore, the *Times* has no qualms about stroking its readership's ego (and thereby its own), at the expense of the black underclass. Because editors, contributors, and writers for the *Times* spend their careers moving through the revolving doors of power—and they lunch with it and marry it—the newspaper will never publish meaningful reporting about the black underclass that critically examines economic, racial, and political hierarchies in America. Instead, America should resign itself to seeing condescending articles that soothe white guilt, that make wealthy readers feel good about their success, and that recycle conventional "wisdom," so as not to rock the boat.[19]

The emergence of black demagogues as a power in American life is directly proportionate to the failure of the political system, of intellectuals, of the media, and of black people themselves to stem the daunting problems threatening black America. In their political stands, black demagogues posit themselves as radicals, but are really conservatives offering regressive visions of black progress. These demagogues might heed this axiom: conservatism is just a worship of dead revolutions.

Black demagogues and the media poison racial discourse just as pit bull trial attorneys gridlock the legal system; they assume the same adversarial and negative stances that trial lawyers typically adopt in personal injury litigation or in criminal prosecution. In a perverse collusion, black demagogues and the negative but uncritical-of-power media keep African Americans in a state of mind hovering between pessimism and nihilism.

Black Americans are in their infancy as a people. Like a young person's, their future should hold more promise than their past. But an extensive survey indicates that blacks' outlook on the situation of black children in America is an abysmal one. A vast majority (83 percent) of adults say that these are either tough times or really bad times for black children. Also,

- 67 percent of black adults think that at least half of all black children will become teenage parents.
- 65 percent think that half or more of all black children will be denied important opportunities because of racial prejudice.

- 62 percent think that at least half of black children will have their lives destroyed by drugs.
- 61 percent think that half or more of black children will get in trouble with the law.[20]

Of course, it is impossible to establish a definitive cause-and-effect relationship between people's attitudes and what they hear and see from demagogues and the irresponsible media. But the virulent nihilism and pessimism among blacks makes very plausible the conclusion that the antagonistic tendencies of black demagogues and the media are being absorbed. Blacks' concern for their future is warranted, but demagogic and print media racial sensationalism is not. Louis Farrakhan, ironically, claims already to have learned this.

I was talking about the devil in 1972 or '73, you know, we were hitting White folk over the head as the devil. We were hitting white folk over the head as the devil. And the Honorable Elijah Muhammad called me on the telephone and said, "I wish you'd stop throwing trash in a well that I am trying to get a drink of water out of." And he hung up the phone. And I couldn't quite understand what he meant. But he was a wise teacher. I guess the well is that there is something of value in America that can be extracted for the good of our people. And you can't consistently keep throwing trash in a well, lest nobody will be able to drink at all."[21]

NOTES

1. Leonard Jeffries of City College, City University of New York, lecturing to a class, as reported in James Traub, *City on a Hill: Testing the American Dream at City College* (1994), p. 242.

2. Khalid Abdul Mohammed, Nation of Islam spokesperson, at Kean College, N. J., November 24, 1993.

3. "Black and Jewish Relations," *The Race Relations Reporter*, April 15, 1994, p. 1.

4. Shabbazz made these comments on February 23 at a Howard Law School rally. The rally was discussed on the March 31 edition of *Eye to Eye with Connie Chung*.

5. "The Fallout from Khalid Abdul Muhammad's Speech at Kean College," *The Journal of Blacks in Higher Education*, Spring 1994, p. 84.

6. Traub, *City on a Hill*, p. 231.

7. Toni Morrison, *Beloved* (1987), p. 246.

8. Evelyn C. White, "Gay Black Men Fighting for Acceptance by Blacks," *Cleveland Plain Dealer*, July 16, 1993, p. 14D.

9. Emanuel McLittle, "Gays Resort to Political Arm Twisting," *National Minority Politics*. August 1993, p. 8.

10. Willie A. Richardson and Guenevere Daye Richardson, "Gays in the Military: Not a Black Cause," *Emerge*, June 1993, p. 64.

11. Kay James, "Hijacking the Freedom Train," *National Minority Politics*, August 1993, p. 12.

12. The most cogent discussion of the similarities between racial and sexual oppression is in Ron Simmons, "Some Thoughts on the Challenges Facing Black Intellectuals," in *Brother to Brother: An Anthology of Gay Black Male Writers*, Essex Hemphill, ed. pp. 211–25.

13. Governor Barbara Roberts of Oregon, cochair of the Human Rights Campaign Fund's Americans Against Discrimination campaign, made these comments to the press.

14. M. V. Lee Badgett, "Economic Evidence of Sexual Orientation Discrimination" (April 1994). The study is available from the author at the School of Public Affairs, University of Maryland, College Park, MD 20742.

15. Felicia R. Lee, "On a Harlem Block Hope Is Swallowed by Decay," *New York Times*, September 8, 1994, pp. A1, B8–9.

16. Felicia R. Lee, "Harlem Family Battles Burden of the Past," *New York Times*. September 9, 1994, pp. A1, B4.

17. Felicia R. Lee, "A Drug Dealer's Rapid Rise and Ugly Fall," *New York Times*. September 10, 1994, pp. A1, 22.

18. In early October 1994, The *Washington Post* published "Rosa Lee's Story: Poverty and Survival in Urban America." A *Philadelphia Inquirer* reporter was forced to return a Pulitzer Prize she had received, after the Pulitzer committee discovered she had fictionalized material in a human interest story about the inner city.

19. In its Whitewater coverage, the *Times* has been in the vanguard of critical investigative reporting. Therefore the *Times* will (gently) goad powerful people under some circumstances, but not for the purpose of objectively critiquing the plight of the "black underclass."

20. Peter D. Hart Research Associates, "Summary of Key Findings from a Nationwide Survey of Blacks on Issues Facing the Black Community," sponsored by the Black Community Crusade for Children. The survey was published in mid-1994.

21. Farrakhan, in George E. Curry, "Farrakhan, Jesse, and Jews," *Emerge*, July/August, 1994, p. 34.

CHAPTER 12

The Political Assault on Affirmative Action: Undermining 50 Years of Progress Toward Equality

The Honorable Gerald W. Heaney

It is not news to you that affirmative action is under attack: several presidential candidates, a majority of the United States Supreme Court, and numerous members of Congress have all taken their shots. What is noteworthy, however, is that this attack by our political leadership marks a dramatic and important shift. Over the past 50 years, affirmative action has enjoyed the support of all three branches of our federal government. This political leadership opened the way for millions of women, African Americans, Hispanics, and other minorities to take their place in academe and the workplace as talented contributors. More important than any single congressional act, executive order, or court decision, this commitment by our political leadership set the standard for individual decision makers at all levels of government, business, and academe. This is where progress was achieved. However, without this political leadership, the momentum of 50 years is undermined.

In my view, affirmative action is nothing more and nothing less than a national policy to bring life to our founding principle: "that all men are created equal, that they are endowed by their Creator with certain unalienable rights, that among those are Life, Liberty and the pursuit of Happiness."[1] So important was this ideal that Abraham Lincoln repeated these words at Gettysburg as the basis for enduring the destruction wrought by the Civil War. Affirmative action is the very essence of our democracy; it is a promise to *all* of us that we will have an equal opportunity for an education, a job, and a home, and that action will be taken to ensure that the promise becomes reality.

One of the many examples of this recent assault is the Supreme Court's decision in *Adarand Constructors, Inc.* v. *Pena*.[2] The opinion, concurrences, and dissents filed by the Justices illustrate the loss of consensus with respect to what had been a national goal. I would not be as concerned with the specific result in *Adarand* or with legislative proposals that are currently being considered to limit affirmative action if these same leaders were clear that they continued to support the underlying goal of equality of opportunity. Unhappily, rather than characterizing these changes as refinements of the manner by which the goal is achieved, many state unequivocally, "We must get rid of affirmative action."

Before focusing on the recent *Adarand* decision as an example of this political shift, I will briefly outline the extent of the past leadership of affirmative action within all three branches of the federal government and the nature of its success. I will also examine the character and causes of the rising opposition to the idea of affirmative action that has, at least in part, caused some of our political leaders to reverse course. Finally, I will discuss briefly a few of the opinions filed in *Adarand*. These opinions, along with a memorandum prepared by the Justice Department in response to the *Adarand* decision, offer insight into the problems faced by our society as well as the issues that remain to be resolved.

From early in our nation's history, discrimination against African Americans was the order of the day. The institution of slavery accompanied early colonists. Even after the abolition of that practice in 1865, the next 100 years of our national history were marked by the denial to black men, women, and children of the opportunity to attend public schools with white children, to work in many jobs, and to live where they desired. Not until 1941, when persons of color were needed in the war effort, were the first steps taken against segregation taken. In that year, Franklin D. Roosevelt issued an executive order declaring it the policy of the United States to encourage full participation in the national defense program by all citizens, regardless of race, creed, color, or national origin.[3] In the belief that the democratic way of life could be successfully defended only with the help and support of all citizens, the order declared it the duty of employers and labor organizations to provide for the full and equitable participation of *all* workers in the defense industry. That order was followed by another in 1943, which established a committee on fair employment practices with the goal of eliminating discrimination in employment.[4] Thus, more than 55 years ago our political leadership took the first steps toward implementing the promise of equality.

In 1948, Hubert Humphrey, then mayor of Minneapolis and a leader in the civil rights movement, made a historic address to the Democratic National Convention calling for equal opportunity in employment for all persons.[5] While Humphrey's speech was successful at the convention, it came to divide the Democratic Party and cost Humphrey Southern support in his bid for the presidency 20 years later when he narrowly lost to Richard Nixon. All polls indicate that the Democratic Party's support of affirmative action continues to cost it millions of votes in the South.

In 1954, the Supreme Court took its first meaningful step to ensure equality of opportunity. In a stunning decision, *Brown* v. *Board of Education*[6] reversed the long-standing doctrine[7] that separate facilities could meet constitutional standards. From the *Brown* decision until the late 1980s, the Supreme Court gave unflinching support to equality of opportunity in all facets of American life.

Presidents Truman and Kennedy followed the lead of President Roosevelt by issuing executive orders renewing the commitment of the United States to equal opportunity in employment.[8] Each order was more comprehensive than the one it succeeded, and each provided for implementing mechanisms to ensure that the policy was more than just policy.

Notwithstanding the executive orders and Supreme Court decision in *Brown* v. *Board of Education*, only limited progress was made toward providing jobs and opportunities in the marketplace for African Americans and other minorities. As a result, tensions within the African American community continued to rise, and on August 28, 1963, the civil rights community sponsored a march on Washington, D.C. demanding strong civil rights legislation. On that occasion the Reverend Martin Luther King made his memorable "I Have a Dream" speech. He proclaimed that 100 years after the Emancipation Proclamation, "the Negro still is not free."[9]

In 1964, the Civil Rights Act was passed under the bipartisan leadership of Senator Everett Dirkson of Illinois and Senator Humphrey. Republicans and Democrats joined forces to overcome a filibuster led by Senator Strom Thurmond of South Carolina. Title VII of the Act prohibited discrimination in employment on the basis of race, color, religion, or national origin, and for the first time, federal law prohibited discrimination on the basis of gender as well. The following year, President Johnson followed up the Civil Rights Act with Executive Order no. 11246.[10] This order, by far the most comprehensive issued by any president, still plays a prominent role in the legal support for affirmative action. The commitment to affirmative action continued in the executive branch during the administrations of Presidents Nixon and Ford and in the judicial branch under the leadership of Chief Justices Warren and Burger.[11]

As a result of this leadership, the people of this nation came to understand the extent of our national commitment to equality of opportunity in academics and the marketplace; its unwavering character made clear that this policy would be implemented. The example set by the political leadership produced a moral suasion that extended beyond the purview of the laws, executive orders, and court decisions. This development was vital. Without individuals making choices and taking action in furtherance of the aims embodied by affirmative action, there would have been only modest success for a promise propelled solely by federal programs.

My greatest concerns now are not the specific changes made by the recent *Adarand* decision, but that the judiciary, along with the other branches, appears poised to weaken the commitment to equality of opportunity. This is particularly apparent in the rhetoric of the presidential candidates and many congressional leaders. In addition to the rollback of the legal framework that would accompany any legislative or executive action, such rhetoric signals the dilution of our goal. Undoubtedly, such a signal will influence the daily decision makers who provided the momentum for our progress.

Let us examine a few results of our national commitment to equality. When I attended the University of Minnesota Law School from 1937 through 1941, there was only one woman in our class, Lorraine O'Donnell. In contrast, when I attended the graduation at the Law School a few months ago, I was pleased to note that 45 percent of the graduates were women. The valedictorian was a woman. In the span of 54 years, women have demonstrated their capacity for success when given an opportunity. Do we really believe that women would have been given this opportunity had our national leadership not been publicly committed to a program of affirmative action?

When I served in the United States Army from 1942 through 1945, African Americans were not permitted to serve in combat units with white men. To be sure, they could be MPs and supply personnel, and segregated black combat units performed magnificently in battle. Today African Americans and other people of color proudly serve in every branch of our armed services. The fact is that without people of color in our military, it is doubtful that we would have an effective defense force. Moreover, military service has provided minorities with skills and training that otherwise would have not been available to them. Do we really believe that minorities would have been given the opportunity to enhance the effectiveness of our armed forces had our national leadership not been publicly committed to a program of affirmative action?

What was true of African Americans in World War II was equally true with respect to women. In that war, women were either nurses or clerical workers. Now women have gained the right to serve in our armed forces, and do so successfully. Indeed, within the last few months it was reported that the number one cadet at West Point was a woman. Do we really believe that women would have been given the opportunity to enhance the effectiveness of our armed forces had our national leadership not been publicly committed to a program of affirmative action?

What is true with respect to government employment is also true with respect to employment in the private sector. As a result of the commitment to affirmative action, millions of women and people of color now hold jobs that were formerly reserved for white men. To illustrate just one of the benefits produced by these changes, our workforce is more productive today than at any time in our history.[12] Acknowledging that diversity has enhanced rather than diminished productivity, executives have made diversity in the workforce a priority. Although these executives were initially reluctant to follow the political lead, they have come to understand, arguably better than their political counterparts, that unless women and minorities are permitted to contribute, American businesses will not be able to succeed in a competitive global economy. Today nearly every major employer in the United States has an affirmative action program.

Of course, not all has been sweetness and light with affirmative action. Dissenting voices, first heard in the 1970s, emboldened opponents of affirmative action to the point that in 1985 Assistant Attorney General W. Bradford Reynolds attempted to eliminate President Johnson's Executive Order 11246. This plot was leaked to the press, however, and abandoned as a result of the public outcry that followed.[13] In 1990, the Supreme Court placed limits for the first time on efforts to fight racial discrimination in employment.[14] Both decisions were later undone by Congress with the Civil Rights Act of 1991.[15] Since then, the opposition to affirmative action within the political arena has grown dramatically; several presidential candidates promised to repeal all affirmative action plans if elected; many congressional representatives and senators have expressed similar attitudes.

What has precipitated this turnabout? In part, the change can be explained as political expediency. The perception among many white men is that women and minorities have been given unfair preferential treatment. Similarly, many small business owners share the fear of reverse discrimination. This perception originated in and is largely perpetuated through anecdotal evidence that is widely reported in the conservative press and on conservative talk shows. The statistics, however, do not support the anecdotal evidence of widespread reverse discrimination. The fact is that of the 90,000 annual complaints of employment discrimination based on race, ethnicity, or gender, less than 3 percent are for reverse discrimination. Moreover, where cases of discrimination against white males are found, relief is provided by the same legal system that protects the rights of minorities.

The most obvious culprit, however, in the ebb of political support for affirmative action is the economic changes that have accompanied the restructuring of American industry since 1960. Not only has manufacturing moved abroad, but American industries have reorganized and downsized. As a result, many men who held good jobs with high wages and excellent benefits in the steel industry, in the automobile industry, and in other manufacturing industries are now looking at jobs that may pay one-third of what they or their fathers had earned. In addition, they now have to compete with women, African Americans, Hispanics, and other minorities.

Let me cite an example from the area in which I live. In the mid-1970s, the taconite industry employed approximately 15,000 men in northeastern Minnesota. These men earned nearly $50,000 per year in current dollars. Now the taconite industry employs 6,000 persons, many of whom are women. In rough terms, this means that 9,000 young men from the Minnesota Iron Range, who had expected to follow in the footsteps of their grandfathers and fathers, are not able to get jobs in the taconite industry. Instead, they are competing for jobs that pay from $5 to $10 per hour. They are not happy. And while the restructuring in response to global market forces seems beyond their control, policies that provide a preference for women or minorities make an easy target for their frustrations.

What is true on the Minnesota Iron Range is equally true throughout the country. The younger generations of men simply do not understand why they cannot have the jobs handed down from their grandfathers to their fathers. Instead, they are forced to compete for less desirable jobs against a broader group of people. I understand their feelings. Indeed, in my own case, and more than likely in your own, every summer job I had during high school and college was obtained through a relative, a friend, or a neighbor. Without a doubt, this practice continues today and will continue tomorrow. It cannot be denied, however, that this practice substantially enhances opportunities for young white men.

No one can blame parents or grandparents for helping their children or grandchildren. But given the effect that this help produces, one cannot reasonably argue that affirmative action deprives white males of their legitimate expectations. Today's white males cannot claim to inherit as their birthright jobs secured by their fathers' and grandfathers' status as white males. Rather, white males, like all others, may claim only an equal opportunity. The human desire to pass on advantages to one's children, however benign in its individual intent, threatens to perpetuate the imbalance left by the discriminatory practices of our past. No one suggests that this desire should or could be curtailed, but given the significance of its impact, it is disingenuous to call for a "color-blind" system in which the status quo is left unaltered. Instead, society has chosen to provide a slight counterbalance as a remedy. Affirmative action provides the same opportunity for African Americans and minorities that white Americans seek for their own children and grandchildren.

Finally, having now sketched the context, I wish to discuss one of the more prominent examples of our leadership's recent change of heart. On June 12, 1995, the Supreme Court handed down a 5–4 decision setting forth a new standard for assessing the constitutionality of federal affirmative action programs. In *Adarand*, the Court considered a Department of Transportation practice that provided contractors with a financial incentive to hire subcontractors certified as small businesses con-rolled by socially and economically disadvantaged individuals. The controversial aspect of this practice was that women and certain minority groups were presumed to qualify for the socially and economically disadvantaged status. In the case before the Court, the prime contractor had awarded a subcontract to a minority-owned company despite the fact that Adarand Constructors had submitted the lowest bid. Adarand filed suit claiming that the race-based presumptions violated its equal protection rights under the Fifth Amendment's due process clause. Assessing the constitution-ality of the federal race-based action under a "lenient" standard resembling intermediate scrutiny, the district court granted summary judgment for the secretary of transportation.[16] The court of appeals affirmed.[17]

In an opinion written by Justice O'Connor, the Supreme Court vacated the lower courts' decisions and held that all race classifications, whether made by federal or state government, would be reviewed by the federal courts under the strictest standard of scrutiny. Thus, to survive judicial review, any classification not only must serve a *compelling* governmental interest but also must be narrowly tailored to further that interest.[18] The Court then remanded the case to the court of appeals to determine whether the strict scrutiny standard required by the opinion had been met. Justice Thomas filed a concurring opinion in which he stated that benign motivations or good intentions are irrelevant in determining whether a governmental classification meets constitutional standards.[19] Justice Stevens, in dissent, sharply disagreed with Justice Thomas, stating that there is no moral equivalence between a policy designed to protect a caste system and one that seeks to eradicate it.[20] Justice Stevens also noted the inconsistency with existing case law whereby courts would apply a stricter standard to cases involving racial classifications than they would to those involving gender classifications. What should be most troubling to any American who supports the principle of equality of opportunity is that not a single justice in the majority expressed support for affirmative action. It remained for the dissenting Justice Ginsburg to set forth a clear rationale for affirmative action. She said that the persistence of racial inequality requires that Congress act affirmatively, "not only to end discrimination, but also to counteract discrimination's lingering effects."[21]

Ironically, the *Adarand* decision, which casts doubt on the constitutionality of many affirmative action programs, was released during the same week that the Southern Baptist Convention apologized to African Americans for its role in perpetuating slavery and segregation. Why is it that at the very time people of goodwill are opening their hearts, their minds, and their arms to their black neighbors, some leaders are moving in the opposite direction? Although I am reluctant to speculate on the legal ramifications of the *Adarand* decision, as undoubtedly our court will be hearing cases on this question in the near future, I will share with you a Justice Department memorandum[22] outlining its perceptions of the extent of the Supreme

Court's shift on affirmative action as well as the important issues that have yet to be answered. The significant points in the Justice Department memorandum are these:

1. While two Justices, Scalia and Thomas, appear to categorically oppose race-based, government affirmative action, a majority of the Court acknowledged that the practice and lingering effects of racial discrimination might justify the use of race-based remedial measures in certain circumstances.
2. The extent to which diversity itself is a permissible justification for affirmative action is uncertain. The memorandum notes the sharp disagreement among the justices. To the extent that diversity itself may not be a permissible justification, the government should seek some further objective beyond diversity, such as enrichment of academic experience or offering a variety of perspectives in other endeavors.[23] [It is unclear to me, however, that the Supreme Court has disavowed diversity as a legitimate basis for federal affirmative action programs. I hope this is not the case.]
3. *Adarand* is not confined to contracting, but is applicable to any race-based classification as a basis for decision-making. *Adarand,* however, does not contemplate predecisional action: outreach and recruitment efforts are not subject to the *Adarand* standards.
4. *Adarand* did not address the appropriate constitutional standard of review for affirmative action programs that use gender classifications as a basis for decision-making. All circuits of the federal judiciary, except the Sixth Circuit, continue to apply *intermediate scrutiny* to affirmative action measures that benefit women. [One hopes that the Supreme Court would recognize the inconsistency of *Adarand* with the standard applied to gender classifications, and return to applying an intermediate standard in both cases.]
5. Finally, a question remains as to whether courts should give greater deference to Congress than to state and local governments when evaluating the congressional findings that form the justification for federal affirmative action programs. The Department of Justice suggests that the Supreme Court would hold such increased deference proper in light of the broad congressional powers granted by the Constitution to remedy discrimination.

It remains my view that even under *Adarand*, carefully designed federal affirmative action programs can be sustained. Furthermore, when read strictly, *Adarand* does not affect the ability of private employers or businesses to continue policies designed to bring more women, more African Americans, more Hispanics and other minorities into the workforce. Thus, private employers can continue to recruit women and minorities, and to give them some preferences, so long as they do not overtly discriminate against more qualified white males in the process. I can say categorically that the court on which I have sat for 30 years has never required an employer, public or private, to hire an unqualified person. The more important question, however, is whether private employers will continue their present efforts to diversify despite the equivocation by our political and legal leadership. I believe they must; to remain competitive in the global economy, businesses need to develop all of the talent that they can recruit.

I want to close by sharing with you my deeply held belief that nothing is more important to the survival of our democracy than a lasting commitment to equality of opportunity for all Americans. Unfortunately, racism is alive and well in the United States. There are many among us who have used and will continue to use race for their personal or political benefit. Thus, we need an effective and continuing program of affirmative action not for the benefit of women, African Americans, Hispanics, Asians, or Native Americans, but for the benefit of all of us, our children, our grandchildren, and for our beloved nation. To effect this goal of equality of opportunity, it is vital that our society, and our leaders, continually reiterate its importance. The alternative to affirmative action is not a utopia of meritocracy, blind to race and gender, but a continuation of the old regime of societal preferences. The alternative will ensure a nation divided by race; we need only listen to the evening news or read our morning paper to understand the consequences of such division. The political damage cannot be overstated. Over the past two years, Europe has demonstrated the consequences of a nation destroyed by ethnic conflict. We cannot permit that to happen. Individually and collectively, we must recommit ourselves to the promise that every American has the opportunity to achieve his or her inalienable right to life, liberty, and the pursuit of happiness.

NOTES

1. The Declaration of Independence (1776).
2. *Adarand Constructors, Inc.* v. *Pena*, 115 S. Ct. 2097 (1995).
3. Executive Order no. 8802, 6 Fed. Reg. 3109 (1941).
4. Executive Order no. 9346, 8 Fed. Reg. 7183 (1943).
5. He stated, "There are those who say—this issue of civil rights is an infringement on the states' rights. The time has arrived for the Democratic Party to get out of the shadow of states' rights and walk forthrightly into the bright sunshine of human rights. . . . For all of us here, for the millions who have sent us, for the whole two billion members of the human family—our land is now, more than ever, the last best hope on earth. I know that we can—I know that we shall begin here the full realization of that hope—that promise of a land where all men are free and equal, and each man uses his freedom wisely and well." Dan Cohen, *Undefeated: The Life of Hubert H. Humphrey.* Lerner Publications, Co.: Minneapolis, MN (1978) p. 144.
6. 347 U.S. 483 (1954).
7. This doctrine was enunciated in *Plessy* v. *Ferguson*, 163 U.S. 537 (1896).
8. Executive Order no. 10308, 16 Fed. Reg. 12303 (1951); Executive Order no. 10925, 26 Fed. Reg. 1977 (1961).
9. Dr. King stated, "The Negro still is not free; one hundred years later, the life of the Negro is still sadly crippled by the manacles of segregation and the chains of discrimination; one hundred years later, the Negro lives on a lonely island of poverty in the midst of a vast ocean of material prosperity; one hundred years later, the Negro is still languishing in the corners of American society and finds himself in exile in his own land." Juan Williams, *Eyes on the Prize: America's Civil Rights Years, 1954–1965* African American Images: Chicago, Ill. (1987) pp. 203–4.
10. Executive order no. 11246, 30 Fed. Reg. 12319 (1965).
11. In 1971, Chief Justice Warren Burger, writing for the Court *in Griggs* v. *Duke Power Co.*, 401 U.S. 424 (1971), held that residual discrimination arising from prior employment practices was not insulated from remedial action. The facts in that case were that after the Civil Rights Act was passed, the Duke Power Company, which had denied employment to African Americans in all but one department, instituted a high school completion requirement and a general intelligence test as conditions of employment. The Court said,

"The facts of this case demonstrate the inadequacy of broad and general testing devices as well as the infirmity of using diplomas or degrees as fixed measures of capability. History is filled with examples of men and women who rendered highly effective performance without the conventional badges of accomplishment in terms of certificates, diplomas, or degrees. Diplomas and tests are useful servants, but Congress has mandated the common sense proposition that they are not to become masters of reality." Ibid. at 433.

12. *Survey of Current Business* (August 1993).

13. Gerald Boyd, "Goals for Hiring to Stay in Place," *New York Times*, August 25, 1986, p. A1.

14. *Wards Cove Packing Co.* v. *Atonio*, 490 U.S. 642 (1989) (5–4 decision); *Patterson* v. *McLean Credit Union*, 491 U.S. 164 (1989) (5–4 decision).

15. P. L. 102-166 (1991), codifying doctrine that Title VII relief is available in cases of disparate impact or mixed motives.

16. 790 F. Supp. 240 (1992).

17. 16 F.3d 1537 (10th Cir. 1994).

18. Justice O'Connor stated, "It is not true that stricter scrutiny is strict in theory but fatal in fact. Government is not disqualified from acting in response to the unhappy persistence of both the practice and lingering effects of racial discrimination against minority groups in this country. When race-based action is necessary to fund a compelling interest, such action is within constitutional constraints if it satisfies the narrow tailoring test set out in this Court's previous cases." No. 93-1841, 1995 U.S. LEXIS 4037, at *6 (June 12, 1995).

19. Justice Thomas states in his concurring opinion, "That these programs may have been motivated, in part, by good intentions cannot provide refuge from the principle that under our Constitution, the government may not make distinctions on the basis of race. As far as the Constitution is concerned, it is irrelevant whether a government's racial classifications are drawn by those who wish to oppress a race or by those who have a sincere desire to help those thought to be disadvantaged. There can be no doubt that the paternalism that appears to lie at the heart of this program is at war with the principle of inherent equality that underlies and infuses our Constitution." Ibid. at *73. He added, "[T]here can be no doubt that racial paternalism and its unintended consequences can be as poisonous and pernicious as any other form of discrimination. So-called 'benign' discrimination teaches many that because of chronic and apparently immutable handicaps, minorities cannot compete with them without their patronizing indulgence. Inevitably, such programs engender attitudes of superiority or, alternatively, provoke resentment among those who believe that they have been wronged by the government's use of race. These programs stamp minorities with a badge of inferiority and may cause them to develop dependencies or to adopt an attitude that they are 'entitled' to preferences. Ibid. at *75.

20. Justice stated, "There is no moral or constitutional equivalence between a policy that is designed to perpetuate a caste system and one that seeks to eradicate racial subordination. Invidious discrimination is an engine of oppression, subjugating a disfavored group to enhance or maintain the power of the majority. Remedial race based preferences reflect the opposite impulse: a desire to foster equality in society. No sensible conception of the government's constitutional obligation to 'govern impartially,' should ignore this distinction." Ibid. at *79 (citation omitted).

21. Justice Ginsburg wrote, "The statutes and regulations at issue, as the Court indicates, were adopted by the political branches in response to an 'unfortunate reality': '[T]he unhappy persistence of both the practice and the lingering effects of racial discrimination against minority groups in this country.' The United States suffers from those lingering effects because, for most of our Nation's history, the idea that 'we are just one race,' was not embraced. For generations, our lawmakers and judges were unprepared to say that there is

in this land no superior race, no race inferior to any other. The divisions in this difficult case should not obscure the Court's recognition of the persistence of racial inequality and a majority's acknowledgment of Congress' authority to act affirmatively, not only to end discrimination, but also to counteract discrimination's lingering effects. Those effects, reflective of a system of racial caste only recently ended, are evident in our workplaces, markets, and neighborhoods. Job applicants with identical resumes, qualifications, and interview styles still experience different receptions, depending on their race. White and African American consumers still encounter different deals. People of color looking for housing still face discriminatory treatment by landlords, real estate agents, and mortgage lenders. Minority entrepreneurs sometimes fail to gain contracts though they are the low bidders, and they are sometimes refused work even after winning contracts. Bias both conscious and unconscious, reflecting traditional and unexamined habits of thought, keeps up barriers that must come down if equal opportunity and nondiscrimination are ever genuinely to become this country's law and practice.

Given this history and its practical consequences, Congress surely can conclude that a carefully designed affirmative action program may help to realize, finally, the 'equal protection of the laws' the Fourteenth Amendment has promised since 1868." Ibid. at *128–30 (citations omitted).

22. Justice Dept. memorandum on Supreme Court's *Adarand* decision, 1995 Daily Lab. Rep. 125th 33 (June 28, 1995), from Assistant Attorney General Walter Dellinger to general counsels.

23. See, e.g., *Regents of Univ. of California* v. *Bakke*, 438 U.S. 265, 314 (1978)—("[T]he interest of diversity is compelling in the context of a university's admissions program" (opinion of J. Powell, giving judgment of the Court); *Metro Broadcasting, Inc.* v. *FCC*, 497 U.S. 547 (1990).

CHAPTER 13

Is Affirmative Action a Quota System?
Barbara R. Bergmann

Are the goals and timetables in affirmative action plans quotas? If they are quotas, what are the implications? On this matter I received enlightenment from President George Bush. Bush loudly and repeatedly opposed the Civil Rights Restoration Act because it permitted judges to use the distribution of employment by race and sex as evidence of discrimination. He said any time the government is allowed to use numbers in that way, it is putting pressure on employers to get the numbers right. And that's the equivalent of requiring employers to fill quotas.

Of course many of the people who are in favor of action to improve the economic position of blacks, of women, of Hispanics said, "No, no, he's got it wrong. Goals are not quotas." They take this position because quotas have been given such a bad name for so long. I believe that honesty is the best policy, and in this case honesty requires us to acknowledge that President Bush was really talking sense. So I don't pretend that goals and timetables are not quotas. We do count people by race and sex. If too many of the privileged are hired, we narrow the search to people of the underprivileged group and put pressure on those doing the hiring to hire some of the latter. How else can you make progress? If you want to desegregate, it is indispensable to count by race and sex, or you end up hiring 30 white men in a row.

This morning the Pillsbury affirmative action executive said you don't make progress by counting, but by inclusion. He says you should broaden the definition of "inclusion," and even make sure you include people who like to fish. He said numbers were not too salient in his operation. He did not make goals known. He just educated people. Well, I've never seen progress made that way. And I'm afraid I have to say I don't believe it can be made that way.

We have to admit that goals and timetables are quotas, and to say in no uncertain terms that quotas are absolutely necessary if there is to be any progress. Those of us who believe in affirmative action need to make that case and to make people understand it. From my own survey research, I conclude that about 50 percent of the white population will understand it.

There are two ways of telling the "affirmative action story." One way is to ask people to think about a firm that has never hired a black person for a certain kind of job. Suppose there are black people available who could do this job. What, exactly, should the firm do to break the previous pattern and hire some black people? Another way to present the affirmative action story is to say that a firm has two applicants, one black and one white. The white candidate has been judged to be the better one. Should the firm give the job to the black person?

The first way of telling the story makes the listener think about what needs to be remedied. The second way (which passes over the question of whether the judgment of the candidates' merit is fair or correct) highlights the alleged unfairness of affirmative action. The first story is never told; the public has been hearing just the second story.

There has been affirmative action. Where do you see it on display? You see it on display in the president's cabinet. You see it on display in the lineup of local news anchors on TV. You see it when you go into an airline terminal and the 15 ticket agents lined up are not all white males, as they used to be. You see it in a row of supermarket checkout clerks. Now what do all those things have in common? Those people are publicly grouped, and it would look funny if they were all one type. Or even if it wouldn't look funny to most white Americans, there are enough people to whom it would look funny so that some kind of protest might be made.

The problem is, we've had very little affirmative action where people are not publicly grouped. An affirmative action plan that contains goals and timetables is a way of artificially grouping hires or promotions. With affirmative action, the employer has somebody look at the hiring record and say, "My gosh, the last 15 people we've hired for this nice job are white males. We've got to do something else." That's taking the next hire and grouping it with the last 15, and saying we've got to have some diversity here.

There has been some very interesting research on this issue in terms of single actions and groupings of actions. Faye Crosby, a psychologist, did an experiment on this issue. She presented fictional resumes of men and women executives supposedly in a single company. The records contained ratings on their education, their efficiency, their experience. The fictitious records showed the males made higher salaries on average, despite having the same ratings, on average, as the females. She found that when she presented these records to people one pair at a time, most of the respondents couldn't see any problem with the men's higher salaries. Unless the female executive was superior to the male she was matched with on every single characteristic, people could rationalize the fact that the male made more money. "Well, he has a better efficiency rating, so it's natural that he should make more money." Then they would look at the next pair, and say, "Well, her efficiency rating is better, and his isn't so good, but he does have more experience." When Crosby, instead of asking people to judge each individual pair, just presented all the data and then asked—"Is this company discriminating against women?"—far more people were willing to say that the company was discriminating than when they were asked to judge the pair of individuals. We live life one episode at a time. So when people view what's going on there is a tendency to rationalize the continuance of awarding the plums to white people who are male.

What justifies quotas? I don't think it has anything to do with slavery, although obviously slavery preceded the present situation and affected it. It is not a lack of aptitude on the part of the blacks or the females. People who are so talented in the areas where they have been permitted to excel have talents in other areas. What justifies quotas is current, ongoing exclusions. Let me tell you about one that is very close to us—right next door. How many of you noticed that 100 percent of the people serving our lunch today were white? Now you may ask who would want those crummy jobs. But whites, who aren't discriminated against on account of race, do want those jobs. So surely there must be some black people who might be enticed to take some of them. How did that exclusion of blacks happen? It happened because each time there is a vacancy, one of these white waitresses brings on a friend. What affirmative action and quotas are for is stopping that.

There are plenty of occupations where we need quotas—where they haven't been applied. Over-the-road trucking is a famous example. Hotel jobs are another. A couple of years ago, the economists had their convention at Disneyland, which is of course very apt. I noticed that there were virtually no black people employed in the hotels. I happened to be outside the hotel at about 6:30 one morning and there was a Hispanic man checking in the laundry workers. I asked him why he didn't have any black people, since Disneyland is very close to LA. He said, "Those people don't want to work." That's a situation that calls for a quota.

Recently, a $108 million settlement was paid by the Lucky supermarket chain in California in a sex discrimination case. They were segregating women, allowing them into some jobs and not others. I am working on a case in the Washington metropolitan area where virtually the same situation persists, despite a 1972 suit that resulted in a consent decree. Under the decree the company was supposed to be doing affirmative action. They didn't do it. The union in that case was complicitous in failing to remedy the situation. I asked a union official why there were so few black employees in the supermarket branches in the Washington, D.C. suburbs. He said that blacks don't like to cross bridges. I assure you that if you have a $17 an hour job at this particular supermarket chain, you can get yourself a jalopy to cross bridges. There is great scope for affirmative action in supermarkets in relieving race and sex discrimination.

Quotas are not without problems, of course. There is a legitimate worry that there will be a balkanization of the labor market. That is, blond Jews will get 1 percent and redheaded Hungarians will get another percent, and so on, and every job will be tabbed for somebody. That would be terrible, but it's not necessary. We should have quotas for a very small number of groups. We have to be on guard against the excessive setting of quotas. But there are some that we obviously need. If it is necessary, we should have quotas for gay people. We need quotas for the disabled and for the most needy.

One alleged problem that is frequently mentioned, especially by black opponents of affirmative action, has to do with the alleged hurt to the beneficiaries. Quotas or affirmative action supposedly marks the black employees as having been hired just to meet the quota, and therefore as inferior. This supposedly louses up their position, ruins their career, and destroys their self-esteem. When I hear that, I'm reminded of what used to be said about a woman who made it into an executive position. It used to be said that she slept her way to the top. So if you got to be a success, you were tabbed as a prostitute. The fact that some nasty people were tabbing the women executives as prostitutes is not a good reason to keep women out of executive positions or for women to decline to be executives.

The people who said that women executives slept their way to the top were sexists, and the people who say that a black hired through affirmative action is not competent are racists. If they didn't have those people to kick around, they would be doing some other racist or sexist thing. It's true that affirmative action provokes racist comments. But they just have to be ignored.

I will close by repeating that we should be honest. There are many situations where pressure has to be applied to diversify the workforce, and people have to be counted by race and sex. Many of them involve occupations for which thousands of excluded people are out there waiting to be hired, who would be competent. If we need quotas to get them a fair chance, then quotas are good things.

CHAPTER 14

Reparations

William A. Darity, Jr.

We can define reparations as compensatory payment for an acknowledged grievous social injustice to a group. The social injustices visited upon African Americans would include the historical experiences of slavery, legally sanctioned apartheid practices, and ongoing discrimination. These three facets constitute the particular pattern of injustice affecting African Americans that has led to advocacy of a scheme of reparations as restitution for those wrongs (see the essays in America, 1990).

These advocates have included black nationalist activists James Forman and "Queen Mother" Audley Moore. In 1969 Forman, one of the founding members of the Student Nonviolent Coordinating Committee (SNCC), interrupted a Sunday morning service at Riverside Church in New York City and read a Black Manifesto that included a demand that churches and synagogues pay $500 million to black Americans as a first phase of reparations for historic oppression (see Forman, 1972; Bittker, 1973; and Carson, 1981).

"Queen Mother" Audley Moore began a campaign in the 1950s for the same sum, again as partial compensation for slavery. She met with President Kennedy at the White House in 1962 in an attempt to advance the cause, and her Reparations Committee of Descendants of U.S. Slaves did file a claim in California. However, her efforts largely were viewed as idiosyncratic and were eclipsed in the public eye by the legislative successes of the civil rights movement. Nevertheless, she never viewed either the Civil Rights Act of 1964 or the Civil Rights Bill of 1965 as measuring up to the intent of her reparations claim (Bair, 1993, pp. 812–813; and Sommerville, 1992, pp. 764–767).

In 1934 the National Movement for the Establishment of a 49th State, based in Chicago, called for the creation of a new state of the union "wherein colored people in the United States can have the opportunity to work out their own destiny, unbridled and unhampered by artificial barriers." The organization offered four major reasons for carving out a separate geographical area for black Americans who would choose to live there, the third of which included the observation that "aid to the Negro in the establishment of his new state offers an opportunity for the nation to reduce its debt to the Negro for past exploitation" ("National Movement," 1992, pp. 84–90).

Realized instances of reparations in the United States include the congressional agreement in the late 1980s to pay $20,000 to each living Japanese American subjected to internment during World War II; the same enabling legislation contained a provision to make payments of $12,000 to 450 living Aleut Indian evacuees, with supplementary funds provided to compensate them for their wartime losses (Dewar, 1988). Even earlier, agreements were reached with the Passamaquoddy Indian tribe in Maine that provided land and monetary compensation in settlements for abrogation of treaties by the U.S. government (Liebman, 1983, p. 14). Similar land and gambling rights agreements have been made with other Indian tribes in the United States.

There are also precedents elsewhere in eh world. In 1988 the German industrial giant Daimler-Benz agreed to pay the equivalent of $11.7 million to victims of Nazi forced labor policies during the war, as well as to their families. On the basis of an agreement signed in Luxembourg in 1952 between West Germany and the World Jewish Congress, the West German government had paid close to $50 billion in reparations to Holocaust survivors by the end of the 1980s (Associated Press, 1988).

In May 1995 the Austrian parliament passed a bill to compensate victims of Nazism there as well. The bill also provides compensation for "those who fled Austria [due to Nazi persecution] and their children born before May 9, 1995." Heinrich Neisser, deputy speaker of the Austrian parliament, estimated that the cost of the reparations program will range from $300 to $500 million (Cohen, 1995).

And there are potential claims to be made elsewhere. In the early 1970s a West Indian economist, Norman Girvan (1974), argued that the comprehensive pattern of European exploitation of the Third World led to European economic development, and therefore all Third World peoples should receive compensation. Girvan's estimate of the value of the exploitation attributable to the use of black slave labor during the period 1790–1860 alone, compounded to the time of his essay, ranged from $448 to $995 million.

In May 1993, at a summit of African and African American leaders held in Libreville, Gabon, Reverend Jesse Jackson proposed that slave reparations be "paid" to the African nations in the form of debt relief. The collective total of African states' external debt was about $255 billion at the time of the summit, owed primarily to multinational organizations, particularly the World Bank and the International Monetary Fund, and to foreign governments. Patently, restitution could be justified for the deleterious impact of slavery and the slave trade on the African continent. The "killing fields" of Cambodia, an instance of genocidal warfare, constitute a case for which reparations may yet be made.

But we are unaware of any instance in which compensatory payments were made to peoples of primarily African descent for their subjugation to slavery—whether to emancipated slaves in the West Indies in the 1830s or to emancipated slaves in the United States in the 1870s. In contrast, in the British West Indies, slave owners were paid for the loss of their human property by the British parliament. The masters were paid two pounds sterling per slave, the total coming to 20 million pounds in 1833, an extraordinary sum. But the ex-slaves themselves received nothing (Marx, 1974, p. 352, n.12).

In the U.S. South, rumors abounded that the ex-slaves would receive 40 acres and a mule. But with the end of radical Reconstruction, prospects for any form of reparations for the ex-slaves evaporated. On the other hand, Abraham Lincoln and the Republican Party earlier had proposed payment to slave owners as a means to emancipate the slaves and avoid civil war; Lincoln's proposal did not include a plan for compensating for the slaves themselves (Lincoln, 1976, pp. 328–329).

Neither has compensation ever been paid to the relatives or descendants of slaves who died during the journey to the African coast from the interior of the continent, who died during the middle passage, who died during the "seasoning period" in the New World, or who lived to labor from sunup to sundown under a regime of forced labor over the course of more than 200 years.

The end of slavery in the United States came with war, and when at last the war had ended, 4 million, largely illiterate, ex-slaves were thrust into a ravished and economically battered region. No effort was made at restitution, nor even any significant effort at investment in the ex-slaves aside form the modest and short-lived activities of the Freedmen's Bureau and the short-lived political actions of the ex-slaves in Southern state legislatures (Du Bois, 1935).

The collapse of slavery and the demise of the Reconstruction gave way to a formal American system of apartheid in the South that lasted roughly from 1873 to 1960, directly affecting the lives of four generations of African Americans beyond slavery. Thereafter the civil rights revolution launched a series of legislative initiatives that dismantled the formal structure of American apartheid. This included the adoption of federal antidiscrimination legislation and the adoption of affirmative action.

Even with the formal structure dismantled, discrimination against blacks still is powerfully operative, particularly in dictating access to occupation and earnings (see Fix and Struyk, 1992; Darity, Guilkey, and Winfrey, 1995). Ongoing discrimination is a persistent obstacle to racial equality.

In establishing the rationale for reparations for African Americans, compensation can be considered on three dimensions: first, compensation for slavery; second, compensation for discrimination in both the Jim Crow and the post-Jim Crow eras; and third, compensation for a cumulative disparity in wealth. We consider each of these in their turn.

COMPENSATION FOR SLAVERY

In recent research, three procedures have been advanced for estimating the magnitude of the compensation that should be paid for the subjugation of African Americans to slavery. These procedures and their associated estimates are presented in papers in a volume edited by Richard F. America, *The Wealth of Races* (1990). These three procedures do not attempt to address the emotional or psychological distress associated with the slave experience, or the mortality and morbidity damage wreaked by the slave regime; but they do try, in a more narrowly economistic fashion, to come up with measures of the cost of slavery for African Americans.

Still, these types of estimates largely omit the general economic development effects of the slave plantation system. For example, no consideration is given to Northern colonial merchants and Northern industrialists who benefited, respectively, from the triangle trade and the development of a textile sector that relied upon slave-grown raw cotton.

The first procedure is to address the potential income lost by Africans, being enslaved. This is based upon the notion of unpaid wages. James Marketti (1990) has pursued this route. He used the average market price of slaves decade by decade from 1790 to 1860 as an estimate of the income Africans could have earned as free laborers in the United States.

Compounded to 1995, using Marketti's procedure, we estimate a total compensation for this "diverted income" ranging from $1.8 trillion to $4.7 trillion, measured in 1983 dollars. The lower figure is based upon the use of a 3 percent interest rate for compounding, while the higher figure is based upon use of an interest rate of 5 percent before 1860 and 3 percent thereafter. The trillion-dollar figures are astronomical, although we will show below that other estimates fall in this range as well. Indeed, a reparations advocacy group in Rockville, Maryland, the Black Reparations Commission, has placed the recommended total payment as high as $4 trillion.

Marketti's approach has its difficulties. He assumes that in the absence of forced migration, African immigrants would have been present in U.S. colonial labor markets in similar numbers which obviously is absurd. He also assumes that wages paid to free laborers would be equal to slave prices, which is highly unlikely in an economy with a vast frontier and prospects for self-sufficiency in agriculture. And finally, he ignores the impact of speculation on slave prices.

Nevertheless, consider the magnitude of these sums in terms of the individual payments that would go to each living African American based upon an equal payout rule. If we assume that there are 30 million African Americans, the corresponding range of payments would run from $60,000 to $156,667 each.

Of course, these results are sensitive not only to the interest rate used for compounding purposes but also to the length of time projected as the relevant period for slavery. An alternative calculation can be performed with a 5 percent interest rate before 1860 and a 3 percent interest rate thereafter that treats the horizon of diverted income as stretching from 1620 to 1860. In 1983 dollars the magnitude of reparations would reach $8 trillion, requiring a payment of $266,667 per African American, or a payment in excess of $1 million for a family of four.

The second procedure used is a concept of net wages. Deducting the cost slave owners incurred in supporting slaves from the market price of slaves, a measure of unpaid wages can be derived. Again the assumption is made that if Africans had been free, they would have been paid wages equivalent to the purchase price of a slave. This approach, developed by Larry Neal (1990), seeks to identify the surplus that the owner captured from the slave.

Neal estimated, by compounding to 1983 at 3 percent, that the present value of unpaid net wages for the interval 1620–1840, after adjusting for inflation, would come to $1.4 trillion. This proves to be a far larger figure than Neal's estimate of the net benefit to American society of free immigrant labor for the period 1790–1912.

Moreover, Neal suggests that his estimate is "low" because he neglects several considerations: (1) the indirect harm to slaves owing to cultural damage, (2) physical and mental suffering, (3) the loss of potential productivity gains, and (4) profits of slavery probably had societal effects on growth and development benefiting whites other than slaveholders.

A third attempt to arrive at a compensation measure for slavery is that of Vedder, Gallaway, and Klingaman (1990). They ask what was the income gain to slave owners from the possession of slaves. They estimate that by 1860, the total wealth accumulated by white Southerners via slavery was approximately $3.27 million. This was on the eve of the Civil War, and it is an estimate calculated in 1859 dollars.

The trio of authors go on to point out (Vedder et al., 1990, p. 129) that "Slave wealth in 1860 was slightly under $500 per white person living in the South. Using only a 6 percent interest rate, this implies about $30 in income for every white Southerner at a time when the national per capita income for free persons was about $144." In addition, they make the following critical observation:

Americans probably receive a roughly equivalent proportion of their total income form ownership of all forms of property today as Southern property owners received from the ownership of slaves in 1860 for all Southern whites (including nonslaveowners) . . . between 3 and 4 to 1. A recent accounting of total net worth of Americans showed that the ratio of net worth to personal income was also between 3 and 4 to 1. The wealth derived from slavery by slaveowners was roughly as high in relation to income as wealth from all sources (real estate, stocks, bonds, insurance policies, bank accounts, etc.) in contemporary America. (Vedder et al., 1990, p. 29)

COMPENSATION FOR DISCRIMINATION AND WEALTH DISPARITY

The most important work in calculating the compensation African Americans should receive for being subjected to racial discrimination has been performed by the economist David Swinton (1990). He estimates that 40–60 percent of the gap in black-white median incomes is due to the cumulative effects of discrimination. In 1983 he found, as a conservative estimate, that it would have required $500 billion to make rapid progress toward equality on the part of black Americans. The 1995 figure would be closer to $650 billion.

A study by Bernadette Chachere, Richard America, and Gerald Udinsky (1990) concludes that between 1929 and 1969, the gains to whites from labor market discrimination amounted to approximately $1.6 trillion. They then argue that that constitutes the appropriate sum to begin construction of the proper estimate of total reparations.

A related case for reparations involves the argument that the key disparity that needs to be addressed is the gap in capital/asset ownership in the United States. Mean net worth of black families is less than 20 percent of mean net worth of nonblack families in the United States. The black savings rate at each income level is at least as high as the nonblack savings rate. Thus racial differences in attitudes toward saving do not explain the gap. The major source of wealth for individuals today in the United States is inheritance, and blacks have had considerably less to pass on to their offspring (Blau and Graham, 1990).

For Swinton (1990) the roles of slavery, Jim Crowism, and discrimination in the accumulation of black wealth—financial, physical, and human capital—are the decisive factors contributing to the persistent gap in income between blacks and whites. It is striking that Vedder and his coauthors (1990 pp. 130–134) estimate that in 1880 the ratio of black to white per capita income was 59 percent and that by 1985 the mean black family income ratio was 62 percent.

Historic patterns of control and repression have limited black wealth accumulation, and the cross-generational consequences are present to this day. Swinton (1990) estimated that in 1983 the value of all private nonhuman assets in the United States was $7.1 trillion, and the total black wealth amounted to no more than 2 percent of that sum (also see Browne, 1974). At that time, for black wealth holdings to match nonblack wealth holdings proportionately, black ownership of U.S. nonhuman assets would have had to have risen from approximately $142 billion to $800 billion, a more than fivefold increase.

Recently Swinton (1992) has proposed a level of reparations requiring payment to the African American population of $700 billion to $1 trillion motivated by the same analysis—as an avenue to redress inherited inequality between the races. This is indicative of the magnitude of the wealth redistribution that would be required to make the proportion of black ownership of the U.S. capital stock equivalent to the black presence in the U.S. population.

The only instance of a legally sanctioned systematic redistribution of private capital ownership based upon ethnicity or race of which we are aware was undertaken under the aegis of the New Economic Policy (1970–1990) in Malaysia. The share of Malaysian corporations owned by native Malays rose under this policy form 2 percent to 20 percent over the course of the two decades (Murphy, 1990).

Corporate shares were held in a government trust on behalf of the native Malays (*bumiputera*). Some notable aspects of this process should be mentioned. Over the course of the 20 years there was a rapid growth in valuation of corporate shares, so the wealth pie grew, which meant there was not a zero-sum game with respect to redistribution of assets. Moreover, to the extent that there was a shift in ethnic patterns of ownership, the decline took place in shares in Malaysian corporations held by foreigners, primarily British nationals. In fact, over the interval the major contestant group in Malaysia, the Malaysians of Chinese ancestry, actually experienced a slight rise in their share of corporate ownership!

A serious persistent issue is the question of the allocation of the shares among the native Malays themselves, that is, the intraethnic distribution of shares. It has been charged that this initiative enriched only those native Malays who were highly placed government officials and bureaucrats, leaving the rest of the "bumi" with a largely unchanged wealth position.

If a racial wealth redistribution were to be executed in the United States, these factors would have to be considered. We believe it is likely that there would be an ongoing growth in the valuation of U.S. corporate shares and that an expanded African

American ownership share could be achieved, at least in part, by reducing foreign ownership. For better or worse, the latter step would be compatible with certain reawakening nativist tendencies, although it is inconsistent with the "globalization" movement.

The question of allocative equity among blacks would have to be addressed if such a redistribution were pursued. Increased wealth customarily enhances maintenance of a secure income, access to advanced educational credentials, the capacity to form sustainable businesses, and, the capability to overcome or bypass the adverse effects of prejudice against blacks.

AFFIRMATIVE ACTION VERSUS REPARATIONS?

It also has been argued that blacks already have been compensated for historic injustices in the form of social programs and affirmative action. So, the argument goes, there is no need for a new reparations initiative; reparations already have been paid.

But social programs in the United States are not race-specific. They are typically means-tested programs directed at assisting low-income persons, regardless of race (Danziger and Gottschalk, 1990). Furthermore, the magnitude of these programs, to the extent that they have been directed toward African Americans, does not approach the scale of the projected reparations bills. Swinton's (1990, pp. 158–160) early 1980s estimate of a $500 billion American social debt to blacks was calculated net of an estimate of $150 billion in the present value of expenditures on social programs.

The money value of the programs created during the Great Depression and extended under Lyndon Johnson's Great Society do not even *consider* the lower ends of the Marketti and Neal estimates of the cost to blacks of slavery. They were not designed even to consider the costs of discrimination or the cumulative effects of slavery and discrimination on the black-white wealth gap.

Then what about affirmative action? Affirmative action does not, in general, rest on the goal of compensation for past injustices, nor does it provide a vehicle for redress of wealth disparity. Until the recent Supreme Court decisions requiring strict scrutiny of race-based programs, affirmative action programs largely have been designed to address the question of present discrimination. Moreover, enforcement always has been problematic with respect to affirmative action; a plaintiff has had to demonstrate intent on the part of those who fail to implement such initiatives. The evidence of the impact on black employment and income prospects is hardly robust.

The most favorable study at the national level is the research of Jonathan Leonard (1984) on government contractors compared with noncontractors after the adoption of equal employment opportunity initiatives at the federal level. Leonard demonstrates that government contractors have a higher rate of hiring blacks than do noncontractors. But the findings are weakened somewhat because the contractors' rate of hiring blacks was significantly higher before affirmative action was inaugurated.

More convincing is the Heckman and Payner (1989) study on state employment practices in South Carolina. This appears to be a case where affirmative action was pursued with some force, and the racial composition of South Carolina's government employees changed dramatically. However, there is little evidence to suggest that the interclass effects of affirmative action among African Americans have been evenly distributed. In fact, Charles Brown's (1984) study from the early 1980s suggested that to the extent that affirmative action had been implemented forcefully enough to benefit blacks, the benefits had fallen disproportionately on blacks already possessing middle-class or near middle-class status.

Regardless, affirmative action is now under heavy assault. Philosophically it is especially disturbing to those who profess the idealized vision of a "color-blind" society. Unfortunately, they never make clear how a society with sharp, historically generated racial inequalities can close the gap without utilizing color-conscious policies.

In the university setting, affirmative action frequently was subverted by the claim that sufficient numbers of "minorities" rarely could be found with the appropriate "qualifications." In a country like India, the thoroughly depressed educational status of the lowest castes can make such a claim valid with respect to the operation of the compensatory discrimination program. Reserved places for the scheduled castes at universities have gone unfilled because insufficient numbers of members of the lower castes have cleared the hurdles of elementary and high school completion that would make them eligible for university training (Galanter, 1984).

Limited research on earnings gaps across castes has tended to demonstrate that virtually all of the earnings deficiencies among members of the Hindu lower castes are due to inferior productivity-linked characteristics (i.e., education, occupational experience, etc.) rather than labor market discrimination (Dhesi and Singh, 1989). Of course, there is no need for the upper castes to bother with discriminatory practices if the lower castes can be readily excluded because they lack the minimal qualifications. Access to such qualifications necessarily has been driven by caste-specific opportunity structures—discriminatory in a more global sense—in India.

In the United States the argument typically is made that at best, universities reshuffle a comparatively small and fixed pool of African American academics and students among institutions. To the extent that there is any truth to this claim, conventional economic theory would suggest that there is a premium for racial scarcity, and this should spur more African Americans to pursue higher education and academic careers. What we actually have observed in recent years has been declining numbers of blacks entering college and subsequently pursuing Ph.D.s.

A related charge is that blacks are overpaid for their qualifications relative to nonblacks with similar curricula vitae. This is, of course, another variant of the "race premium" argument. But are curricula vitae with similar numbers of articles placed in similar journals by a black and a white scholar smoothly comparable in light of deceptive mentoring and negative steering of new black Ph.D.s by some white faculty; in light of the presence of a racial veil over aspects of the journal refereeing process; in light of the systematic under citation of the work of blacks; in light of ongoing presumption of black intellect inferiority by many nonblack colleagues; in light of the discomfiture of students who have never been taught or graded by a black faculty member before, and in light of the burden of serving as counselor and confidant to black students whom white faculty members often have dismissed as intellectually inferior?

This is further aggravated by the perception of departments that once they have one black faculty member, they have enough. They now can view themselves as racially integrated; admittedly, it generally takes two or three white females before the department characterizes itself as integrated on gender grounds.

The existence of affirmative action, it is frequently charged, stigmatizes competent African Americans, who are assumed to have achieved their positions via social policy rather than on the merits of their portfolios. But Claude Steele (1994, pp. 172–182) has argued convincingly that many nonblacks believe blacks are intellectually inferior, regardless of the presence or absence of affirmative action; stigma preceded affirmative action and will outlast affirmative action.

Still, affirmative action may have run its course. For all the furor surrounding it as a policy to redress racial inequality, it has done little to transform the relative economic or social position of African Americans. An additional difficulty that reduces its possible status as a sufficient approach or an alternative to reparations is the further dilution of its application on behalf of African Americans through its appropriation by other groups. To be blunt, affirmative action is not the equivalent of reparations, and it has not proved to be effective in reversing deeply rooted patterns of racial inequality in the United States for a variety of reasons.

At least one vociferous opponent of affirmative action, Charles Krauthammer (1991, p. 18), endorses reparations as a substitute for affirmative action. Arguably both affirmative action and reparations are needed. But, barring the collapse of the U.S. economy, a program of substantial reparations can have a greater effect. If forced to choose—and one hopes the Krauthammer "deal" is not a Faustian bargain —we would take substantial reparations and forgo affirmative action. At minimum the resources from reparations would mitigate racism's effects on the life chances of African Americans. If, as the legal scholar Derrick Bell (1993) has argued, racism is permanent in America, then the question becomes how best to develop a world where racism does not significantly constrain the life chances of black Americans.

One idea, presented by Bell, is embodied in one of his ubiquitous fables. He imagines a United States where a president proposes what Bell calls the Racial Preference Licensing Act. Businesses would be free to exercise their discriminatory preferences at a price. To be able to have the legal right to discriminate, businesses must pay 3 percent of their profits to obtain the appropriate license. Firms with such licenses could put stickers on their products reading "Made by White Hands Only" with impunity, if they believed such information would enhance their sales.

The funds from the licensing fees would go to a Racial Equality Fund that could finance black housing ownership, black education, and so on. In short, the discriminators would de facto compensate their victims directly. How such a scheme would provide compensation to African Americans for discrimination executed by nonprofit institutions like foundations and universities is not evident, but it might be possible if this plan actually became operative to truly put the "equal" in "separate but equal." It would be crucial that effective enforcement of fair hiring practices on the part of the nonlicensees take place, and that is the same tricky issue that arises with respect to compliance with affirmative action.

Nevertheless, the Racial Equality Fund might point, albeit fancifully, toward a means of financing reparations. After all, if we are finally to take reparations seriously as a policy option, we must consider how to pay the bill. Indeed, one of the most obvious political obstacles is how to finance such a large payout in our deficit-ridden times.

There are at least five possibilities that deserve further consideration. First, a reparations tax could be levied on the income of each able-bodied, employed American over a fixed number of years. The revenues could then go into a trust fund for African Americans, and payments could be made out of the trust fund. The payments need not be made as a lump sum; they could be made in a fashion similar to state lotteries, where winners get a part of the total each year.

Second, industries and institutions could pay into a fund to finance regulatory agencies that oversee their hiring practices, and the excess could go into an African American trust fund with a similar payout scheme. A third possibility is to provide reparations in-kind, such as a government guarantee of payment of college tuition for every African American for up to four or five years.

Fourth, a wealth tax could be applied and then a redistribution of that wealth exercised in the form of reparations. Finally, something akin to the Bell plan that makes use of the fees for racial preference licenses could be the means of financing reparations.

Who would be eligible? Rules would have to be set, rather than leaving each American citizen free to "rediscover" his or her black ancestry by creative genealogical inquiry. Birth certificates or other legal documents (e.g., school records) that indicate an individual's race, issued before a particular date, could be used to establish eligibility for reparations—documents that describe the individual as "colored," "Negro," "black," or "African American."

At this stage we have crossed the philosophical barriers to serious consideration of reparations as a viable policy option to redress racial inequality. Now we are down to the brass tacks of the construction of an actual program to put a price tag on oppression. Indeed, put a price tag on oppression, put a large price tag on oppression, and pay the bill. This finally would enable the nation to strip away the question of racial economic inequality and get down to the bare bones of the equally persistent issue of class stratification in America.

BIBLIOGRAPHY

America, Richard F. (ed.). 1990. *The Wealth of Races: The Present Value of Benefits from Past Injustices.* Westport, Conn.: Greenwood Press.
Associated Press. 1988. "West German Firm to Pay WWII Forced Laborers Nearly $12 Million," *Dallas Morning News,* June 12, p. 27A.
Bair, Barbara. 1993. "Moore, Audley (Queen Mother)." In Darlene Clark Hine (ed.), *Black Women in America: An Historical Encyclopedia.* Brooklyn, N.Y.: Carson Publishing.

Bell, Derrick. 1993. Faces at the Bottom of the Well. New York: Basic Books.

Bittker, Boris. 1973. *The Case for Black Reparations*. New York: Random House.

Blau, Francine, and John Graham. 1990. Black-White Differences in Wealth and Asset Composition." *Quarterly Journal of Economics* 105 (May): 321–40.

Brown, Charles. 1984. "Black-White Earnings Ratios Since the Civil Rights Act of 1964: The Importance of Labor Market Dropouts." *Quarterly Journal of Economics* 99 (February): 32–43.

Browne, Robert S. 1974. "Wealth Distribution and Its Impact on Minorities," *Review of Black Political Economy* 4: 27–38.

Carson, Clayborne. 1981. *In Struggle: SNCC and the Black Awakening in the 1960s.* Cambridge, Mass.: Harvard University Press.

Chachere, Bernadette, Richard America, and Gerald Udinsky. 1990. "An Illustrative Estimate: The Present Value of the Benefits from Racial Discrimination, 1929–1969." In Richard F. America (ed.), *The Wealth of Races*. Westport, Conn.: Greenwood Press.

Cohen, Shawn. 1995. "Austrians Provide Reparations to Holocaust Survivors." *Washington Jewish Week*, June 29, p. 22.

Danziger, Sheldon, and Peter Gottschalk. 1990. "Income Transfers: Are They Compensation for Past Debt?" In Richard F. America (ed.), *The Wealth of Races*. Westport, Conn.: Greenwood Press.

Darity, William A., Jr., David Guilkey, and William Winfrey. 1995. "Ethnicity, Race and Earnings." *Economics Letters*. 47: (March): 401–8.

Dewar, Helen. 1988. "Senate Votes to Give Apology, Compensation to Interned Japanese Americans." *Washington Post*, April 21, p. A9.

Dhesi, Autar Singh, and Harbhajan Singh. 1989. "Education, Labour Market Distortions and Relative Earnings of Different Religion-Caste Categories in India: A Case Study of Delhi." *Canadian Journal of Development Studies* 47:1: 75–89.

Du Bois, W. E. B. 1935. *Black Reconstruction in America, 1860–1880*. New York: Atheneum.

Fix, Michael, and Raymond J. Struyk (eds.). 1992. *Clear and Convincing Evidence: Measurement of Discrimination in America*. Washington, D. C.: Urban Institute Press.

Forman, James. 1972. *The Making of Black Revolutionaries*. New York: Macmillan Company.

Galanter, Marc. 1984. *Competing Equalities: Law and the Backward Classes in India*. Berkeley: University of California Press.

Girvan, Norman. 1974, "The Question of Compensation: A Third World Perspective." *Race* 16 (July): 53–82.

Heckman, James, and Brook Payner. 1989. "Determining the Impact of Federal Antidiscrimination Policy on the Economic Status of Blacks: A Study of South Carolina." *American Economic Review* 79 (March): 138–77.

Krauthammer, Charles. 1991. "Reparations for Black Americans." *Time*, December 31, p. 18.

Leonard, Jonathan S. 1984. "Employment and Occupational Advance Under Affirmative Action." *Review of Economics and Statistics* 66 (August): 377–85.

Liebman, Lance. 1983. "Anti-Discrimination Law: Groups and the Modern State." In Nathan Glazer and Ken Young (eds.), *Ethnicity and Public Policy: Achieving Equality in the United States and Britain*. London: Heinemann Educational Books.

Lincoln, Abraham. 1976. "A Plea for Compensated Emancipation." In *The Annals of America*, vol. 9: *1858–1865, The Crisis of the Union*. Chicago: Encyclopaedia Britannica.

Marketti, James. 1990. "Estimated Present Value of Income Diverted During Slavery." In Richard F. America (ed.), *The Wealth of Races*. Westport, Conn.: Greenwood Press.

Marx, Karl. 1974. "The Civil War in the United States." In *Surveys from Exile: Political Writings*, vol. 2. New York: Vintage Books.

Murphy, Cait. 1990. "The Grandest Affirmative Action Failure of All." *Wall Street Journal*,

December 27, editorial page.

"The National Movement for the Establishment of a 49th State." 1992. In Herbert Aptheker (ed.), *A Documentary History of the Negro People in the United States*, vol. 4. Secaucus, N. J.: Carol Publishing.

Neal, Larry. 1990. "A Calculation and Comparison of the Current Benefits of Slavery and an Analysis of Who Benefits." In Richard F. America (ed.), *The Wealth of Races*. Westport, Conn.: Greenwood Press.

Sommerville, Raymond R. 1992. "Queen Mother Audley Moore." In Jessie Carney Smith (ed.), *Notable Black American Women*. Detroit: Gale Research.

Steele, Claude. 1994. "Race and the School of Black Americans." Reprinted in Susan F. Feiner (ed.), *Race and Gender in the American Economy: Views from Across the Spectrum*, Englewood Cliffs, N. J.: Prentice-Hall.

Swinton, David. 1992. "The Economic Status of African Americans: Limited Ownership and Persistent Inequality." In Billy Tidwell (ed.), *The State of Black America 1992*. New York City: National Urban League.

————. 1990. "Racial Inequality and Reparations." In Richard F. America (ed.), *The Wealth of Races*. Westport, Conn.: Greenwood Press.

Vedder, Richard, Lowell Gallaway, and David C. Klingaman. 1990. "Black Exploitation and White Benefits: The Civil War Income Revolution." In Richard F. America (ed.), *The Wealth of Races*. Westport, Conn.: Greenwood Press.

CHAPTER 15

Remedies to Racial Inequality

This discussion followed the presentation of papers by Barbara R. Bergmann, Distinguished Professor of Economics, American University, Washington, D.C., and William A. Darity, Jr., Boshamer Professor of Economics, University of North Carolina at Chapel Hill. The moderator was Chester Hartmann, President and Executive Director of the Poverty and Race Research Action Council. The complete panel consisted of William Spriggs, Senior Economist, Joint Economic Committee, U.S. Congress; Richard America, Adjunct Lecturer, Georgetown University School of Business; Mitchell Pearlstein, President, Center of the American Experiment; and Peter Bell, Executive Vice President, Corporate Community Relations, TCF Bank, Minneapolis. The remarks contained herein are edited and abbreviated.

WILLIAM E. SPRIGGS

Some scholars miss one of the key issues when it comes to talking about affirmative action and its success: that is, the United States military, which is an organization with one of the strictest affirmative action plans and which comes closest, I think, to having goals that in the skewed language of the debate affirmative action opponents label as quotas. And anyone who is objective would not doubt that under Colin Powell, the United States military showed itself to be the most efficient war machine on Earth; that in handling highly sophisticated equipment—more sophisticated than that of any other war machine on Earth—African American officers, Latino officers, Asian-American officers demonstrated that an army that has to operate under affirmative action is not in the least crippled. So any indication that affirmative action is going to hurt some organization, make it less efficient, make it unable to deal in a high-technology area—anyone who is objective could not say that about the United States military. The military's affirmative action now includes stronger efforts to make sure that there is gender equality, and the supply lines that served our troops in the Persian Gulf are clear evidence that having women officers enhances the ability of the military to function. So anyone who says that affirmative action hurts efficiency is just not being objective.

Now even conservatives, I think, agree with the term "quotas." And they believe in quotas—I owe this one to William Raspberry—quotas as they relate to U.S. manufacturers and their interest in the Japanese market. The Japanese say, "Our market is open and consumers can buy anything they want to buy. If you made a better product, we would buy it. You don't make a better product." And the response from the United States government has been, "We don't want to hear that you have opened up your markets. We want results. We want a certain percentage of goods bought in Japan to be made by American companies." That is a quota.

Now, it makes sense for conservatives to argue about a quota when it's American goods sent to Japan because we know that American goods are better than Japanese goods. (audience laughs and claps)

There are African Americans who are troubled by affirmative action and what they have accomplished because of affirmative action. I'd like to personalize this in a way that I explained it to my students, many of whom were first generation college students.

I know for a fact—and there are no statistics that can dispute this—that I am not smarter than either of my grandfathers, both of whom were janitors. I know absolutely, beyond any doubt, that I am not smarter than either of my grandmothers, both of whom were domestics. I am not here because I am smarter than they were. I am not here because I work harder than they did. My mother has reminded me many times that she could work me into the ground any day of the week. I am here because other people made sacrifices, black and white, to ensure that my talents would be rewarded for what they are. And they're good talents. But they aren't superior to the talents of people who went before me on any objective measure of those talents. So any African American who is ashamed because affirmative action gave them an opportunity are being impudent toward their ancestors. They think they are here because they've got some gift and their grandparents didn't.

Now one of the big myths that has been allowed to persist is that somehow our African American youth are deficient. This is something that is promulgated, unfortunately, on both the left and the right. It gets promulgated on the left because of our deep concern for those African American youth who have been left behind; those who do not succeed in school, who drop out, who find themselves in an economy where no legitimate job can be had by someone who drops out of high school without some remedial training or something else to bring them up to speed. But given the low value of the minimum wage and given the structure of our economy, without some additional training a high school dropout is not going to find a legitimate job in this country to let them support a family. Those on the left concentrate on that group because they are in the worst situation. It has never been true in this country since the postdepression era, when we established a minimum wage as a living wage, that we now have a minimum wage that is almost half of what it needs to be to support someone. That was not the case until 1982. So that is a unique situation, and it is right for people on the left to be concerned about that group.

People on the right like to bring up the problems of African American youngsters because it's a way of dealing with pathologies, and that explains why black folks are behind.

The reality is that there is very little difference between African American youth and white youth. The reason why black youth who don't live anywhere near Harlem (and probably really couldn't relate to hip-hop culture if they really came across it), relate to the frustration exhibited in rap music even though they are so distant from the reality of it, is because our youth today are the best-trained, best-educated African Americans we have ever had on this planet. They understand that. But they also understand that, unlike my generation, if you are black and go to college today and finish, you end up with a wage 15 percent lower than a white kid who goes to college. You end up with an unemployment rate twice that of a white kid who goes to college. They have brothers and sisters who go to college, cousins who go to college, somebody in the family who went to college. They understand that. Their frustration is that we don't understand that. Their frustration is that we characterize them as the problem. They won the race fair and square, and there is a referee who is cheating them—and what we're doing is yelling at them.

Now I remember when I played football. You may not believe it, looking at me now, but I did play football. We had a game which we lost because the other team had 12 men on the field. We yelled at the official that there were 12 men on the field. They did what they normally do, which is they think that you're kidding. The other team threw a pass, they scored a touchdown. Afterward, the coach yelled at us—the team—because somebody had missed coverage.

We were young, and good youngsters listen to their leaders. So instead of continuing to yell about the official, we started yelling at the defensive backs, saying, "Why didn't you cover the man who was open?" The reaction of people in a situation where they know they have done their best; they have done what they were supposed to do; and you come back and tell them they're the reason you lost; they're the reason you're behind—there is going to be some sort of nihilistic reaction. You've got to hate yourself. You've got to have dissension within your own ranks. You have to believe that.

Meaningful goals not empty promises make sense today in a way that they did not possibly make sense in the 1960s. We do not give credit that African American youth are economic beings just like anybody else. Every kid has already been told by his or her parents, by the media, by everybody else, "You've got to finish high school." Black kids lowered their dropout rate from the high of 20 percent in the 1960s down to 13 percent—almost the same as white people—today.

If you look at the labor market statistics, the Bureau of Labor statistics, today there are more African-American youths—we're talking about out-of-school youth under 24—who either have finished college or have gone to some college than there are those who are dropouts. Yet we persist in trying to say that black kids can't get ahead is because they're not trained, or some other such pathological reasoning.

Real time tables, without delaying tactics, make more sense today than they did in the 1960s for closing of the gap in the experience of individuals. Affirmative action was meant to address what happens when equally qualified individuals apply for a job.

The sad truth is that economists have not done their job of letting people understand that today there is a huge gap in economic outcomes for equally qualified people that did not exist in 1979. It is the result of what Dr. Anderson pointed out before. The deliberate policies of the last 12 years drove a wedge in the success that we had in the 1970s that closed those gaps. We should not believe that affirmative action never closed any gaps. It closed gaps. In 1979 there was no wage gap between black and white college graduates. So, it is not the case that you cannot close the gaps. It is not the case that there is something inherent in this economy that keeps us from doing it. It can be done if we are serious about enforcing our laws.

So I think it is time that, instead of retreating, we learn how to rephrase the argument to win the day. And I think the way that Dr. Bergmann pointed out may well be the way to show people, as we argue to Japan: "It's all well and good to say that you are making an effort, but you've got to have a bottom line."

RICHARD AMERICA

I will briefly discuss these issues in terms of reparations as Sandy Darity has outlined. We have had a discussion about the history of affirmative action policy, and the shifting political circumstances in which we debate policy. The debate has been distorted and demogogued. Bernard Anderson earlier posited that changing the policy environment is tough, in part because much of the intellectual ground was taken over by conservatives in the last 30 years. But that's because the problem that affirmative action presumably is the solution to, hasn't been properly defined. We need to redefine it properly.

For 40 years we've had a circular, redundant, unresolved discussion about race issues and social injustice. We're familiar with the general evidence on disparities in employment, income, health, educational attainment, crime rates, incarceration, welfare caseloads, teenage parents, school dropouts, and so on. We have a general sense of progress for some, slippage for others, and continuing chronic distress for many.

This conventional wisdom informs the weekend talk shows, the radio call-in shows, political campaigns and public policy decisionmaking in serious forums as well. Civil rights leaders also echo these facts and nonfacts. But now we have a stalemate: a conservative/liberal standoff, frozen dialogue. The problem is thought to be understood by both sides, but it isn't.

We talk about how to make up for past discrimination. The Supreme Court even uses that language. But the problem should be restated.

First, there has been 375 years of slavery and discrimination. Second, income and wealth were coercively diverted interracially by those processes. This results in a current unjust enrichment. That's the problem.

Therefore the issue is to remedy a current injustice, not a past injustice. The top 20 percent—the "haves"—receive 44 percent of earned income. The bottom 5 percent receive 5 percent of earned income. And that disparity is largely explained by past injustice. IQ may be a factor. But the right tries to make that case in order to undermine arguments for redistributive justice.

But a debt is owed. Roughly speaking—whites owe blacks money: 5 to 10 trillion dollars by some estimates. Until we understand that, there will be no policy progress.

The concept of reparations, therefore, is key. Without it, there will be continuing confusion. It is a social accounting problem, first and foremost. It is now possible to perform historical audits; to go back over history and to examine many transactions that occurred under conditions that deviate from current standards of morality and law. And that investigation will produce the crucial information that has been lacking, and provide the basis for redistributive policy on set-asides, affirmative action, and so on.

The results also will shift the psychological ground. Who owes what to whom is important. With that research, it will be clear that we are not talking about compassion, generosity, or charity.

We're subjected to code words; "qualified," "merit," "reverse discrimination," "quotas" (used pejoratively), "tax and spend," "no new taxes," "get government out of our lives." But these debating tricks won't work if the issue is effectively reframed as I suggest.

Once the concept of reparations is analytically established and withstands technical challenge—and that's the first step—then the practical issue is how to pay them. Sandy Darity offered several provocative alternatives. But what's key now is getting the basic principle clear; that the "haves" owe money to the "have-nots," and, generally speaking, whites owe blacks. The debt can be measured, then paid off through the normal workings of the tax and budget processes of government—in the ways that will be least divisive and least painful.

Finally, two points. One, the concept of reparations is a mainstream public policy concept, not a fringe rhetorical idea. Without it, it's not possible to understand and solve the problems of racial injustice, inequality, and dysfunction, or even to manage the economy successfully. We suffer productivity and competitiveness shortfalls, to a significant extent, because of the effects of racism reflected in disparities in income and wealth.

And, second, the concept can be a tool for conflict resolution globally: in Bosnia, Northern Ireland, the Middle East, South Africa, India, Pakistan, and probably in many other cases, where there are chronic, age-old grievances. Conducting a historical audit is the first step toward arriving at a basis for rational discussion of alternative remedies in all these conflicts as well as here at home.

PETER BELL

Mr. Spriggs referenced his grandmother when he spoke, and that inspired me to reference mine. My grandmother, a single black woman who raised three children in the Depression, would have rejected much of what we heard today. She believed in hard work, dedication, education. She did not deny racism, she just refused to overcelebrate it. She understood that the success of black America does not depend on what whites should do for us, but on what we should do for ourselves.

Both proposals that I heard today, regarding quotas and reparations, look to white goodwill to solve the problems in the African-American community. If the only way we can be okay is for white people to change, we will never be okay. To that extent, I am something of a nationalist. Wealth, income, and jobs are not the only problems that beset the African-American community today. I believe in reality, and we have a spiritual and cultural malaise that goes beyond issues of economics. In addition, I believe that we are in a post-civil rights era in this country. The problems in the African-American community, I believe, go significantly and fundamentally beyond affirmative action, quotas, race, norms, test scores, minority set-asides, or the Voting Rights Act. It wasn't too many years ago, that I was told if we elected more Blacks to public office the problems in the black community would be eased. I would ask anyone to go into Harlem and ask the residents there if they think their life was better when David Dinkins was mayor of New York City.

I was told that when the police departments would be comprised of African Americans, there would be less black-on-black crime and better police-community relations. I was told that when we had black school administrators and teachers, reading scores would improve. No serious observer would argue that. That is not an argument against such actions, it is an argument against overpromising what they will produce.

If every white person in this country disappeared today, there would still be many problems besetting the African-American community.

There are a number of questions I would have, particularly regarding the suggestion of quotas. The first question I have is how we will undo them when the time comes about. One of the problems I have with government, period, is that it has a good ability to start things and a questionable ability to stop them. I believe, in essence, that we would need a racial identification board similar to what they had in South Africa. How will we deal with the person who is genetically white but culturally Hispanic? It would, I think, very quickly lead to a racial spoils system. In addition, we would have to set a ceiling for activities. For instance, as Mitch indicated, should we limit the number of Jews in various schools? Affirmative action also, I believe, does little for the underclass. By most measures, the poverty of the bottom third is deeper and more entrenched than ever before.

Investing in the power of government to award benefits on the basis of race, I believe, is a dangerous road to proceed down. I was perplexed by the comment about African Americans who work in minimum-wage jobs. As a matter of fact, it is something that I had exactly the opposite reaction to. I travel across the country, and I am keenly aware of the number of African Americans who work in McDonalds, Burger King, Wendy's, 7-11, Holiday Inn, Taco Bell, Ramada Inn—and am upset by their large number. Twenty-five percent of all the employees at McDonalds in this country are black. The problem, believe me, is not that in this country we don't have enough African Americans working in McDonalds or serving food out here. The problem is that we don't have enough African Americans in the nation's Fortune 500 companies. The concern I have about affirmative action is not how whites view us but, more fundamentally, how we view each other. And I think affirmative action has a corrosive effect on that as well. It heightens the victims' status, which, I think, undermines initiative. For if you are a victim, why should you try? If the white man is omnipotent and all-powerful, why should you delay gratification, get a job, be persistent, and the like?

Finally, I believe strongly—and this is an important point to me—that we will never be seen as equal in the eyes of our fellow citizens as long as we are seen as needing special treatment. That issue of integrity, I think, is key in the African-American community.

MITCH PEARLSTEIN

Let me begin with a concern about the balkanization of the work force and labor market, a concern about the balkanization of the nation. I think we forget how evil the notion of quotas was when it appeared in the 1960s. Talking personally, where Jews are concerned, I must say how truly evil quotas are.

We in this nation who support civil rights went to great pains to distinguish between quotas and affirmative action; between quotas and goals. But slowly over the last-quarter century that stigma has eroded. I agree that Republicans have contributed to this, but I would still argue, for a variety of reasons, that quotas are bad for everyone concerned. They are bad for the nation.

Every time there is a new Republican president, be it President Reagan or President Bush, in about January after the election the president or his lieutenants are proud to announce that there are more women and people of color coming on board in that administration than ever before. And no, no, no—race had nothing to do with it and sex had nothing to do with it. If I give the Clinton administration credit for anything, it is for being more candid about the fact that race and sex have indeed been criteria. Republicans and conservatives, in other words, practice affirmative action all the time. My basic argument is that it is not a choice between affirmative action and no affirmative action; it's pursuing the right kind of affirmative action. And I would argue that the kind we have been talking about today is the wrong kind.

There was a conference in this very room a week and a half ago sponsored by the Humphrey Institute that had as its underlying idea the search for common ground in this nation. Rather than a boiling point we were looking for a melting pot or, at the very least, some unity.

My fundamental point in response to the Bergmann and Darity presentations is that we would have to try very, very hard if we were looking for devices that would do a better job of dividing this nation than is the case with quotas and in reparations. I would argue, more specifically, that one way of looking at the history of race relations and affirmative action in this nation over the last quarter-century, particularly in American higher education, has been that we have attempted to fix problems by affirmative action, by what I would describe as feverish forms of multiculturalism—by segregated dorms, segregated cultural centers, exaggerated preferential admissions. And—surprise, surprise—when we have done these things, they haven't worked as well as we hoped. We have become more divided as a people. So what do we do? We do more of the same. We practice *more* affirmative action.

I would reject arguments that affirmative action has eroded as a policy in this nation. I would argue that despite whatever President Reagan was interested in doing or not interested in doing—and the same thing with President Bush—the idea behind affirmative action (i.e., taking race into account, taking sex into account) is much more ingrained in the very fiber of this nation and its institutions than it was 15 years ago or 25 years ago.

As for Professor Darity's argument, I fully grant that there is something very intoxicating about it. It's reinforced by someone like Charles Krauthammer saying that the idea of reparations, in and of itself, is not beyond the pale of good sense and decency. Yet while fully acknowledging the great sins of the past of this nation and of the world, reinforcing a sense of victimization is about the last thing we need. That can be added to questions of exactly where this money for reparations would come from. It also seems to me that only in the university setting could you have this kind of conversation without great, great masses of people saying, "My gosh. Absolutely not." There's no way they would be willing to shell out more taxes for such an idea. At least half the title of this conference is about race relations. If one were interested in further poisoning race relations, it seems to me that this would be a perfect way to go.

I have two or three very quick comments in closing. Talking about higher education, the lack of Ph.D.s, and moving protected-class faculty—more specifically, black faculty—from one place to another, that pool is small. Sadly, the pool is very small. You can pick disciplines and the numbers would be two in this field, three in that field, half a dozen, three dozen in that field per year. There are over 3,000 universities, including community colleges, in the United States. Is it surprising that the pool is small?

Scarcity would suggest that there would be more people—in this instance more African Americans—doing Ph.D.s. For reasons of scarcity, perhaps a lot of folks are hired away before they finish their degree. If you really want to take a look at the economics of scarcity, then I would suggest you take a look at salary levels for equally qualified faculty, new faculty in similar or identical fields, because different fields pay differently. If there is a consistent gap under those circumstances between white faculty and black faculty, then we do, indeed, have a problem. But I would argue that scarcity indeed works in this area. My educated guess is that quite frequently black faculty benefit financially.

Last point, very personally now: my Ph.D. is in higher education administration. I was for a while, back in the late 1970s and early 1980s, interested in making my career in higher education. I actually worked in higher education here at the University of Minnesota. Let me tell you that if I were in the market right now for an administrative or faculty position, either here or in the academy elsewhere in the nation, I would much prefer to compete with another white male, once it got down to serious competition, than with a protected-class member. Now, I suspect there are any number of people in this room who find that absolutely impossible to believe. They think affirmative action is a sham, in the sense that it's not going to lead to protected-class members' getting preference or even getting a fair shake. I believe, however, that under those circumstances in higher education, I would be at a disadvantage. Affirmative action is the kind of policy that somehow makes everybody mad. And if the idea is to find greater common ground and unity in this nation, practicing a more strident form of affirmative action is about the last route we should take.

Afterword: The Future of Race Relations and Civil Rights[1]

Samuel L. Myers, Jr.

Late in the 1990 North Carolina senate race, a racist television advertising campaign appeared. The first black man elected mayor of Charlotte, North Carolina—Harvey Gantt, was leading in many of the closely watched polls. The lagging opponent: arch-conservative incumbent Jesse Helms. The attack response: a television ad depicting a white man, hands wrenching in pain as he discarded a rejection letter. The background voice told why: This man's rejection was the result of affirmative action. A less-qualified minority obtained a white man's job because of a racial quota. The implication: It could happen to you! It is no wonder that Gantt was defeated and Jesse Helms was reelected. The swell of white resentment towards affirmative action and alleged racial quotas guaranteed that the black challenger would lose.

The opposition to affirmative action and alleged racial quotas is real. One sees it in sports bars; one sees it in classrooms; one sees it in the workplace. In the bars, while white males casually root for nearly all-black NBA teams, they lament the unfairness of civil rights efforts that have retarded their job opportunities. In the classrooms, one hears from middle-class white students hurtful allegations that minorities would not have been admitted or would not have received financial aid but for affirmative action. In the workplace, one hears, "She got promoted only because she was black." One sees it in comments such as Mitch Pearlstein's found in this volume.

Sometimes it is extremely difficult to explain to a white male job applicant how or why he failed to get the job. Consider this scenario: There are 100 applicants for a coveted promotion. Only one promotion slot is open. Ninety nine applicants for that slot are white men. One is a black female. All take an examination, which is one but not the only criterion for weighing the qualifications of the candidates. The top nine scores are received by white men. The tenth highest score is received by the black woman. The black woman gets the job. And 99 white men feel as if they have been discriminated against. Not nine but 99 people might think the process in unfair.

Now let's think about this. Only one person can get promoted. The black woman who gets the job putatively "leap-frogs" over nine "better qualified" applicants. Nobody cares about whether the test—written and calibrated against white male standards is possibly biased against women or minorities. Nobody cares about whether the black woman has to be twice as good as *every* white man in order to score in the top ten-percent of all candidates. Nobody cares whether the black woman brings qualifications that count and are valued, even to the point where those qualifications might more than compensate for her not receiving the highest score. The only thing that the 99 white men might care about is that a "less-qualified" minority got the job. And affirmative action or, worse, racial quotas are the culprit.

Suppose, however, that the same contest consisted of 100 white men. And suppose that the test was still but one factor involved in the final decision. Suppose that seniority, veteran's status, employer's evaluation of interpersonal skills, or similar factors comprised the remaining components of the promotion standard. Now, would 99 men object to the 10th ranked scorer being promoted? Would *all* 99 men assume that the white man who scored in the 90th percentile was "less qualified?" Even if the 9 men who scored higher than the white man scoring 10th on the examination had no knowledge of the promoted person's evaluations on the other criteria, would those 9 men immediately assume that the person who got the promotion was less qualified?

It is curious that vast numbers of white Americans would jump to the conclusion that affirmative action or racial quotas are the cause of rejection in the first instance when many would argue that there is nothing amiss about the second instance. Arguably nine white men could say they were discriminated against in *both* instances if they believed that the test was the only legitimate means for making the promotion decision. Few people would go that far. Few people would deny the value of other compelling factors in making the promotion determination.

But just for argument's sake, let's assume that only the nine men who had higher scores have a claim to be angry about being passed over. How do you explain the anger and feelings of betrayal and distrust among the 90 white men who in either instance would have been passed over? How do you conclude that the problem is affirmative action or racial quotas when the problem of 99 white men being turned down for promotion exists in both cases? How do you conclude that affirmative action and racial quotas are ruining race relations when there must be something amiss about race relations at the outset to lead to the lopsided reasoning observed in the television campaign ads, in the sports bars, in the classroom, and in the workplace?

These questions come to mind when one considers Mitch Pearlstein's claim: "I would prefer to compete with a white male any day, rather than be in the same job pool as a racial minority group member." His comment came in response to American University Distinguished Professor of Economics, Barbara Bergmann, who argues in her forthcoming book, *In Defense of Affirmative Action*, that affirmative action and quotas are the only legitimate devices for reducing racial disparities in the labor market.

Mitch feels that affirmative action is not only unfair to white males like him, he feels that it is bad for race relations. Treating white males unfairly is surely not the best way to reduce mounting tensions and conflicts among different races in society, he argues.

Mitch's concerns come at precisely the time when virtually all of the top administrative slots at the University of Minnesota are held by white males. New searches for numerous vacancies invariably note that "women or minority group members are encouraged to apply"; or at minimum they advertize that the University is an equal opportunity employer. Women and minority faculty complain, however, that the searches also state preferences for persons familiar with internal procedures and state policies. Reasonable expectations on the face, but expectations, nevertheless, that would normally shrink the pool of qualified women and minority candidates. Since there are few women and minorities in the pipeline—in positions as department chairs or deans—there will be few internal candidates in the future for higher coveted leadership positions.

In a survey of the member institutions of the Midwestern Higher Education Commission, Caroline Sotello Viernes Turner and I find that the average number of minority group members who are department chairs at institutions with fewer than 1,000 students is .45. The average number of minority department chairs at institutions with 1,000 to 5,000 students is not much higher at .79. The average number of minority department chairs at institutions with more than 10,000 students is less than 3. These are not numbers that suggest substantial pools for drawing high level administrators.

None of this, of course, is news to those struggling with the problem of under representation of women and minority scholars among the leaders of many major research universities in the nation. The Ford Foundation has funded a major effort to increase minority faculty representation through scholarship programs and mentorship efforts. The McKnight Foundation and St. Paul Companies are funding the last stages of the Midwestern Higher Education Commission's major research project, which is debating strategies for increasing minority presence at membership institutions.

What is new—at least in traditionally liberal Minnesota—is the openness with which white males now contest the goals of diversity.

The recent race relations conference at the University of Minnesota brought together a broad spectrum of researchers and policy makers concerned about reaching a new consensus on future directions for race relations and civil rights. No such consensus emerged for precisely the reason that sparked Mitch Pearlstein's diatribe against affirmative action. The politically charged argument against race-based remedies to racial inequality is not only that they are undeserved by blacks and other protected group members. It is not that these intended beneficiaries may indeed be hurt. Rather, the charge is made that these race-based strategies hurt whites. They hurt the majority. And they hurt in two ways. One way is that they reduce the number of jobs available to white males. Another way is that they create hatred among whites and thus retard race relations.

Unfortunately, as other participants in the conference noted, equal opportunity and race-neutral strategies have not always proved to be effective in reducing racial inequality. Moreover, equal opportunity does nothing to reduce racism and racial hatred. Here the argument becomes: Yes, it may be true that racial quotas will incite racial hatred, but so too does doing nothing. Racism is a fact of life. It will continue with or without quotas.

The *Hungry Mind Review* polled its readers on their attitudes towards race. Sheila Ards, an assistant professor of social policy at the University of Minnesota and Cathi Tactaquin, a researcher at Oakland's Applied Research Center, analyzed these responses. They found troubling signs of deeply embedded racism and hostility towards people of color. They saw fear. They saw intolerance. They observed perplexing levels of bigotry and prejudice, and this among some of the most liberal and liberated white intellectuals in the nation. White privilege, according to University of Florida sociologist Joe Feagin, lies behind these racist themes. And this racism, long submerged in academia under the cloak of tolerance and intellectual freedom, is coming out now in direct response to calls for greater diversity on college campuses.

The new wild card in this debate about diversity in higher education and about race relations in general is nonblack nonwhites. Latinos/Hispanics are often antagonists in the fight to preserve race-based strategies, as witnessed in the *Podersky* vs. *Kirwin* litigation surrounding the Banneker Scholarship program at the University of Maryland. John Poupart, Executive Director of the American Indian Research and Policy Institute, Inc, describes himself as anishinabe, an Indian word for "the people." John refuses to slot Indians into compartments or to accept the customary labeling of the majority population. Poupart recently told a Humphrey Institute seminar that maybe blacks want to be equal to the white man, but many Indians will have none of that. And if the white man doesn't like it, he can go back where he came from!

For many professional Asian Americans the issue is glass ceilings. William Tamayo of the Asian Law Caucus and Margaret Fung of the Asian American Legal Education and Defense Fund report increasing instances of hostility among firms to promote Asian/Pacific Americans to top management positions because of concerns about accents. Patrick Mendis, who holds a Ph.D. in Geography and M.A. in Public Affairs from the University of Minnesota, tells a story about the new wave of racism against Asians in corporate America and in universities as well. Dr. Mendis is from Sri Lanka, although he spent his high school years in northern Minnesota. He applied for an administrative position at the University of Minnesota, did not make the short list, filed suit against the University, and the University solved its embarrassing problem by suspending the search. He eventually began to work for a Fortune 500 company, developing plans for retail outlet locations. He was sent to Texas to present his latest proposal, only to be told that top management preferred someone who had no accent to represent the company.

These and other examples of increasing work place hostility experienced by people of color ought to ignite a unity movement among blacks, Hispanics, Asians, and American Indians. Instead, it has left many policy makers—familiar with the older race-relations problem of black vs. white—confused and unsettled.

There are in fact two confusions that permeate the debate about how to remedy racial inequality. One concerns the coloring of the color line: America is no longer black and white, but tan, bronze, ebony, and various shades of yellow. For practical purposes, nevertheless, this colorization of America leaves white white.

The second confusion which intersects with the new reality of racial diversity from immigration concerns the question of what it is that we are attempting to remedy.

The debate about race-based remedies will not proceed unfettered until the second of these confusions is resolved. Are we attempting to compensate one group for previous wrongs or are we attempting to equalize outcomes *now* based on the notion that unequal outcomes today will lead to escalating costs to society tomorrow? The first of these justifications for remedies is a retrospective justification. The second is a prospective justification. The widely varying types of remedies that are offered in public discourse are often different because of substantial disagreements over why we are attempting to remedy things in the first place.

It is obvious that if the justification for current race-based strategies is to compensate for previous wrongs, then once-and-for-all payments such as reparations for slavery, involuntary servitude, past discrimination, or forced confinement will continue to be demanded by racial minority groups large and small. Yes, whites will have to pay. But that is the whole point, isn't it, of compensatory schemes like reparations?

If the justification is for future parity, it is difficult to see how whites like Mitch Pearlstein will see themselves as winners through affirmative action and similar race-based initiatives.

There is increasingly hostile opposition to any form of redistributive measure designed to make one group better off at the expense of making another group worse off for any reason. This opposition comes not just from Charles Murray and the late Richard Herrnstein. The opposition is now very evident in the inner-circles of the new Democratic Party leadership, a centrist leadership that gained its legitimacy from an appeal to core democratic principles espousing fairness and equity in a society where every voice counts.

The opposition from the new centrists comes about precisely because race-based strategies offend the basic populist sentiment that special interests skew the distribution of outcomes in an unfair manner. This, it is held, even if the special interests are those of a previously discriminated against group. Process matters much in the new centrists' ideology: if the rules are not fair, then the outcomes of the process are suspect. If the rules of the game are fair, then remedies designed to correct the unequal outcomes become suspect. And, particularly when the remedies on their face are unfair to the nonaggrieved party, the centrists are offended.

Many new pragmatists argue that the best hope for reducing racial inequality is to find remedies that are fair to the majority while offering hope of improving the well-being of the minority. These are thought to be non-race based remedies because they can improve the well-being of the minority without consciously making the minority better off at the expense of making the majority worse off.

Unfortunately, there is little hard empirical evidence that non-race-based remedies achieve that very goal. Have admissions policies that eliminate SAT scores and other putatively discriminatory quantitative measures of promise helped to reduce racial gaps in admissions? Have general anti-poverty or welfare policies helped to narrow the gap between blacks and whites? I know of no research that conclusively makes such claims. Indeed, there is much research from econometricians pointing to an illusion effect. This effect states that even the evidence on narrowing of the racial earnings gap between blacks and whites after the 1960s is the result of an illusion created by the selective withdrawal from the labor market of the lowest earners as a result of public transfer and related social programs.

That leads us back to race-based remedies. In the current political environment, the only type of race-based remedy that is likely to emerge is one that makes nonwhites better off without making whites worse off. In other words, a race-based remedy will only survive scrutiny if it is "efficient."

One example of an efficient race-based policy frequently offered in university circles is the "Excellence Through Diversity" strategy. The argument is as follows: Society is changing. Our ability to compete depends on our ability to produce a highly productive workforce that mirrors the social and demographic distribution of the more highly diverse populations of the world, rather than the racially homogeneous populations of many advanced industrialized nations. To achieve diversity in the workforce, however, we must disproportionately allocate resources to the young and growing portions of the population, which for a variety of reasons happen to be disproportionately minority. Indeed, diversity enhances both the quality of the workforce and the productive capacity of the overall economy, according to this view.

To some, this "excellence through diversity" perspective is a smoke screen for permitting the extension of affirmative action programs in the face of continued court and public opposition. That this perspective is frequently promoted within university settings may further implicate universities in charges of attempting to promote "politically correct" strategies.

But to others, it is a sincere attempt to justify redistributive policies on efficiency grounds: "We need to reduce the racial gap if we are to improve our ability to increase the size of the pie." Or, equivalently, "Whites benefit when blacks are made relatively better off."

In other words, "Excellence Through Diversity" strategies are race-based remed-ies that make whites better off while they make nonwhites better off. The Fourth Circuit Court of Appeals did not buy this argument when made by the University of Maryland in defense of its black scholarship program. And probably many white males won't buy it either. Worse, Asians and Hispanics will reject it too.

Now all of this poses specific problems for attempts to reduce racial inequality when we have a diverse group among nonwhites. What happens when Asians have higher test scores on the quantitative section of the SAT than blacks, even though we "lowered" the admissions requirement in order to admit more blacks? Are Asians made worse off at the expense of admitting more blacks with the lowered score? Or, are blacks made worse off when Asians are included in the pool of minorities who are admitted under the lowered standards? Part of the new opposition to remedies like lowering the standards across the board is that some nonwhites gain and others lose.

This also poses problems for the increasingly vocal demands of African Americans and American Indians, who at times justify redistributive policies not on the basis of prospective equity, but based on the notion of retrospective equity. After all it was their bodies, souls, and in the case of Native Americans, their land that was stolen.

It is clear that nonrace-based policies are likely to dominate the landscape for the years ahead. These will include general economic growth strategies, training, employment, health and welfare, and scholarship programs for poor and disadvantaged youth. It is clear that when challenged, as the University of Texas Law School was challenged, the rush will be to eliminate the offending aspects of race-based strategies and to shift to non-race-based efforts laced with good will.

But the impacts of these policies are likely to be uneven across various racial groups for the very reason the African Americans, Asian Americans, Latinos/ Hispanics and American Indians come to the table with varying claims for retrospective equity. The bottom line: race-based policies are under attack; and non-race-based policies might not work since they might increase inequality between different racial groups because of differing access that these groups have to new opportunities.

The solution, then, will have to be to find race-based or outcome driven policies that can survive the new centrists' criterion that they do not make the majority worse off in order to make the minority better off. Beyond that, we can only hope that these strategies make no *minority* worse off at the expense of making *another minority* better off.

The new agenda for people of color in America will have to include this reality: the color line is no longer one that divides black from white alone. It divides white and nonwhites in various degrees and in various ways. Racial minorities must decide to be a united people of color, working tirelessly to develop strategies for improving each group's well-being—while still being mindful of the role that white male opposition can play.

Mitch Pearlstein is still an angry man. He is fighting for fairness and decency, he says. Affirmative action, quotas, racial preferences, set-asides, and other privileges to women and minorities are unfair. He claims his opposition to these efforts is not a sign that he is a racist. Just the opposite, he says. He wants to help improve race relations.

The problem is that almost all remedies to racial inequality create difficulties in reaching a consensus in a society where racial tensions continue to mount. If whites believe that compensatory benefits to racial minorities are unjust and inefficient, then race relations will worsen. On the other hand, in the absence of direct efforts to remedy racial economic inequality, there is little hope for narrowing the persistent gap in well-being between whites and nonwhites in America. Unfortunately, then, there is a possible conflict in the short-run between the goal of improved race relations and the objective of social and economic equality.

Many white males will remain angry at the supposed "reverse discrimination" inherent in affirmative action. Economic expansion policies might help to dismiss these views in the short run. If all 10 of the top scorers in our job promotion parable could be elevated to better jobs, perhaps attention could be redirected away from the presumed unfairness of affirmative action and related civil rights strategies that help minorities at the expense of the majority. The redirection, only fortunately, would be temporary. Unaddressed, unchanged, and unaltered are the very core racial beliefs that hinder implementation of effective civil rights laws. The new agenda for race relations will have to address that reality. Perhaps by openly confronting white racism as a major barrier to future civil rights efforts and by developing sustained, honest discussions, fewer and fewer of the 99 white males will feel an economic threat from efforts to promote equality.

NOTE

1. This essay is based on an article originally published in *Emerge*, Volume 6, Number 6, July/August 1995.

Index

Adarand Constructors, Inc. v. *Pena*, 217, 222, 224

affirmative action, viii, ix, x, xii, xiii, 2, 3, 4, 6, 8, 25, 26, 34, 36, 38, 39, 40, 41, 42, 45, 47-59, 100, 112, 167, 168, 169, 170, 181, 186, 189, 190, 191, 199, 200, 202, 204, 217, 219, 220, 221, 222, 227-230, 233, 237, 238, 239, 240, 241, 243, 244, 245, 246, 247, 248, 249, 250, 251, 252, 253, 255, 256, 257

affirmative action story, 228

affirmative action versus reparations, 233

AFL-CIO, 8, 157-161

African American, 5, 6, 11, 12, 18,30-39, 41, 42, 43, 45, 101, 113, 157, 163, 165, 192, 193, 194, 203, 206, 207, 208, 209, 210, 211, 214, 217, 218, 219, 220, 221, 224, 231-240, 243, 244, 245, 248, 250, 256, 257

African American youth, 207, 245

Agricultural Adjustment Act, 155

aliens, 13, 18-21, 23-26

Alexander, Dr. Will W., 153, 155, 156

Amalgamated Association of Street and Electric Railway Employee, 152

America, Richard F., 235, 240, 241, 242, 243, 246

American Federation of Government Employees, 3, 150, 152, 159, 162

American Federation of Labor, 3, 150

American Federation of Teachers, 152

American Fund for Public Service, 152, 163

American Race Relations Council, 153

Anderson, Bernard E., 47, 58, 242

Angstadt, Ed, 24

Anti-Defamation League, 44

anti-discrimination laws, enforcement of, 40-43, 48, 56, 70, 241

anti-immigrant, 18, 19, 22, 24, 183, 184

apartheid, 231, 233

Association of Colored Railway Trainmen and Locomotive Firemen, 4

backlash, x, 25, 26, 40, 169, 171

Baker, Newton D., 154

Bakke, 3, 4, 49, 56, 59, 226

Baldwin, William, 151

barriers, xii, 14, 16, 33, 37, 38, 47, 151, 226, 231, 240

Becker, Gary, 58

Bell, Derrick, 9, 239

Bennett, William, 21

Bergmann, Barbara, x, 249, 252

black Americans, 2, 31, 32, 37, 40, 42, 146, 206, 208, 214, 231, 235, 239, 241, 242

black labor market, 68

Black Lung Association, 156

black middle class, viii

Black Reparations Commission, 234
black underclass, viii, 30, 206, 212, 213, 214, 216
black wealth accumulation, 232
black workers, x, 4, 5, 33, 50, 51, 54, 62, 67, 70, 101, 102, 106-110, 112, 149-154, 156, 157, 159, 161
Black Workers in White Unions: Job Discrimination in the United States, 157, 161, 164
black working class, 7
Black-Asian tension, 22
Black-Latino tension, 23
Blackmun, Justice Harry, 49
blacks, viii, x, xii, 1-6, 9, 13, 30-32, 34, 36, 38, 39, 54, 59, 61, 62, 65-68, 147, 149-151, 153-159, 162, 175, 177, 180, 181, 183, 184, 188-190, 201, 206-211, 213, 214, 215, 216, 227, 229, 233, 236-239, 241, 247, 248, 253-256
Blauner, Robert, 5, 9
Blumrosen, Alfred, 39
Boxer, Senator Barbara, 19, 20
bracero, 15, 24
Bradley, Senator Bill, ix, x
Brooks, Charles, 146
Brown v. *Board of Education*, 2, 7, 47, 159, 218, 219
Brown, Kathleen, 19, 20
Buchanan, Pat, 20, 208
Bunche, Ralph, 151
Bureau of Labor Statistics, 62, 63, 245
Bureau of National Affairs, 39, 54, 58
Bush, President George, 6, 9, 16, 41, 223, 245, 246
Bush administration, 57, 163
Business Roundtable, 56

California Civil Rights Initiative, vii, 1
Carter administration, 55
Chavez, Linda, 21, 24
Chicago Teachers Union, 158
Chinese, ix, 12, 13, 15, 21, 173, 236
Chinese Exclusion Act, 15
CIO, 6, 153, 154, 159, 161
Civil Rights, vii-xiii, 1, 2, 5-7, 11, 15, 17, 25, 32, 34, 35, 40-43, 47, 49-51, 53, 55, 56, 59, 157-160, 167, 172-174, 184, 185, 194, 205, 206, 209-211, 218, 219, 224, 231, 233, 241, 246, 248, 249,
251-257
Civil Rights Act of 1964, 2, 5, 7, 51, 157, 174, 231, 241
Civil Rights Act of 1991, 220
Civil Rights Bill of 1965, 231
civil rights movement, vii, 6, 17, 40, 47, 157, 158, 185, 194, 209, 218, 231
Civil Rights Restoration Act, 227
civil rights struggle, 211
Clinton, President, 16, 20, 21, 24, 205
Clinton administration, ix, 41, 206, 214, 249
Coalition of Black Trade Unionists, 159
cold war, 16, 18
Collapse of the Cotton Tenancy, 155
Colored National Labor Union, 150
coloring of the color line, 252
Commission on Immigration Reform, 19, 22, 26, 41, 42, 53, 149, 151, 155, 159
Commission on Interracial Cooperation, 155, 159
Committee on Farm Tenancy, 156
Committee on Government Contracts, 50, 58
Committee on Negroes in the Economic Reconstruction, 153
compensation for discrimination and wealth disparity, 235
compensatory benefits, 257
competition, 4-6, 48, 112, 171, 257
consequences, 2, 5, 38, 40, 113, 224-226, 236
continuing discrimination, x
Contracts, viii, 5, 15, 50, 52, 58, 105, 217
Corporation, 33, 53, 54, 154
cost of slavery, 234
costs of discrimination, 33, 36, 237
Crosby, Faye, 228
Croson, vi, 42
cumulative effects, 237

Darity, William A., Jr., 8, 233, 243, 245, 246, 257
decomposition, 100, 104-108, 110, 111, 113
DeFunis, 4
demographic changes, 17
denial, 24, 29, 30, 33, 47, 49, 218
differential industrial impact, 103
differentials, 58, 153
Disabled Miners & Widows of Southern

West Virginia, 156
disadvantages, 68, 70
discrimination, vii-xiii, 2-6, 9, 26, 31-43,
    47-52, 55, 57, 58, 99-100, 103, 104,
    147, 151-153, 155, 157, 161, 173, 174,
    182, 194, 202, 207, 210, 211, 216, 218,
    219-227, 229, 231, 233, 235-239, 241,
    246, 255
discussions of race, 205
distribution of wealth, 183, 201
diversity, viii, 12, 13, 36, 104, 106,
    167-175, 196, 202, 203, 220, 223, 226,
    228, 253, 254, 256
Dred Scott, 1

economic inequity, 189, 240, 257
economic status, 6, 7, 48, 149, 153, 154,
    196, 197, 200, 208, 227, 239, 242
Embree, Edward, 153, 155
employment, vii-ix, 3-6, 9, 14, 18, 32, 33,
    38-42, 47-55, 58, 59, 61-70, 96-106,
    146, 147, 150, 157, 173, 175, 218-221,
    224, 227, 237, 246, 257; by race, 51,
    66, 224
employment opportunities, ix, 61, 70, 106
enforcement, vii, 6, 32, 40-43, 48, 51, 52,
    55-57, 69, 70, 92, 93, 105, 147, 234,
    236
English-only, 173, 174
Equal Employment, 33, 40, 41, 50-52, 106,
    157, 218, 237
Equal Employment Opportunity (EEO),
    50, 53, 58, 61-70, 100-102, 105, 107,
    113, 170
Equal Employment Opportunity Commis-
    sion (EEOC), 41, 53-55, 58, 66, 173
equal opportunity in employment, 100,
    113, 157, 218, 237
equal rights, vii, 29, 32, 202
equality of opportunity, 41, 42, 219, 222,
    223, 224
Establishment of a 49th State, 231, 242
Executive Order 10925, 49, 50
Executive Order 11246, vii, 47, 51, 54, 56,
    219
Executive Order Program, 53
Ezell, Harold, 22, 24

fair employment, 4, 49, 50, 218
Fair Employment Committee, 4, 49, 50,
218
farm tenancy, 155, 156
Feagin, Joe, ix, xi, xii, 254
federal affirmative action programs, 220-
    222
Federation for American   Immigration
    Reform, 22
Fair Employment Practices Commission
    (FEPC), 49, 50
15th Amendment, 1
Field Foundation, 156, 190
fishing, 14, 168
Fix, Michael, 17, 23, 24, 26, 147, 233, 241
Ford, Gerald R., 219
Ford Foundation, 150, 157, 158, 161, 253
Forman, James, 231
foundation interest, 149
foundations, viii, 43, 149-165, 239
14th Amendment, 1, 2, 13, 14, 21, 226
Fugitive Slave Acts, 1

gangs, 19, 29
Garland Fund, 152, 155
general assistance, 23
Georgia Workers Education Service, 159
Glass Ceiling Commission, 37, 38
glass ceilings, 252
Government Employees, 162, 238
grassroots, 22, 156, 160
"guest worker," 14

Harlan, Justice John Marshall, 2
Heritage Foundation, 24
homophobia, x, 206, 209, 210
homophobic rhetoric, 208
House Un-American Activities Committee,
    152
Human Rights, 16, 20, 25, 42, 43, 216, 224
Hungry Mind Review, x, 179, 180, 182,
    189-204, 254

Immigration Act of 1917, 14
Immigration Reform, 15, 16, 18, 19, 21, 22
Immigration Reform and Control Act, 18
inclusiveness, 169
Indians, viii, xi, 12, 256, 257
industries, 14, 52, 54, 55, 63, 66, 67,
    101-103, 105, 106, 150, 153, 154, 159,
    221, 240
inequality, viii-x, xiii, 1, 3, 9, 48, 189, 200,

201, 213, 222, 236, 239, 240, 242, 253-257; remedies to racial, 243-251
initiative, vii, xiii, 15, 20-22, 25, 26, 65, 189, 236, 237, 248, 255
inner city, 212-213, 216
institutionalized racism, 39
integration, 65, 153, 156, 190, 194-197, 202, 202
interclass effects of affirmative action, 234

Jackson, Rev. Jesse, 232
Jackson, Michael, 211
Japanese American, 221
job ceilings, 47
job creation, 22, 24
job discrimination, 5, 6, 50, 157, 161, 210
Job Discrimination in the United States, 157, 161
job seniority, 6
Johnson, Charles, S., 153
Johnson, James Weldon, 42, 155
Johnson, Josie, 167
Johnson, Lyndon B., 58, 219, 220, 237
Johnson, Magic, 209
Jones v. *Mayer*, 2
Jordan, Barbara, 20, 21
Julius Rosenwald Fund, 153, 159
justification, 49, 59, 223, 255

Kagan, Donald, 26
Kemp, Jack, 21
Kennedy, John F., 49, 50, 52, 218, 231
Kerr, Clark, 162, 165
King, Rodney, 182
King, The Rev. Dr. Martin Luther, 151, 157, 187, 219, 224
King, W. L. Mackenzie, 151
Knights of Labor, 150
Korn/Ferry, 54, 55, 58
Krauthammer, Charles, 239, 250

Labor Apprenticeship and Education Program, 158
labor market position, 53
labor markets, vii, viii, 67, 104, 230
labor organizations, 3, 4, 150, 218
labor organizers, 14, 15, 152
labor unions, viii, 4, 5, 149, 150, 153, 154, 162
Lamm, Richard, 22

Laura Spelman Rockefeller Memorial (LSRM), 151, 152
League for Industrial Democracy, 155
legal permanent residents, 17, 19
legal support for affirmative action, 219
legislation, v, vii, 40, 55, 157, 158, 169, 219, 232, 233
Leonard, Jonathan, 58, 146, 241
Lincoln, Abraham, 241
Loury, Glenn, 58
Lucy, William, 159
Ludlow Massacre, 151
Lyndon Johnson's Great Society, 237

Malaysia, 236
Manhattan Institute, 22, 26
Marketti, James, 238
Marshall, Ray, 52
Marshall, Justice Thurgood, 3, 40
McCarran-Walter Act, 15
McKinnon, Mark, 20
media, viii, x, 18, 19, 29, 31, 32, 55, 183, 185, 205-209, 211-215, 245
melting pot, xi, 3, 183, 189, 200, 249
The Messenger, 152
middle class, viii, xiii, 17, 18, 22, 214
middle management, 55
middle passage, 208, 233
midwest, xii, 14, 99, 100, 161
Midwest Center for Labor Research, 161
Midwestern Higher Education Commission, 253
Miners for Democracy (MFD), 156
Minnesota, viii, xii, 1, 167, 168, 179, 182, 219, 221, 250, 253, 254
minorities, viii, x, xi, 2, 6, 17, 32, 38, 47-49, 52-55, 59, 65-67, 70, 112, 113, 161, 162, 171, 177, 203, 211, 217, 219, 220, 221, 223, 225, 238, 241, 251-253, 256, 257
Mitchell, George M., 153, 159
Mitchell, H. L., 155
Mitchell, Reginald J., Sr., 189
Moore, "Queen Mother" Audley, 231
Muhammad, Elijah, 210, 211
Muhammad, Khalid, 208, 215
multiculturalism, ix, 17, 25, 194, 249
Murray, Charles, 255
Myrdal, Gunnar, 153, 154, 155

NAACP Legal Defense and Education Fund, 6
NAFTA, 20
National Association of Manufacturers, 161
national employment, 96, 97
National Farm Labor, 156
National Immigration Forum, 22
National Labor Relations Board, 161
National Labor Union, 150
National Miners' Union, 156
National Negro Congress, 154
national origin discrimination, 174
National Recovery Administration, 153
Native Americans, 12, 96, 183, 186, 189, 191, 201
nativism, ix, 11, 18, 25
nativist movement, 14, 18
Naturalization Law, 1, 12, 13, 21
Neal, Larry, 241
Nearing, Scott, 152
Nelson, Alan, 22, 23
Neufeld, Maurice N., 162
New Economic Policy, 236
new globalism, 25
New World Order, ix, 11, 16, 20, 25
New York Community Trust, 161
Nixon, Richard M., 50, 216, 219
Nogren, Paul, 154
North, Oliver, 205
Northwest, 14
Nourse, Edwin, 156

obstacles to black participation in education, 36, 148, 196
Office of Federal Contract Compliance Programs (OFCCP), 53-59, 112, 157
Office of Federal Contract Compliance (OFCC), 51, 146, 147
organized labor, 3, 5, 9, 58, 151, 155, 157-162

Palmer Raids, 14
Passel, Jeffrey, 17, 23, 24
pathologies, 209, 211, 213, 245
Payne, Robert, 156
Pearlstein, Mitch, 243, 249, 251, 252, 253, 255, 257
Podersky v. *Kirwin*, 254
portrayal of blacks, 206

Post Reagan-Bush Era, 211
Poupart, John, 254
Powell, Gen. Colin B., 50, 243
powell, john, 179, 185, 226
preferences, vii, xi, 48, 55, 56, 65, 223, 224, 225, 239, 253, 257
preferential treatment, ix, 5, 42, 49, 59, 220
prejudice, 31, 187, 206, 215, 237, 254
President's Committee for Equal Employment Opportunity, 50
Proposition 187, 20, 21, 22, 189
prospective justification, 255
protection under the law, 209, 210
public accommodations, 38
Puerto Rico, 15
Pullman Company, 152

quotas, vii, ix, 3, 13, 15, 52, 53, 55, 227-230, 243, 244, 247, 248, 249, 251, 252, 253, 254, 257

race, vii, xiii, 1-7, 9, 11, 13, 15, 25, 26, 30, 33, 34, 47-51, 55, 59, 61-69, 103-108, 111, 113, 150, 153, 154, 157, 160, 168, 175, 176, 179-183, 179-188, 189-197, 199-205, 211, 212, 218, 219, 221-227, 229, 230, 236, 237, 240, 243, 245, 246, 248, 254
race relations, viii, ix, x, xi, xiii, 153, 154, 160, 182, 187, 206, 215, 249, 250, 251-257
race-based remedial measures, 223
race-based strategies, 252-257
racial and ethnic differences, ix, x, xiii, 43, 61, 70
racial attitudes, 30, 32, 34
racial beliefs, 194, 196, 200, 257
racial discourse, x, 205, 208, 211,
racial discrimination, vii, ix, xi, xii, 2, 6, 31-35, 37-41, 147, 152, 155, 157, 161, 182, 200, 223, 225, 235
racial disparities in the labor market, 252
racial diversity, xii, 13, 200, 203, 254
racial earnings gap, 255
racial equality, vii, viii, 69, 191, 233, 239, 240
racial inequality, ix, x, xiii, 1, 3, 9, 48, 189, 199, 200, 201, 202, 213, 222, 238, 239, 240, 242, 243-250, 251, 252, 253, 257
racial inequities, 190, 201

racial preference licensing, 240
racial preferences, vii, x, 236, 257
racial quotas, 251-253
racial segregation, ix, 4, 6, 64, 196
racially diverse, vii, 199
racism, vii, viiii, ix, xi, xii, 1-3, 5-7, 15,
    29-32, 34-43, 49, 51, 169, 171, 172,
    180, 185-187, 202, 206, 208, 210, 223,
    229, 239, 247, 253, 254, 257
Rand Corporation, 54, 59
Randolph, A. Phillip, 151, 152, 158
Raspberry, William, 244
Reagan, Ronald, 6, 22, 40, 41, 55, 56, 57,
    58, 249
Reagan administration, 40, 55-57, 173
Reagan-Bush Era, viii, 41, 43, 88, 211
recession, ix, 16, 18, 62, 66, 67, 70, 97, 98,
    100-106, 147
reconstruction, 2, 6, 7, 9, 10, 150, 153,
    233, 241
redistributive policies, 254, 256
refugees, 16, 17, 19, 24, 172
reparations, x, 231-242, 246, 247, 249,
    250, 255
Reparations Committee of Descendants of
    U. S. Slaves, 231
reparations in-kind, 240
residential and psychological discrimin-
    ation, 210
retrospective justification, 255
reverse discrimination, vii, 45, 247, 257
revolving door strategy, 15
Reynolds, William Bradford, 55, 220
Richards, Ann, 20
Rights, vii-xiii, 1, 2, 5-8, 11-27, 29-55 , 66,
    69, 96, 100, 150, 157-160, 162, 167,
    172-174, 181, 184, 185, 194, 205, 206,
    209-210, 211, 217-222, 227, 231, 232,
    231, 232, 246, 248, 249, 251-257
riots, 26, 40, 150
Rodriguez, Richard, 26
Rogan, Don, 22
Rosenthal, A. M., 21, 22, 23, 24
Roosevelt, Franklin D., 49, 50, 155, 156,
    218
Russell Sage Foundation, 15

Safire, William, 22
Samson, Gloria Garrett, 152
"Save Our State" ballot, 20, 22

Saxton, Alexander, 10, 27
school desegregation, 6
Second Reconstruction, 2, 6
segregated neighborhoods, 196
segregation, ix, 2, 4, 6, 35, 39, 43, 47, 61,
    62, 64, 65, 69, 70, 151, 195, 202, 218,
    222
seniority, 5, 6, 99, 101, 106-108, 111, 112,
    157, 252
set-asides, xiii, 247, 248, 257
Sharry, Frank, 27
Simpson-Mazzoli Bill, 191
Simpson, O. J., 211
Sjoberg, Gideon, 43
slave labor, 232
slavery, ix, 1-3, 10, 186, 201, 208, 211,
    218, 222, 229, 231-237, 239, 246, 255
slaves, ix, 11, 12, 21, 150, 208, 231, 231-
    237, 239, 246, 255
Smith, James, 59
social position, 239
Social Sciences Research Council, 152
Social Security, 21, 23, 40
Southern Baptist Convention, 222
Southern blacks, 149
Southern Regional Council
    (SRC), 159
Southern Tenant Farmers Union, 155
Southerners for Economic Justice
    (SEJ), 160
Southwest, 14, 18
Sowell, Thomas, 52, 53, 55
Spatial Mismatch Hypothesis, 67, 68
Special Analysis J, 40
Spriggs, William, 146, 243, 247
Steele, Claude, 239
Steelworkers Fight Back, 156
Stein, Dan, 22
Stern Family Fund, 156, 160, 161
Stevens, Justice, 222
strategies for reducing racial and ethnic in-
    equality, x
Stokes, Anson Phelps, 151, 154
Strikers Emergency Relief Committee, 155
Student Nonviolent Coordinating Commit-
    tee (SNCC), 231
Supplementary Security Income, 23
surveys, xi, xii, 30-33, 36, 58, 61, 162,
    171, 175, 180, 181, 184, 189-192, 201,
    204, 206, 216, 227, 253

Sviredoff, Michael, 151, 164
Swinton, David, 238

Tamayo, William, 21, 27, 167, 172, 176, 254
Taylor, William, 41
Teamsters for a Democratic Union, 156
tenant farmers, 155
13th Amendment, 1, 2
Title VII, viii, 5, 51, 54, 157, 174, 219

Ueda, Reed, 13, 15, 27
unemployment, 14, 23, 39, 245
unemployment insurance, 23, 92
union, 3, 5, 6, 16, 24, 26, 149-152, 154-162, 229, 231
United Mine Workers, 5, 152
U.S. Naturalization Law, 12, 21
United States v. *Bethlehem Steel Corporation*, 5
United States v. *Wong Kim Ark*, 13, 21
Universal Declaration of Human Rights, 42
universities, 6, 17, 36, 37, 182, 239, 250, 253, 254, 256
University of Texas Law School, 257
Urban Institute, 23, 26, 33, 146, 147, 241
urban violence, 29

Vanguard Press of Negro Labor, 152
Vaughn, Ted, 43
Via, Emory, 160, 167
Voter Fraud Task Force, 24

Warren, Chief Justice Earl, 219
Washington, Booker T., 150
Wasserstrom, Richard, 59
Watts riot, 18, 150
wealth redistribution, 236, 240
Welch, Finis, 54
welfare benefits, 19, 22, 24
"welfare magnet," 21
welfare reform, 24, 26
Wesley, Charles H., 10, 152
West, Cornel, 185
white backlash, 40
white privilege, viii, ix, xi, 254
white racism, ix, xi, xii, 5, 29-32, 37-42, 257
white supremacists, 187
Wilson, Kirke, 162

Wilson, Governor Pete, 18, 19, 21, 22, 23, 24
Wise, Leah, 160
Wood, Thomas, vii
workers, x, 3-6, 9, 12, 14, 15, 21, 23, 26, 33, 41, 48, 50, 51, 54, 57, 58, 62, 64, 67, 70, 99, 101, 102, 106-113, 149-161, 172, 173, 218, 220, 229
Workers Defense League, 158

Zero Population Growth, 22

About the Contributors

Bernard E. Anderson is Assistant Secretary, Employment Standards Administration, Department of Labor.

M. V. Lee Badgett earned her undergraduate degree in economics at the University of Chicago and her Ph.D. at the University of California-Berkeley in 1990. Most recently she served as visiting assistant professor, Lesbian and Gay Studies, Yale University. She is an assistant professor in the School of Public Affairs at the University of Maryland, College Park.

Richard M. Benjamin is a former senior editor of *The Race Relations Reporter* and *The Journal of Blacks in Higher Education*, both in New York City. He is currently a doctoral fellow in the Program of Modern Thought and Literature at Stanford University.

Barbara R. Bergmann, Distinguished Professor of Economics, American University, received her Ph.D. in economics from Harvard University. Her academic and public career includes faculty positions at the University of Maryland and at Brandeis and staff positions at the Bureau of Labor Statistics, the President's Council of Economic Advisers (during the Kennedy administration), and (as Senior Economic Adviser) the U.S. Agency for International Development. Her most recent book is *In Defense of Affirmative Action*.

William A. Darity, Jr. is Boshamer Professor of Economics at the University of North Carolina at Chapel Hill. He has also been on the faculty at the University of Texas at Austin; visiting professor at Grinnell College, the University of Tulsa, the University of Maryland at College Park, and the London School of Economics; and a visitor at the Board of Governors of the Federal Reserve. His most recent book is an edited two-volume work, *Economics and Discrimination.*

Joe R. Feagin is Graduate Research Professor in the Department of Sociology, University of Florida. Dr. Feagin received his Ph.D. at Harvard University and has served as Scholar-in-Residence for the U.S. Commission on Civil Rights and as professor at the University of Texas, Austin, before joining the University of Florida. Dr. Feagin's books include *Ghetto Revolts, White Racism: The Basics,* and *Living with Racism: The Black Middle Class Experience.*

The Honorable Gerald W. Heaney was appointed judge of the U.S. Court of Appeals for the Eighth Circuit in 1966. In addition to being a decorated veteran Judge Heaney has served on several committees for the United States Judicial Conference and the Board of Regents of the University of Minnesota.

Herbert Hill is Evjue-Bascom Professor of African-American Studies and Professor of Industrial Relations at the University of Wisconsin-Madison. He is the former National Labor Secretary of the NAACP and author of *Black Labor and the American Legal System* and other books. Professor Hill has been a special consultant to the Economic and Social Council of the United Nations and to the United States Equal Employment Opportunity Commission. He has presented testimony before congressional committees and frequently appears as an expert witness in federal court litigation involving employment discrimination.

Betsy Hubbard, Rebecca Kelleher-Reeth, Dartrell Lipscomb, and Michelle Revels are Humphrey Institute graduates. **Kathleen Kalina** is a doctoral student, Department of Fisheries & Wildlife, University of Minnesota, and **Reginald J. Mitchell, Sr.,** is a graduate of the Carlson School of Management and the University of Minnesota Law School. These coauthors were students in PA5493, Racial Inequality and Public Policy, at the Humphrey Institute, Fall 1994.

Evelyn Hu-DeHart is Professor of History and Director of the Center for Studies of Ethnicity and Race in America at the University of Colorado at Boulder. She lectures, testifies, consults, and conducts workshops on Latin America/Caribbean history, politics, and contemporary affairs, race, ethnic, and gender relations and issues; multicultural education and the politics of multiculturalism; ethnic studies and curriculum reform; Asian-American history and the Asian diaspora worldwide; refugee and immigration issues; recruitment and retention of students and faculty of color.

Richard Magat has worked at the Ford Foundation's Communications Department, the Edward W. Hazen Foundation, and as editor of a series of 114 volumes in the Philanthropy and Society series for Transaction Publishers. He is the author of *An Agile Servant: Community Leadership by Community Foundations* and has conducted extensive research on organized labor and philanthropic foundations.

Samuel L. Myers, Jr., Roy Wilkins Professor of Human Relations and Social Justice at the Hubert H. Humphrey Institute of Public Affairs, University of Minnesota, convened the 1994 National Conference on Civil Rights in the Post Reagan-Bush Era from which this volume emerged. A graduate of Morgan State University, Myers received his Ph.D. in economics from Massachusetts Institute of Technology. Prior to joining the University of Minnesota's Humphrey Institute, Myers was a faculty member at Cuttington University College, Liberia, the University of Texas, the University of Pittsburgh and the University of Maryland-College Park and from 1980-82, Senior Economist with the Federal Trade Commission. His most recent book is *The Black Underclass: Critical Essays on Race and Unwantedness* with William A. Darity, Jr., William Sabol, and Emmett Carson.

William M. Rodgers III is Assistant Professor of Economics at the College of William and Mary. A graduate of Dartmouth College, Rodgers earned his M.A. at the University of California at Santa Barbara and his Ph.D. in economics from Harvard University. In 1993 he was a Visiting Fellow at the W. E. B. Du Bois Institute for Afro-American Research in 1992-93, and most recently Consultant to the Chief Economist, Office of the Secretary, U.S. Department of Labor.

This book grew out of the 1994 conference on Race Relations and Civil Rights in the Post Reagan-Bush Era, funded by The Honeywell Foundation, Medtronic, Inc., The McKnight Foundation, General Mills Foundation, Otto Bremer Foundation, Roy Wilkins Foundation, and the University of Minnesota's Distinguished Carlson Lecture Series. The conference drew upon the talents and skills of Coordinator Jennifer Williams and other staff of the University of Minnesota's Roy Wilkins Center, Humphrey Institute of Public Affairs. Lan Pham and Judy Leahy helped with early preparation of the manuscript. Claire Cohen contributed valuable editorial assistance. Final editing and manuscript preparation were provided by Leone Carstens, University of Minnesota, and Lynn Zelem, Greenwood Publishing.

ISBN 0-275-95621-0

90000>

EAN

9 780275 956219

HARDCOVER BAR CODE